Essential Bible Background

What you should know *before* you read the Bible

J. Carl Laney

For Ezra had set his heart to study the Torah of Yahweh and to practice it, and to teach His statutes and ordinances in Israel.
Ezra 7:10

Dedicated to the students I have had the privilege of teaching
during my career at Western Seminary
Philippians 1:3

Copies available from CreateSpace.com,
Amazon.com and Amazon.co.uk
Copyright 2016 by J. Carl Laney
ISBN 9781539635048
Printed in the United States of America

Essential Bible Background

Table of Contents

INTRODUCTION:	7
An Invitation	7
The Essential Story of the Bible	9
The Essential Question for Bible Readers	12
CHAPTER 1 The Books of Moses	15
Genesis	17
Exodus	21
Leviticus	24
Numbers	27
Deuteronomy	31
CHAPTER 2 The Historical Books	35
Joshua	36
Judges	40
Ruth	43
Samuel	47
Kings	50
Chronicles	55
Ezra	58
Nehemiah	62
Esther	66
CHAPTER 3 The Wisdom Books	71
Job	72
Psalms	76
Proverbs	79
Ecclesiastes	83
Song of Solomon	87

CHAPTER 4 The Major Prophets	91
Isaiah	92
Jeremiah	97
Lamentations	100
Ezekiel	103
Daniel	107
CHAPTER 5 The Minor Prophets	112
Hosea	115
Joel	118
Amos	122
Obadiah	125
Jonah	128
Micah	131
Nahum	135
Habakkuk	138
Zephaniah	141
Haggai	144
Zechariah	147
Malachi	148
CHAPTER 6 The Gospels	155
Matthew	159
Mark	162
Luke	167
John	170
CHAPTER 7 Acts of the Apostles	175
Book of Acts	177
CHAPTER 8 The Pauline Epistles	182
Romans	186
First Corinthians	189
Second Corinthians	194

Galatians	198
Ephesians	202
Philippians	206
Colossians	210
First Thessalonians	213
Second Thessalonians	217
First Timothy	220
Second Timothy	225
Titus	228
Philemon	232
CHAPTER 9 The General Epistles	**236**
Hebrews	237
James	241
First Peter	245
Second Peter	249
First John	253
Second John	256
Third John	260
Jude	263
CHAPTER 10 The Apocalypse	**268**
The Book of Revelation	269
CHAPTER 11 The Most Asked Questions About the Bible	**274**

Appendices

APPENDIX 1 How to Study the Bible Study	283
APPENDIX 2 The Most Important Events of the Bible	290
APPENDIX 3 Who's Who in the Bible?	296

APPENDIX 4	Important Dates to Remember	302
APPENDIX 5	The Best Known Bible Quotations	306
APPENDIX 6	Classic Prayers of the Bible	311
APPENDIX 7	Bible Definitions You Should Know	313
APPENDIX 8	Index of Biblical Theology	332
APPENDIX 9	Fun with Bible Trivia	337
APPENDIX 10	What Happened After Acts?	342
APPENDIX 11	What is the Apocrypha?	346
APPENDIX 12	Is there Humor in the Bible?	350

Scripture taken from the New American Standard Bible, Copyright (1997) by the Lockman Foundation. Used by permission.

INTRODUCTION

AN INVITATION TO READERS

From the account of creation in Genesis to the prophecies of future events in Revelation, the Bible gives us a sweeping picture of God's dealings with humankind. This holy book, revered by Jews, Christians and Moslems, is not just a record of what people think about God, but what God has to say to people. Here we discover what God has to say about Himself, about sin and its consequences, about justice and forgiveness, about mercy and love. Here we also learn about the Promised One who was sent from heaven to reconcile the relationship between God and alienated humanity.

It has been my privilege to study and teach the Bible for the last 40 years. It all began at Western Seminary where I earned my Masters of Divinity (1973) and Masters of Theology (1974). I then went on to Dallas Theological Seminary for doctoral studies, earning my Th.D. in Bible Exposition. Since 1977 I have had the privilege of teaching Biblical Literature at Western Seminary in Portland, Oregon. And while some would consider me an expert on this subject, I know better. I'm still a student–a student of Scripture. And the more I study, the more I discover what I have yet to learn! As a young seminary graduate, I thought I knew the Bible. Only now do I realize that my training in biblical studies was just *beginning* of my educational adventure.

In this book I would like to share with you the highlights of what I've learned on my journey. I would like you to know the essential Bible background information which I have discovered over my years of study and teaching. Perhaps you are familiar with the Bible but don't fully understand its message. Or perhaps you want to know more about a particular book of the Bible. Or maybe you would like to know where Jesus fits in to the grand story recorded in the Bible. I believe that the book in your hands has the answers you are seeking.

I recently read a book about the Bible which was written by a bestselling author. And while it was interesting reading, he viewed the Bible merely as religious literature, not as divinely revealed truth. His explanations about the Bible were entertaining and humorous. But he didn't present the essential facts of the Bible as reliable or trustworthy.

This book is different. I believe that the Bible is the Word of God revealed by God's Spirit to human writers who recorded a divinely inspired message. The Bible is God's truth and serves as a reliable guide for salvation and life. You may not have the same regard for the Bible, but I hope that reading my book will elevate both your appreciation and understanding of God's Word.

I'm extending to you a personal invitation to join me in a study of the Bible. If you choose to accept, you will begin a great learning adventure. My prayer is that we may be enlightened and encouraged by the truths of the Bible. We join the psalmist in praying, "Open my eyes to see the wonderful truths in your instructions" (Psalm 119:18 NLT).

THE ESSENTIAL STORY OF THE BIBLE

I remember my grandmother reading me stories when I was little. And if I close my eyes and recall her face, I can still hear her soft, gentle voice reading me the story of *Peter Pan*. I enjoyed having stories read to me as a child. The only thing better is the joy of reading them to my own children!

Everyone loves a good story. And the Bible is the greatest story ever told. It is the story of good and evil, grace and glory, redemption and judgment. It is the story of a cosmic conflict that is full of serious setbacks, awesome comebacks and surprising finishes. The Bible is the story of human failure, God's gracious intervention and deliverance, His ultimate judgment on sin and Satan, and the establishment of His righteous, eternal rule.

The best thing about the Bible is that it is not like the story of *Peter Pan*–fiction or myth. The story of the Bible is very real and true! And it is our story--the story of humanity–our past, present and future. It is a story that will answer the basic questions of life: Who am I? Why am I here? Where am I going? And what is life on planet earth all about anyway?

To understand the story of the Bible, we must begin in eternity past. The psalm writer declares, "The LORD is King forever and ever!" (Ps. 10:16). The prophet Jeremiah adds, "He is the living God and the everlasting King" (Jer. 10:10). But God could not rightly be called "King" without a recognized throne and a realm. So David acknowledges, "The LORD has established His throne in heaven and His kingdom rules over all" (Ps. 103:19).

As Creator, God has always possessed absolute sovereignty over His creation. He rules the heavens and the earth. God's rule over creation has often been delegated to authorities that are raised up by God to officiate over His dominion. Earthly kings, priests, and judges served in this capacity.

God's rule over creation was going nicely when there arose an angelic challenger. A created being known as "Satan" or the "Devil" rebelled against the sovereign authority of God. As part of his rebellion, Satan instituted a counterfeit kingdom to parallel God's eternal rule and to challenge His authority. Satan is an usurper who has no right to infringe on God's kingdom rule. Yet even Jesus recognized that he exercises a limited authority over God's sin alienated creation (Matt. 4:8-9). The apostle Paul referred to him as the "god of this age" (2 Cor. 4:4), the "prince of the power of the air" (Eph. 2:2).

Every ruler needs subjects, and Satan is no different. In order to gain a following, Satan tempted the first human couple to join in his rebellion. God's instruction to Adam and Eve was clear. He said, "Of every tree of the garden you may freely eat; but of the tree of the knowledge of good and evil you shall not eat, for in the day you eat of it you shall surely die" (Gen. 2:17). Sadly, Adam and Eve were tempted by Satan to reject God's command. They chose the way of evil and ate of the fruit that was forbidden to them.

The effect on Adam and Eve was immediate and conclusive. For the first time in human history, fellowship with God was broken and the human couple was separated from God by their sins. This was spiritual death. In addition, both Adam and Eve and their descendants became subject to physical death. Paul summarizes the consequences of their sin in Romans 5:12, "Therefore, just as through one man sin entered the world, and death through sin, and so death spread to all people, because all sinned."

What a mess! God created a perfect world for the first human couple. But they followed Satan in rebelling against God. Now God's kingdom authority has been challenged. Humanity has fallen into sin. And the world, under Satan's sway, is in open rebellion against God.

Now this is where the story gets really good. Because of His love and grace, God has inaugurated a program to bring this sin marred creation back into the blessings of His glorious reign. Like a fine jewel with many bright facets, God's program to restore blessing to His creation has several aspects. God has determined to restore fallen humanity, reestablish His kingdom authority, and deal justly with sin. God's program of redemption, kingdom and judgment are three aspects of His ultimate plan to reverse the curse which came on this earth because of sin. Most of the story of the Bible can be understood as the outworking of these three aspects of God's marvelous plan.

Although God didn't have to, yet because of His infinite grace and love, He chose to redeem rebel people and provide a way of deliverance from the fate of spiritual death. The story of the Bible traces this program of redemption from the first announcement of God's plan (Gen. 3:15) to its culmination with the crucifixion of Jesus. God's plan of redemption is illustrated by the sacrifices brought to the Jerusalem temple. This plan is anticipated by the words of John the baptizer, "Behold, the Lamb of God who takes away the sins of the world!" (Jn. 1:29). God's plan of redemption is memorialized at the communion table (1 Cor. 11:23-26). The "good news" of the Bible is God's plan of redemption. As we read the Bible, we learn more of the details of this plan from Genesis through Revelation.

But God didn't stop there. A sovereign God cannot let His kingly authority be successfully challenged. To do so would be to demonstrate that the King is not really sovereign. So God set about a plan to reclaim His kingdom and reassert His sovereign authority here on this earth–the very place where it was challenged. God's Kingdom program is based on promises which were made to Abraham (Gen. 12:1-2) and David (2 Sam. 7:12-16). The kingdom program revealed through the promises and prophecies of God was announced by Jesus when he declared, "Repent, for the kingdom of heaven is at hand!" (Matt. 4:17). Although His kingdom offer was rejected by Israel, entrance into God's kingdom is possible today for any who will place themselves under the King's authority. And someday, the prophets predict, the kingdom rule of God will be fully and physically reestablished on this earth (Zech. 14:9).

There is one more aspect of God's plan which is traced through the story of the Bible. Every major project requires some "clean-up," and God's program is no exception. Because God is holy, He cannot look upon sin and rebellion with indifference. He must execute judgment on Satan and his followers and purge the earth of the effects of sin. Like God's plan of redemption, this program can be traced through the Bible from Genesis 3:15 to Revelation 22:3. The Apostle Peter wrote how this present earth, the place of Satan's rebellion, will be purged by fire in preparation for eternity. This judgment will remove all the effects of sin and the fall. Then the words of John in Revelation 22:3 will be fulfilled, "And there shall no longer be any curse."

Genesis begins with a curse because of sin. Revelation concludes with the removal of the effects of sin, bringing an end to the curse. This is God's plan for the ages–to reverse the curse.

Believers today are living between the first and second coming of Jesus under the blessings and provisions of the New Covenant. They are participating in God's kingdom, but are yet awaiting its full consummation. Someday the story of life on this earth will be over, but the story of God's people will go on as they enjoy their Heavenly Father's presence forever.

God's plan for the ages is revealed in the story of the Bible. He knows the end of the story as well as the beginning (Isa. 46:9-10). All of history and human existence is under His rule and divine design. As you read the Bible, keep the story in mind and look for evidences of God's plan. Most of the verses of the Bible relate to one of the three great themes introduced here: (1) His plan to redeem fallen humanity; (2) His plan to reassert His kingdom authority; and (3) His plan to judge rebellion and sin. This is the story of the Bible--the story of a glorious beginning, a devastating fall, a remarkable rescue, and an indescribable future. And it is all by God's grace and for His glory.

THE ESSENTIAL QUESTION FOR READERS:
WHERE'S JESUS?

On the day of His resurrection, Jesus met two of his disciples who were traveling along a road to the village of Emmaus. Strangely, they did not recognize their fellow-traveler and began telling him about the events which had recently taken place in Jerusalem–the arrest, crucifixion, and resurrection of Jesus. He responded with a mild rebuke, "O foolish men and slow of heart to believe in all that the prophets have spoken" (Luke 24:25). Luke then records, "And beginning with Moses and with all the prophets, He explained to them the things concerning Himself in all the Scriptures" (24:27). Readers might expect to find the story of Jesus revealed in the New Testament. Yet Jesus was telling the two Emmaus bound disciples that story of his life, death and resurrection could be found in the Hebrew Bible!

Someone has said, "In the Hebrew Bible, Jesus is predicted. In the Gospels Jesus is revealed. In the Book of Acts, Jesus is preached. In the epistles, Jesus is explained. And in the book of Revelation, Jesus is expected."

This is not to suggest that every chapter and verse of the Hebrew Bible is about Jesus. Take the prohibition in Exodus 23:19 for example, "You are not to boil a young goat in the milk of its mother." I am not proposing that the young goat represents Jesus and its mother is the virgin Mary! Nor would I want to suggest that the fate of Jephthah's daughter (Judges 11:30-40) contains a veiled reference to the death and resurrection of Jesus. On the other hand, there is abundant evidence that the central message of Scripture from Genesis to Malachi is about Jesus. While not every text in the Bible is *about* Jesus, I believe that every book of the Bible *points* to Jesus.

Jesus is the promised descendant of Eve (Gen. 3:15), who comes through the line of Abraham (Gen. 12:2-3) and David (2 Sam. 7:12-16), is born of a virgin (Isa. 7:14) in the village of Bethlehem (Mic. 5:2). According to the prophets He would suffer, die and be resurrected (Isaiah 52:13-53:12) to reconcile sinful humanity with a holy God.

We do not need to resort to unusual or questionable methods of Bible interpretation to discover that the overarching message of the Bible centers on the person and work of God's Promised One, Jesus. While not every biblical text reveals some truth about Jesus, we may safely say that the message of the Bible, from Genesis to Revelation, is about Jesus—His coming, His redemptive work, and His return and rule over all creation.

What we need to ask as we examine a biblical text is, "How does each little story advance the *big* story of God's purpose to save the human race through Jesus?" Jesus is the Prophet greater than Moses, the Priest greater than Aaron, and the King greater than David. So when we study the lives of these leaders in the Hebrew Bible we must understand them in the greater context of the coming of the One who completely and perfectly fulfills the offices of prophet, priest, and king.

I am discovering through my continuing study of Scripture that all the stories of the Bible contribute to telling the one *mega*-story—the story of God's gracious intention to save the fallen human race through His Son, Jesus Christ. John Calvin, one of the major theologians of the Protestant Reformation, said "The Scriptures should be read with the aim of finding Christ in them." As we study the books of the Bible, I invite you to join me in a search for Jesus, looking along the way for where and how He is revealed.

Luke records that after appearing to His disciples on the day of His resurrection, Jesus "opened their minds to understand the Scriptures" (Luke 24:45). May we experience a similar enlightenment by the illuminating ministry of the Holy Spirit as we search the Scriptures for Jesus.

CHAPTER ONE

The Torah
(Books of Moses)

Most of the books I read are divided into chapters. The chapters help me understand and follow the story line as it advances step by step. The Bible is different. Instead of being divided into chapters, the Bible is divided into books. But the sixty-six books of the Bible can be divided into two major sections—the Hebrew Bible and the New Testament. There are ten major sections of the complete Bible based on the literary form of the books and their content.

The Hebrew Bible:

The Torah	History Books	Wisdom Books	Minor Prophets	Major Prophets

The New Testament:

Gospels	Book of Acts	Paul's Epistles	General Epistles	Revelation

We will appreciate the story of the Bible better if we understand how each section of the Bible advances the story.

The first five books of the Bible form "chapter one." This section of Scripture is known as the Pentateuch, a Greek word meaning "five books." The Hebrew Bible refers to this section as the Torah, a Hebrew word that means "instruction." I prefer the Hebrew name because it says more about the content of this section. The Torah is God's "instruction." Here God reveals the beginnings of the human race, how humankind fell into sin, the consequences of sin, and what God has undertaken to restore His blessing on a creation cursed by sin.

The Torah also instructs us about God Himself. Here God reaches out His hand to humanity and says, "Here I AM" (Exodus 3:14). Then He proceeds to tell us about Himself. The first thing God wants us to know is that He is sovereign. This truth is revealed in Genesis by God's work of creation and His providential involvement in the lives of Abraham, Isaac and Jacob. God speaks and things happen; God commands and people obey; God promises and His promises are fulfilled. God is the King of His creation! He is sovereign over all.

Next, God wants us to know that He is the Savior of His people. God demonstrates this truth in Exodus by His work of delivering the people of Israel from bondage in Egypt. Moses and the Israelites left Egypt singing, "Yahweh is my strength and song, and He has become my salvation! (Exodus 15:2). The holiness of God is introduced in the next book, Leviticus. God declares to His people, "You shall be holy, for I the LORD your God am holy" (Leviticus 19:2). Leviticus reveals the sacrificial means of approaching a holy God and the kind of conduct a holy God expects of His people. The Lord instructed Israel to set aside special days and seasons as "holy convocations" to receive instruction in holiness and provide cleansing through the ritual of temple sacrifice.

The next thing God wanted to say about Himself in the Torah is that His holiness demands that sin and wickedness be judged by divine wrath. This is the focus of the book of Numbers. God's wrath is the natural expression of His holiness in the face of willful sin. Numbers also teaches that God's wrath may be propitiated or satisfied by the offering of a sacrifice or by intercessory prayer.

The other side of God's wrath is revealed in the last book of the Torah, Deuteronomy. Here we learn that since God has demonstrated His love through the deliverance of His people, the redeemed are obligated to demonstrate their love for God in return (Deuteronomy 6:5). This love is best expressed in terms of loyalty, service and obedience to God.

The Torah begins with humanity's sin and failure (Genesis 3), but throughout this section of the Bible we see evidence of God's gracious plan to redeem fallen humanity and restore blessing to the earth (Gen. 3:15, 12:2-3, Exod. 6:2-7, Lev. 26:3-5, Num. 23:20, 24:9, Deut. 30:1-6).

Many people are confused by the laws and regulations that fill the pages of the Torah. We should understand that these laws were never intended as a means of securing salvation. They were given to a people who had already experienced redemption from bondage and simply needed to know how to live and prosper as the people of God. The laws, or better "instructions," provide counsel and direction for a redeemed community who want to enjoy the fullness of God's blessing and avoid the devastating consequences of going their own way.

The Torah ends with the death of Moses which marks the end of a great era of the people of God. Now Joshua, a man "filled with the spirit of wisdom" (Deut. 34:9), assumes leadership of the nation. Joshua will bring us into the next chapter in the story of the Bible. But first, let's explore the five books of the Torah!

GENESIS

According to the psalm writer David, God has revealed Himself to people in two ways. First is His revelation in nature (Psa. 19:1-6). Without words or voice, all creation joyfully proclaims the existence of a glorious Creator. Second is God's revelation through His Word, the Bible (Psa. 19:7-11). The Word of God further reveals the character and attributes of God and explains how we can enjoy a personal relationship with Him.

The book of Genesis is the beginning of God's self-revelation through the Bible. In this book that the eternal Creator extends His hand into our times and says, "Hello. Let me introduce myself. I'd really like to get to know you."

The Book of Genesis not only introduces us to God. The book reveals something of God's plan for His creation. We discover in Genesis that God has a wonderful plan to bless His creation, the people of Israel, and to extend His blessing to all the nations of the earth.

God's plan for blessing His creation starts in Genesis and can be traced through all sixty-six books of the Bible. So Genesis is a great place to meet God and to discover His plan for world blessing.

What's the title?

The title, "Genesis," is the Greek word for "beginning." This title is quite appropriate since Genesis *is* the book of beginnings. Here we read of the beginnings of the world, the human race, and the Hebrew nation. Genesis also tells us of the beginnings of sin, suffering, death and the beginnings of God's plans to resolve these issues and restore blessing to His creation.

Who wrote it?

While Genesis is an anonymous work, many scholars believe that it was written by Moses. His education in pharaoh's court (Acts 7:22, Exod. 24:4) and acquaintance with the land of Egypt provided Moses with good background for writing the book.

The writers of the New Testament lend their support to the opinion that Moses wrote Genesis (Jn. 1:17, Matt. 9:7, Mk. 1:44, 7:10, 10:3, 12:26, Lk. 5:14, Acts 3:22, and 1 Cor. 9:9).

Affirming the Mosaic authorship of Genesis does not necessarily mean that Moses could not have gathered much of his material from other ancient sources.

When was it written?

Moses probably compiled and wrote Genesis during the forty years he spent with the people of Israel in the wilderness (1446-1406 B.C.) on their journey to Canaan.

What is the historical setting?

The book includes events from creation of the world to the death of Joseph in Egypt (1805 B.C.). Geographically, the events of the narrative took place in the Fertile Crescent which includes the valleys of the Tigris and Euphrates rivers in Mesopotamia, the land of Canaan, and the fertile region along the Nile River.

Taking 931 B.C. as the date of the division of Israel's monarchy into the Northern and Southern Kingdoms, we can calculate that the birth of Abraham took place around 2166 B.C. Dates for other key figures in Genesis may be calculated as follows:

Abraham	2166-1991	Lived 175 years
Isaac	2066-1886	Lived 180 years
Jacob	2006-1859	Lived 147 years
Joseph	1915-1805	Lived 110 years

Why was it written?

The purpose of Genesis is to preserve an accurate record of the beginnings of the human race and the Hebrew nation. In addition, the book tells of mankind's initial rebellion against God and the beginnings of His program to redeem His people and restore their blessing.

What's the theme?

The theme of Genesis is the "sovereignty (rule) of God"

over His people and all creation (Gen. 50:20).

What's it about?

Beginnings of the Human Race Chapters 1-11	Beginnings of the Hebrew Nation Chapters 12-50
Creation 1-2 Fall 3:1-6:4 Flood 6:5-11:32 New Beginnings 8:5-11:32	Life of Abraham 12:1-25:18 Life of Isaac 25:19-26:35 Life of Jacob 27-36 Life of Joseph 37-50

What does it teach us?

Genesis teaches that God rules over all creation and that His sovereign authority will be established over every area of rebellion. The sovereignty of God is seen in His act of creation (1:1-2:13), His regulation of man's existence (2:16-17), and his condemnation and judgment of mankind's sin (3:14-19). The sovereignty of God is also evidenced by God's destruction of the wicked world (7:21-23), His promise to Abraham (12:1-3), and His preservation of Abraham's offspring (22:1-9).

The story of Joseph contains one of the greatest lessons in the Bible on the sovereignty of God. The sale of Joseph into Egypt, his promotion to prime minister, and his provision for his family were all part of God's sovereign plan to preserve and provide for Joseph and his family.

What Joseph's brothers did was evil, but God used it for good (Gen. 50:20)! Amazingly, God can use the evil actions of evil people to accomplish something good. Now that's serious sovereignty!

Where's Jesus?

Where is Jesus in the book of Genesis? Jesus is the promised "seed" born of woman (Gen. 3:15), the descendant of Abraham through whom the world will be blessed (Gen. 12:3) and the "ruler" from the tribe of Judah (Gen. 49:10). You will also find Jesus in Genesis 22:8. Before being bound and placed upon the altar, Isaac asked his father Abraham, "Where is the lamb for the burnt offering?" Abraham replied, "God will provide for Himself the lamb for the burnt offering, my son."

That day on Mt. Moriah God provided a *ram* to sacrifice in place of Isaac. Two-thousand years later, Jesus came as "the lamb of God who takes away the sin of the world" (Jn. 1:29).

EXODUS

A birth is one of the most exciting events for any family. Birthdays are so special that we celebrate them annually with cards, presents, cake and ice cream. I would prefer that my own birthday be ignored. But in view of the sobering alternative, I'm glad to be still having them!

The book of Exodus is one of the most important books in the Old Testament because it celebrates the "birth" of the nation of Israel. The people of Israel were "born" as a nation through their travails in Egypt and the waters of the Red Sea. The book of Exodus goes on to record how the new nation was led by Moses to Mt. Sinai where they received the Law (Torah) and instruction on how to build the Tabernacle.

The exodus made Israel a nation with their own leader and laws. Just as the crucifixion of Jesus stands out as the key event in the New Testament, so the exodus from Egypt is the defining event for the people of Israel. And the Book of Exodus tells their great story!

What's the title?

The title of the book comes from the Greek translation of the Bible (the Septuagint) which named this book "Exodus" (a Greek word meaning "exit" or "departure"). This title captures the principle event of the book, Israel's *exit* from Egypt.

Who wrote it?

Exodus has traditionally been ascribed to Moses who names himself several times in connection with the Lord's command to write (17:14, 24:4, 34:27). The Mosaic authorship of Exodus is confirmed by the fact that Jesus attributes quotations from the book to Moses (Mark 7:10, 12:26).

When was it written?

Exodus was probably written shortly after Genesis during Israel's time in the wilderness (1446-1406 B.C.) after leaving Egypt.

What is the historical setting?

The date of the exodus is crucial to the historical setting of the book. According to 1 Kings 6:1 Solomon began to build the temple in the 4th year of his reign (966 B.C.), 480 years after the exodus. Thus, the date of the exodus may be calculated at 1446 B.C. (966 + 480). Although questioned by some scholars, this date has been confirmed by biblical and archaeological evidence.

The Hebrews sojourned in Egypt 430 years after Jacob's entrance into the land in 1876 B.C. (Exod. 12:40). For 200 years after Joseph's death (1805 B.C.) the Israelites lived in relative peace and prosperity. Then there arose a pharaoh, probably Ahmose I, founder of the 18 dynasty, who "knew not Joseph" (Exod. 1:8). Oppressive measures began to be carried out against the Hebrews (Exod. 1:22).

Why was it written?

The purpose of Exodus is to recount the birth of the nation of Israel which came about through the exodus from Egypt and the giving of the law at Mt. Sinai.

What's the theme?

The theme of Exodus is God's salvation (Exod. 15:2). God is the Savior and Deliverer of His people.

What's it about?

Bondage 1-12	Exodus 13-18	Law 19-24	Tabernacle 25-40
Suffering of the people 1-12 Preparation for Departure 3-11 First Passover 12	Miracle of the Exodus 13-15 Journey to Mount Sinai 16-18	Historical Setting 19 Ten Commands 20 Details and Applications 21-24	What to build 25-27 How to Worship 28-31 How Israel Obeyed 32-40

What does it teach us?

The book of Exodus teaches a great deal about God and His dealings with people. Through the first Passover, God revealed that redemption takes place through the offering of a substitute. On the night of Passover those under the sentence of death were delivered through the shed blood of the innocent lamb. The death of the Passover lamb anticipates Jesus, the Lamb of God, who gave His life in behalf of those under a death sentence because of sin (Rom. 5:12).

God's power, holiness and plan for redemption are highlighted in the book of Exodus. Through the exodus and deliverance of the people from Egypt, God revealed His *power*. Moses told the people, "Do not fear! Stand by and see the salvation of the LORD which He will accomplish for you today" (Exod. 14:13). Through the law given at Mt. Sinai, God revealed his *holiness*. And through the instructions about the Tabernacle, God gave His people a powerful illustration of His plan for *redemption* through His Promised One, the Messiah.

Where's Jesus?

If you read carefully Exodus 25-31, you'll find Jesus in God's instruction about the Tabernacle. The bronze altar in the court of the Tabernacle points to Jesus and His perfect sacrifice on the cross (Heb. 9:14). The laver illustrates Christ's provision for continual cleansing from sin (1 Jn. 1:9, Eph. 5:22-27). The lampstand in the tent of the Tabernacle points to Christ as the "light of the world" (Jn. 8:12, 9:5). The table of showbread typifies Christ, "the bread of life" (Jn. 6:35,48). The inner veil reminds that the sacrifice of Christ's own body provides a way of access to God (Heb. 10:20, Mk, 15:38). The incense altar illustrates Christ's present ministry of intercessory prayer (Heb. 7:25). Finally, the ark of the covenant, where the blood was applied on the Day of Atonement, reminds us of Christ's completed atonement at the cross (Heb. 9:5).

LEVITICUS

Leviticus is among the least read and least understood books of the Bible. The laws about sacrifice, priestly duties and ceremonial regulations seem so distant from our religious experience and western culture. We wonder why certain discharges from the body render a person "unclean" and others don't. And why is ritual cleansing necessary for a woman after an event as special as childbirth? This book just doesn't seem to be relevant for Christians living in the 21st century. Yet when we take a careful look, you will discover that the book of

Leviticus lays an important foundation for our understanding of God as the Holy One who desires that His people share in His holiness.

If you were going to write a Christian hymn, the book of Leviticus would probably not be the place you would turn for inspiration. But Leviticus must have a relevant message since Charles Wesley wrote *sixteen* hymns based on its texts! The book of Leviticus reminds us that personal holiness is essential, not optional, for those who desire to honor God.

What's the title?

The translators of the Septuagint gave the third book of the Torah the title "The Levitical Book" because of its emphasis on Levitical and priestly regulations. This comes into English (through the Latin Vulgate) as "Leviticus."

Who wrote it?

The author of Leviticus is not named. But the Lord repeatedly addresses Moses (1:1, 4:1, 6:1,8,19,24, 7:22) and he is the most likely person to have recorded these words. Jesus acknowledged the Mosaic authorship of Leviticus when He referred to the laws concerning cleansing from leprosy (Lev. 14:2-32) as that which "Moses commanded" (Matt. 8:4, Mk. 1:44).

When was it written?

Leviticus was probably written shortly after Exodus during Israel's wilderness wanderings (1446-1406 B.C.)

What is the historical setting?

The events and legislation of Leviticus have their geographical setting in the wilderness at the foot of Mount Sinai located in the southern region of the Sinai Peninsula. Mount Sinai has been traditionally identified with 7,363 foot Jebul

Musa where the Roman emperor Justinian built the monastery of St. Catherine around A.D. 527. The time period of the book extends from the setting up of the Tabernacle to the departure from Sinai about one month and twenty days later (Exod. 40:17, Num. 10:11) in the year 1445 B.C.

Why was it written?

Leviticus shows us that the way of access to God is by sacrifice, and that the way of fellowship with God is by separation from all that is contrary to God's holiness.

What's the theme?

The theme of Leviticus is the holiness of God (19:2) as indicated by the 90 occurrences of the term "holy" in the book.

What's it about?

The Sacrificial Means of Approaching God 1-17	The Separation of God's People 18-27
Law of Offerings and Sacrifices 1-7 Consecration of the Priests 8-10 Separation from Defilement 11-15 Day of Atonement 16 Law of the Altar 17	Practical Holiness for God's People 18-20 Priestly Holiness and Duties 21-22 Israel's Holy Convocations 23 Parenthetical Regulations 24 Regulations Concerning the Land 25-27

What does it teach us?

Leviticus teaches us about holiness. This concept is derived from the Hebrew *qodesh* and has the basic meaning of "separateness" (Lev. 20:26). Holiness is the opposite of *hol* ("profane"), meaning "not separate" or "common." That which is holy is marked off, separated, and withdrawn from ordinary use. When holiness means separation to God, a morally righteous being, the concept takes on the implication of moral purity-- conformity to God's righteous standards and statutes (Lev. 20:7-8).

Those who are associated with a holy God are called to be holy ("separated") even as God Himself is holy. How does someone become holy? *First*, people become holy based on new birth through faith in Christ. The Corinthian believers were "saints" by position (1 Cor. 1:2) even though they were struggling with some serious spiritual problems. *Second*, Christians are becoming holy through the process of growing in Christ-likeness. This is what sanctification is all about (Rom. 6:12-13). Finally, the process of growing in holiness will be complete when Christ returns and believers are glorified as He is (1 Jn. 3:2).

Where's Jesus?

You will find Jesus in Leviticus 16:20 where Moses records God's instruction to the High Priest about the Day of Atonement. "When he finishes atoning for the holy place, and the tent of meeting and the altar, he shall offer the live goat [scapegoat]" which was then released into the wilderness. Although the New Testament doesn't identify the scapegoat with Jesus, there is a clear parallel. The scapegoat was designated to carry away the sins of the people. This is exactly what Jesus did through His sacrifice on the cross (Heb. 9:13-14). The scapegoat offered on the Day of Atonement points us to Jesus, the Lamb of God.

NUMBERS

Have you ever started out on a long trip and before you have gone a hundred miles several members of the family have started grumbling? Being cramped up in a hot car with five other people for a day or two does put some stress on one's patience! But you can't turn back once you have started on a journey! And so you drive on trying to make the best of a bad situation.

That experience shares a lot in common with the book Moses wrote next. Numbers is the story of a grumbling people. They were just three days into their journey when the people began complaining. They complained about their desert diet of manna (11:4-6). They complained against Moses and Aaron (12:1-2, 14:1,36). They complained against the Lord (14:27-29).

By murmuring against the Lord the Israelites were breaking the covenant with God which they had promised to uphold. Their unrelenting murmuring was a major factor in the judgment which fell upon the generation which died outside the land.

What's the title?

The title "Arithmoi" was given to the book by the translators of the Septuagint because of the prominence of census figures in the book. The English title, "Numbers," is derived from the Latin Vulgate, "Numeri."

Who wrote it?

Only in Numbers 33:2 is there an indication that Moses recorded the details of the Israelite's journey reported here. But there are many references to that fact that God spoke these words to Moses (1:1, 2:1, 3:5,14,40), and it is most likely that Moses himself recorded this revelation. Local color, authentic wilderness background, and antiquity of the material lends support to the Mosaic authorship of Numbers.

When was it written?

Numbers was written or at least completed after the death of Aaron (20:28) which took place during the fortieth year after the exodus (33:38-39) or 1407 B.C.

What is the historical setting?

There are four geographical settings for the events recorded in the book of Numbers:

<u>At Sinai</u>. The book begins with the numbering of the people at Sinai just one month after the completion of the Tabernacle (Num. 1:1, Exod. 40:17), Iyyar (April-May) 1, 1445 B.C.

<u>To Kadesh-barnea</u>. Twenty days later Israel broke camp (10:11) and began following the pillar of cloud north in the direction of Canaan to Kadesh-barnea (13:26).

<u>In the Wilderness</u>. The refusal of Israel to enter the land (13-14) resulted in the judgment of 37 1/2 years of fruitless wandering in the Sinai desert (15-19).

<u>To Transjordan</u>. After the old generation had died off, the children of Israel journeyed to the plains of Moab near the Jordan River where they received the final instruction from Moses before their entrance into the land.

Why was it written?

First, Numbers was written to give an account of the wilderness experience of Israel. Secondly, the book was intended to demonstrate that God's love for His people did not preclude severe judgment upon sin, apostasy, and rebellion.

What's the theme?

The theological theme of Numbers is the wrath of God. While God's love never ceases, there comes a point when His holiness must respond to sin and disobedience with an expression of divine judgment (Num. 11:1-3). The wrath of God is not a popular message in today's post-Christian culture, but it is a thoroughly biblical one.

What does it teach us?

The wrath of God is emphasized and illustrated throughout Numbers. God's wrath is the natural expression of His holiness as He interacts with the willful sin and rebellion of mankind (1:53, 11:1,10,33, 12:9). Numbers teaches that Yahweh's wrath may be turned away from His people by the offer of a sacrifice (16:46-47) or through intercessory prayer (14:11-20).

The book of Numbers also teaches us that our Lord is a promise keeping God. God's faithfulness to His promise to give Abraham a land, nation and blessing (Gen. 12:1-3) is illustrated throughout the book. In spite of the fact that God must judge sinful and disobedient people, He anticipates the day when they will enter the promised land (15:1). The numbering of the people in chapters 1 and 26 illustrate the fact that God fulfilled His promise to make Israel a great nation. And the story of Balaam teaches that God is determined to bless His people in spite of the hostilities of an unbelieving world.

What's it about?

Preparation at Sinai 1-10	Wandering in the Desert 11-20	Advance to the Land 21-36
Israel's Numbering 1-4 Israel's Purity 5-6 Israel's Worship 7:1-9:14 Israel's Advance 9:15-10:36	Israel's Defection and God's Rejection 11-14 Israel's Years of Fruitless Wanderings 15-20	Journey to Moab 21-25 Second Census 26-30 Preparations to Enter Canaan 31-35

Where's Jesus?

We can find Jesus in Numbers 20:11, "Then Moses lifted up his hand and struck the rock twice with his rod; and water came forth abundantly, and the congregation and their beasts drank." This was the second time in the wilderness that God provided water from a rock. Paul writes in 1 Corinthians 10:4 that the "rock" which quenched the thirst of the Israelites in the wilderness was none other than Christ! Jesus is our source of spiritual refreshment in a dry and desolate land!

DEUTERONOMY

It is not surprising that of the English poets, William Shakespeare is reputed to be the most frequently quoted. But you will probably be surprised to learn that the obscure Book of Deuteronomy is one of the most widely quoted books in the Bible! It is quoted 356 times in later Old Testament books and 80 times in the New Testament. Jesus quoted Deuteronomy to confirm His messiahship, summarize the law, and refute the devil.

Besides being noted for its quotations, the book of Deuteronomy is a richly devotional book, encouraging believers to love God with all their hearts, fear the Lord, and keep His commandments. It is here that we find the ancient confession of God's people, the *Sh'ma,* "Hear O, Israel! The LORD is our God, the LORD alone!" (Deut. 6:4).

What's the title?

The title Deuteronomy is a Greek word which means "second law." The book was given this name based on the words in Deuteronomy 17:18 which are more accurately rendered "a copy of the law" rather than "second law." Deuteronomy is not really a second law but a *restatement* of the law for the benefit of those who were children at Mt. Sinai when the law was first given.

Who wrote it?

The Mosaic authorship of Deuteronomy is affirmed by Deut. 31:9 which states, "Moses wrote this law." The Jews of Jesus' day believed that Moses wrote Deuteronomy (Matt. 22:24, Mark 10:3-4, 12:19), and Jesus Himself refers to Deut. 24:1-4 as the teaching of Moses (Matt. 19:7-8). Chapter 34, the account of Moses' death, may have been written by Joshua.

When was it written?

Deuteronomy was written by Moses in the fortieth year after the exodus from Egypt. The work was probably completed just before the entrance of the second generation of Israelites into the land and Moses' death on Mount Nebo (1406 B.C.)

What is the historical setting?

Deuteronomy contains a restatement of the law for the generation of Israelites who were children at Mt. Sinai. It was given by Moses in the plains of Moab across the Jordan River from Jericho (Deut. 1:5, Num. 36:13) in the fortieth year since the exodus. The giving of the law by Moses was followed by his death and thirty days of mourning for the great leader.

Why was it written?

Deuteronomy was written to (1) remind the second generation of their redemption out of Egypt and of God's discipline in the wilderness, (2) restate the law given at Mt. Sinai for the benefit of the new generation, and (3) call God's people to keep the covenant, emphasizing the blessings of obedience and consequences of disobedience.

What's the theme?

The theme of Deuteronomy is its restatement of the law

for the new generation. Its theological emphasis is the love of God for Israel (Deut. 7:7-8).

What does it teach us?

It has been said that the book of Deuteronomy contains more about the love of God than the Gospel of John! Certainly, the love of God is prominent in Deuteronomy. The book presents God's love for His people and the imperative necessity of Israel's love for God in return.

A key passage on the love of God is found in Deut. 7:7-11. Here we discover that God's love is an undeserved, selective affection by which He binds Himself to His people. This binding commitment then compels Him to reach out in love to His people and redeem them from bondage.

Because God has demonstrated His love in the act of redemption, the redeemed are thus obligated to demonstrate their love for God in return (Deut. 6:5, 10:12, 11:1,13,22). Our love for God should involve our heart, our soul and our might-- our total being! Such love is best expressed not so much by words, but by loyalty, service and obedience.

The book of Deuteronomy makes it clear that God's relationship with His people under the Old Covenant was one of *love* rather than legalism. In light of this background, the words of Jesus have even greater significance, "If you love me, you will keep my commandments" (John 14:15).

What's it about?

Historical Setting 1:1-5	Reminders of the Past 1:6-4:49	Guidelines for Living 5-26	Blessings of Obedience 27-30	Moses' last words 31-34

Where's Jesus?

If you are looking for Jesus, you will find Him in Deuteronomy 18:15 where Moses declares, "The LORD your God will raise up for you a prophet like me from among you, from your countrymen, you shall listen to him." The apostle Peter understood the "prophet" mentioned here to refer to Jesus (Acts 3:22). Like Moses, Jesus was a prophet or a "spokesman" for God. Stephen the evangelist acknowledged in his witness to the high priest and leaders of Israel that Jesus was the prophet whose coming Moses had foretold (Acts 7:37).

At the completion of their reading of Deuteronomy, a Jewish congregation exclaims, "Be strong, be strong, and let us strengthen one another." They are saying one another, "be strong and encourage each other to obey the teachings of the Torah." Having read the last verses of Deuteronomy, they roll the Hebrew scroll back to Genesis and start reading the Torah again.

CHAPTER TWO

The Historical Books

The historical books cover about one-thousand years of Israel's history, beginning with the conquest of Canaan and ending with the return from Babylonian captivity. Israel's conquest of Canaan was the first step in experiencing the fulfillment of God's promise to give His people a land. Like so many blessings in the Bible, the land was a gift, but it had to be received by faith. The conquest of Canaan was not so much a demonstration of Israel's military prowess, but of God's grace and faithfulness to His promise.

You would expect that entering into the Promised Land would be the beginning of a time of great blessing for the people of Israel. But the book of Judges shows how the people of Israel failed to be the distinctive people God intended them to be. Instead of worshiping their true God and deliverer, they turned aside to worship the Canaanite deities. Idolatry ran rampant during the period of the judges and the people of Israel experienced the devastating consequences of their foolish disobedience. But God remained faithful to Israel and raised up judges to lead and deliver them when the people repented.

The period of the judges is followed by the Israelite monarchy during which God ruled His people through his chosen representatives, the kings. The monarchy began around 1050 B.C. when God directed Samuel to anoint Saul as Israel's first monarch. Saul was followed by David, and David by Solomon.

At the end of Solomon's forty-year reign, the northern tribes broke off from Judah and Benjamin and the Israelites entered into a period of divided rule. David's descendants continued ruling in the south. Rule over the northern tribes was chaotic as one ruler after another usurped the throne, was eventually overthrown and then replaced by another.

The northern kingdom of Israel eventually succumbed to the Assyrians in 722 B.C. The southern kingdom of Judah fell to the Babylonians in 586 B.C. The history of the monarchy is the story of sin and failure. It is also the story of God's faithfulness to the promise He had made to the line of David (2 Samuel 7:12-16). Just as God had promised, the dynasty of David was preserved.

The period of the monarchy was followed by seventy years of Babylonian captivity. During this time, the people of God experienced the just consequences of disobeying God and breaking their covenant commitment. But God never lost sight of His people during their seventy-year captivity. The book of Esther illustrates how God protected and preserved the Jewish people during their time of exile. And once again, God was faithful and brought His people back to their homeland just as He had promised (Jeremiah 29:10).

In 537 B.C. Cyrus, the new king of Persia, gave authorization for the Jews to return to Jerusalem and rebuild their holy Temple. The books of Ezra and Nehemiah tell the exciting story of the return to Judah and reestablishment of a Jewish presence in the Promised Land.

JOSHUA

Although I have not been in the military, I deeply appreciate the sacrifices made by those serving in our armed forces to ensure the freedoms that Americans enjoy today. I drive my restored WWII jeeps in Veterans' Day parades. I salute my dad, my cousins, my son and all those soldiers, sailors and flyers who have served and are serving our country.

The book of Joshua is of particular interest to me because it records the military conquest of Canaan, bringing to reality God's promise to give Israel a national homeland. But while much of the book deals with Israel's military conquest of the land, we discover in Joshua that the victories Israel experienced were not due so much to their military superiority, but to the power and presence of God. The narrative makes it clear that the credit for the conquest belongs not to the Israelite soldiers, but to God alone (Josh. 21:44, 23:3,9-10).

What's the title?

The book is named for its principal character, Joshua, Moses' successor. Joshua's name was originally Hoshea (Num. 13:16), meaning "salvation," but Moses changed his name to Joshua meaning "Yahweh is salvation."

Who wrote it?

While Joshua is an anonymous work, it is reasonable to conclude that is was composed by Joshua. First, there are intimate biographical details given which only Joshua could have known. Second, the first person plural occurs in 5:1,6 which indicates that the author was an eyewitness who had participated in the events. Third, Joshua wrote his own farewell address (24:26), and this would suggest that he probably wrote the whole book as well. Later editorial work is evidenced by the inclusion of events which occurred after Joshua's death (24:29-31, 15:13-17, 19:47).

When was it written?

Evidence of an early date of writing is seen in the reference to Canaanite cities by their early, archaic names (15:9,13,49). In addition, the references to Sidon (13:4-6, 19:28) suggests a time before the twelfth century B.C. when Tyre began gaining prominence.

If Joshua was about the age of his brother Caleb, who was 40 years old at the time of the spy mission into Canaan (1445 B.C.), then he would have died about 1375 B.C. being 110 years old (24:29). The book was probably written just prior to Joshua's death and edited shortly thereafter.

What is the historical setting?

The events of the book cover about 31 years from the beginning of the conquest (1406 B.C.) to the death of Joshua about 1375 B.C. The crossing of the Jordan took place in the spring of the year (3:15), 1406 B.C.

The conquest of Canaan took approximately 7 years to complete. Caleb was 40 at the time the spies were sent into the land (1445 B.C.) and 85 at the time of Joshua's division of the land (14:7-10). So the final division was around 1400 B.C., 6 or 7 years after the 1406 B.C. entrance into the land. The elders of Israel served as leaders and ruled the land until around 1375 B.C. (Josh. 24:31).

What's the purpose?

Joshua was written to record how the Israelites ultimately conquered and occupied the Promised Land (11:23), demonstrating God's faithfulness to His covenant promises (Deut. 9:5).

What's the theme?

The book of Joshua shows how God's people can overcome the world and take possession of their inheritance through faith in Yahweh. The theme is the venture and victory of faith (1:8).

What does it teach us?

The book of Joshua is the culmination of God's covenant promise to give Abraham's descendants a land--the land of Israel (Gen. 12:1, 13:15, 17:8). The provision of a land demonstrates God's faithfulness to His covenant with the patriarchs and people of Israel. Joshua 11:23 sums up this message well, "So Joshua took the whole land, according to all that the LORD had spoken to Moses" (Josh. 11:23). Later

Joshua acknowledged, "Not one of the good promises which the LORD had made to the house of Israel failed; all came to pass" (Josh. 21:45). The book of Joshua emphasizes God's faithfulness to accomplish all that He had promised His people.

What's it about?

Conquering the Land 1-12	Dividing the Inheritance 13-21	Final Days of Joshua 23-24
Entering the Land 1-5 Central Conquest 6-9 Southern Conquest 10 Northern Conquest 11:1-15 Reviewing the Conquest 11:16-12:24	Distributing the Land 13-21 Controversy with the Transjordan Tribes 22	Joshua's Farewell 23 Covenant Renewal at Shechem 24

Where's Jesus?

You will find Jesus in Joshua 5:14 where Joshua encountered a man with a drawn sword who announced, "I indeed come now as captain of the host of the LORD." Joshua immediately fell on his face before this figure and asked, "What has my Lord to say to his servant?"

Most Christian commentators agree that the "captain of the LORD's host" was Jesus who temporarily took on human form to reveal Himself to Joshua. While Jesus was born in Bethlehem, His encounter with Joshua before the conquest reflects His eternal existence (Jn. 1:30; 8:58)..

JUDGES

Have you ever started out on a family outing only to have a well-planned and long anticipated event turn into utter chaos? First, someone gets sick and doesn't get the window down in time. Next, someone urgently needs the bathroom and the next rest stop is 60 miles away. Some kind of car trouble usually follows. As the children began to quarrel, you begin wondering, "Why did we ever think this was going to be fun?"

The book of Judges reminds us that things don't always go as planned. Under the leadership of Joshua, the Israelites conquered the Promised Land. And you would think that this would mark the beginning of a period of great blessing for Israel.

Wrong! Within a very short time the Israelites were in a worse state of bondage than they had experienced in Egypt! And it was all because of their own sinful actions.

The book of judges dramatically illustrates Proverbs 14:34, "Righteousness exalts a nation, but sin is a disgrace to any people."

What's the title?

The title of the book is taken from the Hebrew term *shophetim* ("judges") used to describe the Spirit empowered deliverers who gave leadership to the tribes of Israel before the rise of the monarchy.

Who wrote it?

There is no clear indication from the book itself as to the identity of the author. But Jewish tradition attributes the book to Samuel. Internal evidence would suggest that if the book wasn't written by Samuel, it was probably written by one of his contemporaries.

When was it written?

The evidence suggests that Judges was written sometime during the early monarchy. First, the Jebusites were still living in Jerusalem, 1:21, cf. 2 Sam. 5:4-7. Second, the Canaanites were still living in Gezer, 1:29, cf. 1 Kings 9:16. Third, Sidon, rather than Tyre, was the chief city of Phoenicia, 3:3. Fourth, the references to the absence of a king (17:6, 18:1, 21:25) point to a time when the monarchy was being regarded as a blessing.

What is the historical setting?

After the death of Joshua (c. 1375 B.C.), life in Israel became increasingly chaotic due to the failure to drive out the Canaanites, the people's involvement in Canaanite worship, and the attacks of foreign oppressors. This period was characterized by religious, political, and moral chaos, as indicated by the key verse, "In those days there was no king in Israel; everyone did what was right in his own eyes" (17:6, 21:25).

In response to their prayers for deliverance, God raised up judges to function in both a military and supervisory role in Israel (2:16, 3:9,15). If all the terms of service performed by the judges are added together, they total 410 years. This is about 85 years too long to fit between the conquest and the monarchy. It is likely that some of the judges were contemporaneous (10:1-5,7), ruling over different parts of the country at the same time. The period of the judges covers about 325 years, from 1375 to 1050 B.C.

Why was it written?

Judges was written to record the history of Israel's failure, thus demonstrating why the nation was not blessed by God during this period.

What's the theme?

Apostasy and idolatry are inevitably followed by chastening from the Lord. This theme is illustrated through the book by seven cycles of relapse into sin, ruin, repentance, and restoration followed by a period of rest (2:16-19).

What does it teach us?

The book of Judges teaches an important truth about God. His character is clearly revealed through his relationship with the people of Israel. God is seen to be faithful to His covenant promise while the people of Israel are unfaithful to Him and turning to false gods (2:1-2). God's righteous wrath is seen in His judgments on His disobedient and rebellious people (2:12,20, 3:8).

God's mercy and patience are evidenced throughout the book as He raises up judges and provides deliverance for the people when they cry out to Him (2:18, 3:9,15, 4:3, 6:6).

The book of Judges also teaches us about the importance of repentance. When the people did evil, God disciplined them by bringing plunderers into the land. After a time of misery and suffering, they would "return" to the Lord. Then he would raise up a judge to bring deliverance and restore blessing.

The cycles of failure, followed by repentance and restoration, are used to highlight the doctrine of repentance (see also Deut. 30:1-10 where the catchword "return" is used three times).

Repentance is a genuine change of the heart and mind that leads to a change in conduct. This change of heart is exemplified by the Thessalonians who "turned to God from idols to serve a living and true God" (1 Thess. 1:9). Such a turnaround is the prerequisite for any new work and blessing after a time of spiritual failure.

What's it about?

Causes of Israel's Apostasy 1:1-3:4	Cycles of Israel's Apostasy 3:5-16:31	Culmination of Israel's Apostasy 17-21
Military Failure: Incomplete Occupation 1:1-2:5 *Religious Failure*: Spiritual Apostasy 2:6-3:4	Seven Cycles of Relapse, Ruin, Repentance, Restoration and Rest	Idolatry of Micah and the Danites 17-18 Atrocity at Gibeah 19 War on Benjamin 20-21

Where's Jesus?

It is not easy to find Jesus in the Book of Judges, but I think He is revealed in the person who appeared to Gideon as "the Angel of the Lord" (Judges 6:11-24). This figure is identified as "the LORD" (6:14). As in Joshua 5:14, most scholars understand "the Angel of the Lord" to refer to God, specifically Jesus Christ before His incarnation and birth in Bethlehem. Manoah, the father of Samson, had a similar encounter with the Angel of the Lord and feared that he would die because he had "seen God" (13:21-22).

RUTH

Everyone enjoys a love story. My all-time favorite is "The Princess Bride," a story of how *true love* endures and prevails over dangers, villains, and even death. The book of Ruth is a love story–a true romance. America's best known radio preacher, J. Vernon McGee called it God's great "Romance of

Redemption." But more than a romantic story, the book illustrates God's love for us and what Jesus went through to provide our redemption.

The book of Ruth is the bright spot in the spiritually dark and dreary period of the judges. It is like the breath of fresh air that provides such relief after having to visit a long neglected outhouse. The book illustrates the fact that no matter how bad things get, there is always a place where goodness and godliness prevail.

What's the title?

The title of the book is taken from the name of the principle character, Ruth, a Moabite immigrant to Israel who became the great-grandmother of King David.

Who wrote it?

Although the book is anonymous, Jewish tradition recorded in the Talmud attributes the book to Samuel (<u>Baba Bathra</u> 14b). This is unlikely, however, since the concluding genealogy implies that David was well known at the time of writing. While it is possible that the genealogy was added sometime after the time of Samuel, we must conclude that the author of the Book of Ruth remains unknown.

When was it written?

The book appears to have been written during David's reign (1010-970 B.C.). It could not have been written earlier than the time of King David since he is mentioned by name (4:22), unless the genealogy was added later. Had the book been written after the time of David, his famous son Solomon would have probably been listed among Ruth's descendants.

What is the historical setting?

The events of the book transpired sometime during the

period of the judges (1375-1050 B.C.). This was a time of political, religious, and moral chaos (Judg. 21:25). The political chaos of this period is seen in the seven cycles of apostasy which resulted in Israelite oppression by foreign powers. The religious chaos is reflected in the person of Micah who set up his own house priest instead of going to worship at Shiloh (Judg. 17:5-13). The moral chaos is illustrated in the homosexuality, degeneracy, and abuse of the Levite's concubine recorded in Judges 19. The book of Ruth is an oasis of fidelity in a time of idolatry, sin, and infidelity.

Why was it written?

The book was written to document the providential workings of God in the ancestry of David which accounted for the non-Israelite in his family line. The book was also intended to provide a beautiful illustration of the biblical concept of redemption.

What's the theme?

The book of Ruth reveals that redemption requires a kinsman-redeemer (3:13).

What does it teach us?

Ruth is a little book, but it teaches some great truths about how God's people should regard and respond to the law. The story of Ruth and her entrance into the ancestry of David elevates the place of the spirit of the law over the letter of the law. The letter of the law said that the widow and foreigner could glean in the fields (Lev. 19:9-10). But Boaz went far beyond what the letter of the law required when he invited Ruth to glean among the sheaves, even requiring the workers to drop grain for her (2:15,16).

Again, the letter of the law said that no Moabite could enter the assembly of Yahweh, nor any of his descendants, even to the tenth generation (Deut. 23:3). David, however, was the third generation descendant of Ruth. Yet he became king of Israel, built an altar, and sacrificed on the altar to God (2 Sam. 24:25). Through God's grace, the spirit of the law was elevated over the letter of the law, allowing David to serve as king!

While the Bible's moral precepts are absolute and must never be compromised, the book of Ruth illustrates a legitimate exception to Israel's ceremonial regulations based on faith, love and service for God. Jesus affirms this same principle when responding to the Pharisees who accused His disciples of breaking the Sabbath (Matt. 12:1-8). The book of Ruth teaches that when it comes to the ceremonial regulations given to Israel, God is more concerned with the spirit than the letter. He clearly values the attitude of the heart worship more than legalistic adherence to tradition and ceremony.

What's it about?

Ruth's Choice for Naomi	Ruth's Chance to Glean	Ruth's Claim on a Kinsman	Ruth's Conception of Obed
1	2	3	4

Where's Jesus?

Jesus can be found in the person of Boaz who functioned as Ruth's kinsman-redeemer (2:1, 2:20, 3:2). The qualifications and function of the kinsman-redeemer are demonstrated by Boaz who illustrates the person and work of Jesus Christ. *First*, the kinsman-redeemer had to be a blood relative to have the right of redemption, even as Christ was a blood relative of mankind through the virgin birth (Jn. 1:14, 1 Tim. 2:15). *Second*, the kinsman-redeemer had to have the resources to accomplish redemption, even as Christ had the resource of His own precious blood (1 Pet. 1:18-19). *Third*, the kinsman-redeemer had to have the resolve to redeem, just as

Jesus resolved to lay down his life for sinful humanity (Mk. 10:45).

SAMUEL

I owe my life to my godly, praying mother. When I was stricken with polio at the age of 5, she prayed through that first painful night asking God to let me live. I am here today because God answered my mother's prayer.

The prophet Samuel owed his existence to the prayers of his once barren mother, Hannah. Before Samuel was born Hannah poured out her heart before the Lord asking that He would give her a son. God answered her prayer and gave her a son who became a prophet and judge in Israel.

What I appreciate most about Samuel is that, like his mother, he was a man of fervent prayer. Again and again we see him interceding in behalf of his people and leading them to prayer (1 Sam. 7:5-8, 12:23, 15:11). I suspect that Samuel learned of the importance of prayer from his godly mother (1 Sam. 1:15, 2:1-10). Samuel's words to the people of Israel reflect what he regarded as his top ministry priority: "Moreover, as for me, far be it from me that I should sin against the LORD by ceasing to pray for you" (1 Sam. 12:23).

What's the title?

The books of First and Second Samuel were originally one book. The two-fold division was first introduced about the time of Martin Luther by the Venetian printer, Daniel Bomberg, in his first edition of the Hebrew Bible (1516). The book is named for Samuel, the principal character of the early narratives.

Who wrote it?

While the Book of Samuel is anonymous, Jewish tradition attributes 1 Sam. 1-25 to Samuel. The rest of the book may have been composed by Nathan and Gad, as perhaps indicated in 1 Chron. 29:29.

When was it written?

There are indications that parts of the book would have been written after the death of Samuel (1 Sam. 25:1, 28:13) and after the division of the kingdom (1 Sam. 27:6). Since the author seems to be ignorant of the fall of Samaria in 722 B.C., it is reasonable to date the book between 931 and 722 B.C.

What is the historical setting?

The events of the book of Samuel cover the period from the ministry of Eli to the close of David's reign. Samuel is the central character of the early narratives of the book. He was the last of the judges and the first of a series of great prophets who ministered in Israel. His date of birth may be determined by the fact that he had sons old enough to be judges in Beersheba (1 Sam. 8:1-2) before Saul began to reign in 1050 B.C. This places Samuel's birth around 1100 B.C.

Samuel had the privilege of anointing the first two rulers of Israel, Saul and David. Taking 931 B.C. as the date of the division of the kingdom, the following dates for Israel's first kings may be calculated:

Saul	40 years (Acts 13:21)	1050-1010 B.C.
David	40 years (2 Sam. 5:4)	1010-970 B.C.

Gibeah (Tell el-Ful), several miles north of Jerusalem, was Saul's fortress and capital. David reigned seven-and-a-half years in Hebron before he established his capital in Jerusalem after being appointed king over all Israel (2 Sam. 5:3-5).

Why was it written?

The book provides an official account of the ministry of Samuel along with the rise and development of the monarchy.

The book was written to show the sovereignty of God as He raises up, commands, and removes the leaders of Israel.

What's the theme?

The theme of the books of Samuel is the establishment of the kingdom of Israel (1 Sam. 8:22).

What's it about?

First Samuel	Second Samuel
Ministry of Samuel 1-7 Reign of Saul 8-15 Rise of David 16-31	Triumphs of David 1-10 Troubles of David 11-20 End of David's Career 21-24

What does it teach?

The Book of Samuel introduces one of the great themes of the Bible--the theocracy. A "theocracy" is a government in which God rules as supreme monarch. God's program to manifest His sovereign rule on earth may be called the "theocratic kingdom."

In a theocracy, God rules, but He does so through divinely chosen representatives who speak and act for Him. The theocratic kingdom of God demonstrates God's universal sovereignty as he sets up (1 Sam. 9:16-17), commands (1 Sam. 15:2-3) and deposes (1 Sam. 15:26-28) the rulers of Israel.

The theme of God's theocratic kingdom is advanced in 2 Samuel 7:12-16 where the Lord announced to David that he would have a son who would succeed him and build God's temple. God promised David that although his son's sins would justify chastening, the Davidic dynasty would not terminate as did Saul's. David's line would endure. God said, "And your house and your kingdom shall endure before Me forever; your throne shall be established forever" (2 Sam. 7:16).

This promise, known as the "Davidic Covenant," assures David and his descendants of an eternal house, an eternal throne, and an eternal kingdom. It guarantees that the right to rule over Israel will always belong to one of David's descendants.

The implications of the Davidic Covenant are extremely significant. The promise means that Israel must be preserved as a nation and that one of David's descendants must someday reign over an earthly, eternal kingdom. The Davidic Covenant is the theological foundation for the belief that God's kingdom will one day be literally and physically established on earth.

Where's Jesus?

You will find Jesus in the promise God gave David in 2 Samuel 7:16. God promised that one of David's descendants would rule over an earthly kingdom forever. When the angel Gabriel told Mary that she would bear a son, she was also told that her son would be the heir to the throne of David! Gabriel announced, "He will be great and be called the Son of the Most High; and the Lord God will give Him the throne of His father David; and He will reign over the house of Jacob forever, and His kingdom will have no end" (Lk. 1:32-33). Jesus is the Davidic descendant who will rule God's earthly kingdom forever!

KINGS

Have you ever looked back and wondered how things might have turned out if you had done something differently? I recall the cold January morning when I was riding my bicycle and turned right instead of going straight. Either way would take me home, but I chose to turn right. Making a sharp turn I hit a patch of ice and landed on the pavement breaking my hip. Decisions which may seem rather insignificant at the time can often be critical turning points.

Reflecting on Israel's monarchy, I wonder how differently things might have turned out if the kings had followed the simple instructions in Deuteronomy 17. God commanded the rulers of His people to write for themselves a personal copy of the law so that they might read and obey it. There is no indication that any of Israel's kings did what God instructed. What a difference their obedience in this matter might have made!

What's the title?

The Hebrew title for this book is simply *Melekim* or "Kings." Like the books of Samuel, it was originally one book in the Hebrew Bible.

Who wrote it?

Jewish tradition recorded in the Talmud asserts that Jeremiah was the author of Kings. Since the author writes from a consistently prophetic standpoint and is a man of literary ability, the tradition may be accurate. Jeremiah, or perhaps one of his contemporaries, probably authored the book.

When was it written?

The author drew material from written sources dating from as early as the reign of Solomon (1 Kings 11:41). Events recorded in the 2 Kings 25 would indicate that the writing was completed after the fall of Jerusalem (586 B.C.) and release of Jehoiachin (560 B.C.). The book of Kings was probably written late in the monarchy and completed around 560 B.C.

What is the historical setting?

Kings contains a record of the kings of Israel and Judah

from the death of David (970 B.C.) to the destruction of Jerusalem in 586 B.C. This was a time of great growth and development for the monarchy politically. Saul had fashioned the tribes of Israel into a nation. Through alliances and military actions, David strengthened the nation and established his capital in Jerusalem. When David died in 970 B.C., Solomon inherited a kingdom.

Sadly, what began as a united kingdom divided into two kingdoms in 931 B.C. after King Solomon's death. The division of the monarchy constituted God's discipline on Solomon (1 Kings 11:31-33) but the revolt of the ten northern tribes was precipitated by Rehoboam's unwillingness to lift the heavy tax burden his father Solomon had placed on the people (1 Kings 12:1-15). The Northern Kingdom of Israel established its capital at Samaria and continued until 722 B.C. when it was crushed by the Assyrians and the Israelites exiled. The Southern Kingdom of Judah survived the Assyrian onslaught, but succumbed to the Babylonians in 586 B.C.

On the international scene, the early part of the monarchy was paralleled by the growth of the great Assyrian Empire (c. 900-612 B.C). But with the decline of the Assyrian Empire, Babylon inherited most of the Assyrian territory. The Babylonian Empire began with the alliance of the Medes and the Babylonians in 626 B.C. After overthrowing Assyria and defeating Egypt at Carchemish in 605 B.C., Nebuchadnezzar became the undisputed ruler of the eastern Mediterranean world. Babylonian rule ended in 539 B.C. when Cyrus captured the city of Babylon.

Religiously, the period began with the construction of the Solomonic temple, but idolatry soon became prominent among both the rulers and people. Jeroboam instituted golden calf worship in the Northern Kingdom and this idolatry continued in the reigns of his successors. Judah had 19 kings, eight of which were good. Israel had 19 kings also, but all of them were evil!

Why was it written?

The book of Kings was written (1) to record the history of the monarchy from Solomon to the Babylonian captivity, and (2) to show how each ruler functioned in relationship to God and his covenant responsibilities. Each ruler is judged not on the basis of political accomplishments, but on religious and spiritual grounds. The intent is to present Israel's history from a divine perspective.

What's the theme?

The theme of Kings is the blessings of obeying God and the consequences of disobedience (1 Kings 9:4-9).

What's it about?

United Kingdom Under Solomon 1Kings 1-11	Divided Kingdoms of Israel and Judah 1 Kings 12 - 2 Kings 17	Solitary Kingdom of Judah 2 Kings 18-25
Sol's Kingdom 1-4 Sol's Temple 5-9 Sol's Splendor 10 Sol's Decline 11	Conflict 1 K 12:1-16:28 Alliance 1 K 16:29-2 K 11:16 Independence 2 K 11:17-15:26 Assyrian Domination 2 Kings 15:27-17:41	Assyrian Domination 2 K 18-21 Egyptian Domination 2 K 22-23 Babylonian Domination 2 K 24-25

What does it teach us?

The primary teaching of the book of Kings is that violating the stipulations of the Mosaic Covenant (the law) has severe consequences! The author makes is clear that the division of the kingdom, the destruction and exile of the Northern Kingdom by Assyria, and the destruction and exile of the Southern Kingdom by Babylon were the direct results of forsaking God and His covenant (1 Kings 11:11,31-33, 2 Kings 17:7-18, 21:10-15, 23:27).

The exile should not have surprised the citizens of Israel and Judah, for such judgment had been announced beforehand. God had told His people that their disobedience would be judged by scattering and exile from the land (Deut. 28:32-33,41,49-57,64).

The book of Kings teaches that God is not to be trifled with. Those who ignore God and neglect His warnings reap the sobering consequences. The Lord disciplines His people (Prov. 3:11, Heb. 12:6). Israel's choice determined her destiny and accounts for the record of God's discipline in the book of Kings.

Where's Jesus?

God had promised David that he would have a righteous descendant who would sit on his throne and rule and reign forever (2 Sam. 7:16). The Book of Kings reveal that none of the rulers during the period of the monarchy measured up and fulfilled the prophecy. At the end of the monarchy the people of Israel had to understand that the good and righteous king was yet to come!

You may have to look hard to find Jesus in the Book of Kings. But I think you will find Him illustrated in the life of King Solomon. Not everything about Solomon's life points to Jesus, but Solomon was a man of peace. His name is derived from the Hebrew word for "peace" (*shalom*). Solomon raised a strong army, but never fought any wars. His life points us to Jesus Christ who "preached peace" (Eph. 2:17), "made peace" (Col. 1:20), and "is our peace" (Eph. 2:14). In Jesus, God and mankind meet in peace.

CHRONICLES

I have been asked, "How did you learn the Bible so well?" My answer is simple: "Repetition with variety is the key to learning." I studied the Bible at Western Seminary. I studied the Bible again at Dallas Seminary. I studied the Bible in Israel at the Jerusalem University College. For the last forty-five years I have been a student of the Bible. Reading or studying the Bible *once* is never enough! Reviewing it again and again in a variety of contexts is the key to learning its truths.

Maybe that is why God gave us both Kings and Chronicles! He figured that a review lesson would be helpful! But Chronicles is really more than a repeat of the history of the monarchy which is recorded in Kings. The history we find in 1 and 2 Chronicles is more focused. Here we have an account of the Davidic kings who ruled Judah. And the emphasis is not on political events, but rather the spiritual successes (and failures) of these rulers.

What's the title?

The Greek translators gave this book the title "things omitted," suggesting that the material here supplements the books of Samuel and Kings. Jerome suggested the title, "Chronicle of the Whole Sacred History." The title "Chronicles" used by English versions is taken from Jerome's proposal. The book of Chronicles was a single volume in the Hebrew Bible, but was divided into two parts by the translators of the Septuagint.

Who wrote it?

Talmudic tradition assigns the book to Ezra. As a scribe (Ezra 7:6) and spiritual leader during the Restoration Period, no one would be more qualified to write the book. The style and verbal link between Chronicles and Ezra (2 Chron. 36:22-23, Ezra 1:1-3) suggests that whoever wrote Ezra also wrote Chronicles. It should be noted, however, that the author was really a researcher and compiler. He made free use of earlier works, drawing from sixteen other sources.

When was it written?

The close relationship between Chronicles and Ezra, both of which recount the decree of Cyrus, seems to indicate that the two books were one consecutive history (cf. 2 Chron. 36:22-23, Ezra 1:1-3). Since Ezra returned to Jerusalem in 458 B.C., it is reasonable to assume that he wrote Chronicles sometime between 450 and 425 B.C.

What is the historical setting?

The Book of Chronicles records a history of the Hebrew people from Adam to the time of Cyrus providing material paralleling Genesis through Kings with the first two verses of Ezra forming the conclusion to Chronicles. The historical period covered by the books extends from the beginning of king David's reign (1010 B.C.), following the death of Saul, until the decree of Cyrus (538 B.C.).

The religious community under the leadership of Ezra and Nehemiah between 450 and 425 B.C. is the background of the book. Nehemiah 8-10 records how the Feast of Tabernacles was observed in an unprecedented manner in Jerusalem. It may have been at that or a similar occasion that Ezra provided the people with an account of their past which gave them a religious and political background for the re-established Jewish state.

Why was it written?

The purpose of Chronicles is to review the history of the nation of Israel showing God's blessing on obedience and chastening for disobedience. This record is designed to give the Jewish remnant which had returned from the Babylonian captivity a spiritual foundation on which to rebuild the nation. Chronicles was written to encourage the Jews of the

Restoration Period in their faithfulness to God during the new era ahead.

To gain the maximum benefit from Chronicles, put yourself in the place of one of the exiles recently returned from Babylon. Then as you read, ask yourself, "How would this account serve to motivate me in my spiritual life and obedience to God?"

What's the theme?

The theme of Chronicles is basically the same as that of Kings. Ezra writes to emphasize the blessings of obedience and discipline that results from disobedience to the Mosaic covenant (2 Chron. 6:36-39).

What's it about?

Genealogies from Adam to David	History of David's Reign	History of Solomon's Reign	History of the Kings of Judah
1 Chron. 1-9	1 Chron. 10-29	2 Chron. 1-9	2 Chron. 10-36

What does it teach us?

The Book of Chronicles serves as a divine commentary on Israel's history. But beyond that, it instructs us concerning God's judgment and mercy. Repeatedly the author attributes calamity to the sovereign hand of Yahweh who brings judgment on sin and spiritual defection (1 Chron. 10:13-14, 2 Chron. 36:15-17). God allows the kings of Judah to experience the law of the harvest. They reaped what they had sowed. The rulers of Judah were blessed according to their spiritual character and judged according to their disobedience and apostasy.

In addition to teaching us about God's justice and judgment, Chronicles also gives us a glimpse of God's mercy and compassion. Even after sin and apostasy, God is always ready to restore and bless His people when they seek Him and turn from their wicked ways (2 Chron. 7:14). As the prophet Micah acknowledged, "Who is a God like You, who pardons iniquity and passes over the rebellious acts of the remnant of His possession? He does not retain His anger forever, because He delights in unchanging love" (Micah 7:18). While God must hold His people accountable, He would sooner restore and bless them than judge them.

Where's Jesus?

Can Jesus be found in the books of Chronicles? I think you will find Him in a psalm of thanksgiving which celebrated David's bringing the Ark of the Covenant to Jerusalem. In 1 Chron. 16:31, the psalmist declares, "Let the heavens be glad, and let the earth rejoice; and let them say among the nations, 'The Lord reigns!'" These words anticipate Jesus' return to Jerusalem when He comes to claim His throne and crown.

EZRA

It is encouraging to know that we serve a God of new beginnings. His plan for us includes a New Covenant, a new birth, a new creation, a new song, a new commandment, and a new Jerusalem! God's willingness to provide us with new opportunities for obedience and blessing is nowhere more evident than in the book before us now.

The book of Ezra brings us to the time of the return of the Jews from the Babylonian captivity. This Restoration Period, as it is called, offered the returned exiles a unique opportunity to begin again, rebuilding their Temple and re-establishing Jerusalem on spiritual foundations. But while this period brought new opportunities, it also brought new temptations and potential for spiritual disaster. New beginnings are exciting, but they bring new challenges and hazards.

What's the title?

The book is named for Ezra, the principle character of the narrative. Ezra was a Jewish scribe who led a small group of Jews from Babylon back to Jerusalem in 458 B.C.

Who wrote it?

Ezra the priest and scribe compiled and authored the book of Ezra as indicated by his use of the first person (7:28-9:15). The evidence suggests that Ezra also wrote Chronicles.

When was it written?

Ezra served his people during the reign of Artaxerxes I Longimanus, king of Persia (464-424 B.C.). His ministry during the years 458 and 457 B.C. is recorded in Ezra 7-10. Ezra was also active in Jerusalem during Nehemiah's governorship between 444 and 432 B.C. (Neh. 8:1-9, 12:36). The book of Ezra was probably completed before Chronicles, perhaps between 450 and 430 B.C.

What is the historical setting?

As the Old Testament prophets had predicted the captivity, so they predicted the return to the land. Jeremiah prophesied that the nation would serve seventy years of captivity in the land of Babylon (Jer. 25:11-12, 29:10). After Babylon fell to Persia (539 B.C.), the way was prepared for the restoration of the Judeans to their homeland.

In 538 B.C., Cyrus issued a decree providing for a renewal of the worship of Israel's God in Jerusalem and the return of the exiles to Judah (Ezra 1:1-4). Ancient Persian documents record Cyrus' own boasting of how he returned exiled peoples to their cities and authorized them to rebuild temples for their gods.

"I returned to these sacred cities on the other side of the Tigris, the sanctuaries of which have been ruins for a long time, the images which used to live therein and established for them permanent sanctuaries. I also gathered all their former inhabitants and returned to them their habitations." (James B. Pritchard, ed., The Ancient Near East, Princeton, NJ: Princeton University Press, 1971, p. 208).

In 537 B.C. a group of Jews returned to their homeland under the leadership of the prince of Judah, Sheshbazzar (Ezra 1:8). Back in Jerusalem, they attempted to rebuild the Temple, but faced considerable opposition from certain enemies who had taken over Jewish land. After a lengthy delay, the prophets Haggai and Zechariah exhorted the people to finish the project and the Temple was eventually completed in 515 B.C.

A second group of Jews returned to Judah in 458 B.C. under the leadership of Ezra about 58 years after the completion of the Temple. Ezra worked mainly as a spiritual leader and teacher to enhance worship in the Temple.

A third return to Judah took place in 444 B.C. under the leadership of Nehemiah for the purpose of rebuilding the walls of Jerusalem. The following chart provides a brief summary of the Restoration Period:

Return #	Date	Leader	Purpose
First	537 B.C.	Sheshbazzar	To rebuild the temple (Ezra 1-6)
Second	458 B.C.	Ezra	To establish worship (Ezra 7-10)
Third	444 B.C.	Nehemiah	To rebuild the walls (Nehemiah)

Why was it written?

Before the exile, God announced that His people would spend seventy years in Babylon and then return to their homeland (Jeremiah 25:11, 29:10). Ezra was written to record the events of the first and second return of the Judeans to the land of Israel in fulfillment of Jeremiah's prophecy.

What's the theme?

Ezra reports that God did not leave His people in exile but returned them to their homeland just as He had promised. The theme of Ezra is the faithfulness of God to fulfill His promises (Ezra 1:1-3).

What's it about?

First Return Under Sheshbazzar 1-6	Second Return Under Ezra 7-10
Return of the Jews from Babylon 1-2 Temple Construction Begins 3-4 Temple Construction Completed 5-6	Ezra's Return to Jerusalem 7-8 Ezra's Ministry in Jerusalem 9-10

What does it teach?

The book of Ezra provides an opportunity to review a great truth which was introduced during the conquest of Canaan. Like the book of Joshua, Ezra reveals that God is faithful in keeping His promises. The decree of Cyrus authorizing the return to Jerusalem and rebuilding of the Temple was divinely intended to fulfill the word of the Lord by the mouth of Jeremiah (Ezra 1:1).

Jeremiah had prophesied that the Judeans would spend seventy years in captivity and then God would bring them back to their homeland (Jer. 25:11-12, 29:10). Ezra records how God used a Persian ruler, Cyrus, to issue the decree which brought an end to the exile and provided for the return of the Jews. How encouraging to know that God can be trusted. His Word is absolutely reliable. God is the original Promise Keeper.

Where's Jesus?

It is easy to miss Jesus in the book of Ezra since He is illustrated in the person and work of an unbelieving ruler, Cyrus king of Persia. It was Cyrus who welded Media and Persia into a duel monarchy and overthrew Babylon in 539 B.C. After capturing Babylon, he decreed the release of the Jews in Babylon, allowing them to return to Jerusalem and rebuild their holy temple.

The prophet Isaiah calls Cyrus God's *anointed*, literally, "His messiah" (Isa. 45:1). Although Cyrus was not a believer in the one true God of Israel, his release of the Jewish exiles from Babylon typifies the work of Jesus whom God sent "to proclaim release to the captives" and "set the downtrodden free" (Luke 4:18).

NEHEMIAH

Western Seminary, where I teach the Bible, is an educational institution committed to nurturing godly leaders for Christ's kingdom work throughout the world. It is exciting to realize that many of the next generation of Christian leaders have been my students! As someone involved in training leaders, I have often pondered the subject of Christian leadership. "What does it mean to be a leader?" "What qualities should characterize a leader?" "How to people become Christian leaders?"

The book of Nehemiah provides us with a biblical, case study of leadership. Nehemiah exemplifies a number of timeless leadership qualities that enabled him to do great things for the Lord. As you study Nehemiah, be alert to the principles of leadership which are relevant to your personal life and ministry. God may use these principles to prepare you for future leadership opportunities.

What's the title?

The book receives its title from the name of the principle character of the narrative, Nehemiah. The Jewish Masoretes who copied and preserved the Scripture considered Ezra and Nehemiah as one unified composition, but internal evidence does not support this tradition.

Who wrote it?

The author of the book was Nehemiah, as indicated by the use of the first person throughout the narrative. There is little reason not to regard this work as the authentic memoirs of Nehemiah, the wall builder and governor of Judea during the Restoration.

When was it written?

Nehemiah ministered during the reign of Artaxerxes I (464-424 B.C.). His later reforms (13:4-31) came after a brief stay in Babylon in 432 B.C. (13:6) and his memoirs in the book that bears his name were probably written shortly thereafter, around 430 to 425 B.C.

What is the historical setting?

The book covers a period of about fifteen years from 444 B.C. to around 430 B.C. Nehemiah was the cup-bearer for Artaxerxes, king of Persia (464-424 B.C.) and received the king's permission to go to Jerusalem to rebuild the city walls (Neh. 2:1-8). The third return of the exiles from Babylon took place under Nehemiah's leadership in the twentieth year of Artaxerxes (Neh. 2:1) or 432 B.C.

Nehemiah's immediate task as governor of Judah was rebuilding the ruined walls and gates of Jerusalem which was completed in an amazing fifty-two days (Neh. 6:15). Although Josephus reports that the project took two years and four months (Antiquities XI. 179), the biblical record is clear. Nehemiah acknowledges that the work was accomplished "with the help of our God" (Neh. 6:16).

Nehemiah left Jerusalem to visit Artaxerxes in Babylon during the thirty-second year of his reign (Neh. 13:6) or 432 B.C. Things appear to have fallen apart spiritually in Jerusalem while he was away so God raised up the prophet Malachi to challenge and correct the people of Jerusalem. Many of the evils Malachi denounced are the focus of Nehemiah's later reforms:

Priestly Laxity	Neh. 13:4-9,29	Malachi 1:6-11
Neglect of Tithes	Neh. 13:10-13	Malachi 3:7-12
Intermarriage with Foreigners	Neh. 13:23-28	Malachi 2:10-16

Nehemiah's primary achievements as governor were rebuilding the walls of Jerusalem (6:15) and initiating civil and religious reform (13:4-31).

Why was it written?

The book was written to record the events of the third return under Nehemiah, and to give the date of the decree to rebuild Jerusalem (444 B.C.) which marks the beginning of prophetic period in Daniel known as the "seventy weeks" (Dan. 9:25).

What's the theme?

The theme of Nehemiah is the rebuilding of the wall and renewing of the covenant (6:15, 10:28-29).

What's it about?

Restoration of the City Walls 1-7	Reformation of the People 8-13
Return of Nehemiah to Rebuild 1:1-2:20 Rebuilding the Walls of Jerusalem 3:1-7:4 Register of the Returned Exiles 7:5-73	Public Reading of the Law 8 Mosaic Covenant Renewed 9-10 Cities of Judah Re-Populated 11 Register of the Priests & Levites 12:1-26 Dedication of the City Walls 12:27-13:3 Later Reforms under Nehemiah 13:4-31

What does it teach?

Nehemiah exemplifies a number of leadership qualities which enabled him to do great things for God. He was a man of prayer (1:4-11) and vision (2:4-5). His caution as a leader is evidenced by the fact that he analyzed the situation he faced before he confronted the people with the challenge before them (2:11-20). Chapter three demonstrates that Nehemiah was a man who had organizational skill and an ability to delegate tasks to others. His response to enemy attack demonstrates that he knew how to balance the principles of faith and hard work (4:20,22).

Nehemiah's personal integrity is evidenced by the fact that he did not use his office as a means of personal enrichment, but rather gave liberally of his own resources (5:14-16). The record of his work with Ezra demonstrates that Nehemiah was able and willing to work together with other leaders without resenting their distinctive gifts and ministries (8:1-8).Nehemiah models a biblical style of leadership that is greatly needed in the church today.

Where's Jesus?

In the prayer of confession by the Levites, they acknowledge that during years of God's patient working with His people, they were admonished "by His Spirit" through the prophets (Neh. 9:30). The "Spirit" to whom they refer is identified more specifically by the Apostle Peter who records that the prophets were seeking to know more completely "what person or time the Spirit *of Christ* within them was indicating" (1 Pet. 1:11). Jesus was ministering *in His Spirit* (before His incarnation) through the prophets. Where's Jesus? Right there in Nehemiah 9:30! Additionally, the godly leadership of Nehemiah points to perfect leader and shepherd of God's people, Jesus, the promised Messiah.

ESTHER

Hannah Senesh was a Hungarian Jew who trained with the British army to parachute into Yugoslavia during WWII in order to help save the Jews of Hungary who were being deported to German death camps. She was arrested at the Hungarian border and was eventually executed by a firing squad for her refusal to reveal the details of her mission.

Hannah Senesh willingly gave her life to secure the safety and freedom of her countrymen. Her sacrifice reminds me of the book of Esther–an ancient story of the heroic actions of another young Jewish woman who risked her life to intervene in behalf of her people during their exile in Babylon.

The story of wicked Haman, his decree against the Jews and Esther's intervention in behalf of her people provides the historical background for the Jewish celebration known as Purim. The name Purim means "lots" and refers to the lots cast by Haman (Esther 3:7) to determine the best day on which to destroy the Jews.

The Feast of Purim, though secular in its origin and celebration, is an important part of Jewish culture and heritage. According to Jewish tradition, the book of Esther is read to celebrate Purim. During the reading, it is customary to "boo" and "hiss" at the mention of Haman. Some participants use noisemakers for the same purpose. Special foods like *Hamantashen* ("Haman's pocket") add to the merriment of this secular Jewish holiday.

What's the title?

The title of the book is taken from the name of the principle figure, Esther. The name Esther is derived from the Persian word for "star." Esther's Hebrew name was Hadassah, meaning "myrtle."

Who wrote it?

The book of Esther is an anonymous work. It was attributed by the Talmud to the men of the Great Synagogue (Baba Bathra 15a). Josephus, on the other hand, held that Mordecai authored the book (Antiquities. XI. 184-303, cf. Esther 9:20,23). This may be the case since the author demonstrates an intimate knowledge of Persian customs and appears to have been an eyewitness of the events recorded.

When was it written?

Internal evidence (10:1-2) indicates that Ahasuerus died

before the book was written. The earliest date for the writing would be the death of Xerxes I (464 B.C.) and the latest date would be around 330 B.C. for there is no trace of Greek language or thought in the book. The book of Esther was probably written between 450 and 350 B.C.

What's the historical setting?

The events of Esther took place during the reign of King Ahasuerus of Persia who is commonly associated with Xerxes I (486-464 B.C.). More specifically, the events of the narrative cover a ten-year period dating from the third year of Ahasuerus (483 B.C.) to the Feast of Purim in the twelfth year of the king (473 B.C.). The events of the book of Esther fit nicely between chapters 6 and 7 of Ezra.

The story of Esther takes place in the city of Susa (Hebrew *Shushan*) located at the foot of the Zagros Mountains 150 miles north of the Persian Gulf. Susa became the winter capital of the Persian kings after the rule of Cyrus. The city is noted for its royal palace begun by Darius I and enlarged and adorned by later kings. Nehemiah later served as cupbearer for King Artaxerxes I (464-424 B.C.) in Susa.

Why was it written?

The primary purpose of the book is to relate the origin of the Feast of Purim (3:7, 9:24,26). The book of Esther was also intended to encourage the Jewish people by illustrating the providence of God in delivering and preserving His people during the Babylonian captivity.

What's the theme?

Although the personal name of God (Yahweh) is not mentioned in Esther, the narrative shows that He is active behind the scenes. The theme of Esther is the sovereignty of God in watching over and preserving His people (4:15). As the psalmist wrote, "Behold, He who keeps Israel will neither slumber nor sleep" (Psa. 121:4).

What's it about?

Removal of Vashti 1	Intercession by Esther 5-7
Selection of Esther 2	Edict of Deliverance 8
Plot of Haman 3	Institution of Purim 9
Decision of Esther 4	Greatness of Mordecai 10

What does it teach?

The book of Esther serves as a powerful illustration of God's providence in preserving His chosen people. The story of Esther shows how God uses seemingly insignificant events in people's lives to accomplish His purposes. The removal of Queen Vashti allowed for the selection of a Jewish woman– Esther–as queen. Her position as queen enabled her to appeal to King Ahasuerus to preserve the Jews. God's sovereignty is evidenced by the precise timing of events which God orchestrated to protect and preserve His people.

The oversight of failing to reward Mordecai allowed him to be honored at a more opportune time. The insomnia of the king and discovery of Mordecai's unrewarded favor to the king was timed precisely to coincide with Haman's plan to have Mordecai hanged. The sequence of events led to some unusual reversals which reflect the sovereign "hand of God in the glove of history."

The book not only illustrates God's providential care for

His own, but also demonstrates His faithfulness to His covenant with Abraham and his descendants. God promised Abraham, "the one who curses you I will curse" (Gen. 12:3). Wicked Haman, the enemy of the Jews, certainly experienced that curse!

Where's Jesus?

Where is Jesus in the book of Esther? I think you will find Him where you would least expect—in the submission of Esther. Esther realized that God had providentially placed her in a position to deliver her people from the wicked Haman's death decree. She also knew that her actions in behalf of the Jews could cost her life. But she willingly submitted and said, "If I perish, I perish" (Esther 4:16). And so Jesus faced His costly sacrifice with the words, "My Father, if this cannot pass away unless I drink it, Your will be done" (Matt. 26:42). Esther depicts the attitude of self-sacrifice that led Jesus to the cross.

CHAPTER THREE

The Wisdom Books

The third major chapter of the Bible turns from history to reflection. Some scholars call Job, Psalms, Proverbs, Ecclesiastes and the Song of Songs the "Poetic Books." They certainly are poetic in the Hebrew sense of parallel thought or expression of ideas. But the thematic focus of these books is worship and wisdom. The Psalms, known in Hebrew as "the book of praises," promote worship by declaring the works and attributes of God. Job, Proverbs, Ecclesiastes and the Song of Solomon promote wisdom, telling God's people how to live.

As the ancient Israelites looked to the priests for instruction from the Torah, so they looked to wise men and women for guidance and counsel on how to live life successfully. Together the sages of Israel declare, "Wisdom has the advantage of giving success" (Ecclesiastes 10:10). In other words, if you want to live a happy and successful life, then follow the words of the wise. And the secret of success, according to the wisdom writers, is to practice "the fear of the Lord" (Proverbs 1:7, Ecclesiastes 12:13). The "fear of the Lord" characterizes both the ideal woman (Proverbs 31:30) and the successful man (Psalm 115:13, 147:11).

The fear of the Lord has been a greatly misunderstood concept. Most people think this involves dread, apprehension, and trembling before God. But this is not the fundamental response of one who truly fears God. The wisdom writers tell us that "fearing God" begins with knowing God (Prov. 2:5). If you know that He is holy, just, sovereign, all powerful and eternal, you can't help but respect Him and want to please Him. The fear of the Lord is really an action oriented response to God which is sourced in a knowledge of God's will and a whole-hearted response to it. The fear of the Lord involves departing from evil (Job 28:28), obeying God's commandments (Psa. 111:10), and sharing God's attitude toward sin Prov. 8:13).

By the fear of the Lord we walk in His ways, avoid the complications of sin, and enjoy the blessings that come with successful living. Like the tree planted by streams of water (Psalm 1:3), the wise and god-fearing person will prosper. This is a chapter of the story of the Bible which you can't afford to miss!

JOB

Have you ever wondered why God allows those who love and serve Him to suffer? I have asked myself that question many times. I asked it when my younger brother was killed in an automobile accident while returning from a skiing trip. I asked it when I learned that the wife of one of my students had died of cancer on Christmas day. I asked that question again when I read of how Muslim fanatics had attacked Christian seminary students in Indonesia and how one brave student was beaten to death because he refused to recant his faith. Why? Why? Why, Lord, do you allow the righteous to suffer?

The book of Job helps us to reflect on this burning question but leaves us with a surprising answer. The story of Job helps us realize that God does not have to give us a reason for everything He does. One of life's great challenges is to live by faith with unanswered questions.

What's the title?

The book of Job derives its title from the name of the central character, Job, a man known in biblical history for his great suffering.

Who wrote it?

The book of Job is anonymous. Although the Talmud attributes the work to Moses, there does not seem to be any internal evidence to support this tradition.

When was it written?

There is a wide divergence of opinion concerning the date of composition. Five main views are held by biblical scholars:

1. The patriarchal age, before the time of Moses.
2. The reign of Solomon (10th century B.C.)
3. The reign of Manasseh (seventh century B.C.)
4. The time of Jeremiah (late seventh century B.C.)
5. The Babylonian exile (6th century B.C.)

A number of biblical scholars date the writing during the reign of Solomon who was noted for his literary activity.

What's the historical setting?

Evidence within the book suggests that the age of the patriarchs (2000-1000 B.C.) provides the most likely historical setting for Job. This accounts for Job's patriarchal family-clan organization and sacrifice, and his longevity. He lived 140 plus years! This would also account for the lack of reference to Israel, the exodus, or the Mosaic Law. The events of the book reflect a non-Hebraic background, for Job lived in the district of Uz located in northern Arabia, far from the land of Israel.

Why was it written?

Many believe that Job was written to consider the problem, "Why do the righteous suffer?" While the problem of suffering may provide the historical setting for the book, the author presents an even more significant issue--the problem of faith and doubt.

The story of Job leads the reader to consider, "How do you maintain faith in God in the face of such devastating trials? How do you go on believing in God in times of His apparent absence?" The book of Job is intended to demonstrate that it is possible to keep faith through trial (2:10).

What's the theme?

The theme of Job is keeping faith during times of trial (1:20-21).

What's it about?

The Tragedy of Job 1-2	The Struggle of Job 3:1-42:6	The Triumph of Job 42:7-17
Job's Character 1:1-5	Job's Lament 3 Eliphaz the Mystic 4-7	Job's Friends 42:7-9
Satan's Challenge 1:6-12	Bildad the Traditionalist 8-10 Zophar the Rationalist 11-14	Job's Fortune 42:10-17
First Assault 1:13-22	Second Time Around 15-21 Third Time Around 22-31	
Second Assault 2:1-10	Elihu the Young Man 32-37 Yahweh the Creator 38-41 Job's Response 42:1-6	

What does it teach?

The message of the book of Job is set in the context of great suffering. After enjoying years of prosperity from the hand of God, Job experienced the loss of his ten children, his property, and personal health. Job's three friends held to the thesis that all suffering is punishment for sin (4:7-8, 8:3-4, 11:4-

6). They concluded that since Job was suffering greatly, he must be a great sinner. But the encounter between Satan and the Lord recorded in the preface of the story shows that this is not the case. Job is not suffering because of any particular sin. Rather, the suffering that God allowed Satan to bring upon Job was designed to prove the genuineness of Job's faith. Job was not being good simply because God was being good to him. Job was living as a righteous man because he loved God!

The book of Job does not provide us with a mechanical answer as to why people suffer. The problem of suffering does not lend itself to being easily simplified. The book of Job demonstrates that God's people may experience suffering which has a hidden purpose in the plan of God--a plan which may never be revealed to the one who is suffering. But we see through Job's experience that there is something more important than knowing the reason for our suffering. More important than knowing the reason is *knowing God!*

There may be suffering in your life or mine which is beyond human explanation. We wonder, "Why?" But no answer is forthcoming. In these situations, we must remember that God is in control (Rom. 8:28). And we don't need to know "why?" if we know God! The book of Job teaches the practical lesson that it *is* possible to continue believing in God in the face of devastating trials. Our hope is not in our circumstances. Our hope is not in our healing. Our hope is in God alone!

Where's Jesus?

You will find Jesus in Job 19:25 where Job exclaims, "And as for me, I know that my Redeemer lives, and at the last He will take His stand on the earth." A "redeemer" in biblical times was a person who provided legal protection for a close relative who could not do so for himself. Despite his terrible circumstances, Job he knew that his Redeemer was alive and would eventually vindicate him. Job's Redeemer is none other than *our* Redeemer, Jesus Christ, who "redeemed" us with His "precious blood" (1 Peter 1:18-19).

PSALMS

People sometimes ask me, "What is your favorite book in the Bible?" My standard reply is, "whichever book I happen to be teaching." Each book of the Bible is "my favorite," but the one I would have the most difficulty living without is the book of Psalms. Reading a psalm is the best way to begin my devotions. Reading a psalm is the best way to conclude my day. Reading a psalm is one of the best ways to have a mini-worship experience with God.

I took a group of students on backpacking in Oregon's Cascade Mountains where I spent a week teaching the Psalms. It was such a great experience that I held the class the following summer on the Oregon coast. Enjoying the Psalms for a week in the beauty of God's creation, I felt like the Kingdom had arrived! The Psalms have a way of bringing us into the very presence of God. I'm truly glad that I don't have to live life without the Book of Psalms!

What's the title?

The Hebrew title for Psalms is, *Sefer Tehillim*, the "Book of Praises." The Greek name, *Psalmoi*, appearing in the Septuagint, means "songs sung to the accompaniment of a stringed instrument," like a guitar. And you thought contemporary music was a recent innovation!

Who wrote it?

Although many psalms are anonymous, a number of the psalms identify the author. The authors and their psalms include:

1. David (3-9, 11-32, 34-41, 51-65, 68-70, 86, 101, 103, 108-110, 122, 124, 131, 133, 138-145). 73
2. Asaph (50, 73-83). 12 total
3. Sons of Korah (42, 44-45, 47-49, 84-85, 87). 9 total

4. Solomon (72, 127). 2 total
5. Heman the Ezrahite (88). 1
6. Ethan the Ezrahite (89). 1
7. Moses (90). 1

When was it written?

The earliest of the psalms would be Psalm 90, written by Moses (c. 1440 B.C.). The Davidic psalms would have been composed between 1020 and 975 B.C. and those of Asaph during approximately the same period. Psalms 72 and 127 date from Solomon's reign, around 950 B.C. The psalms of the descendants of Korah and the two Ezrahites were probably written before the exile. Psalm 126 and 137 date from the return of the exiles. There is little evidence for dating any of the psalms later than around 500 B.C.

What is the historical setting?

Thirteen psalms record in their preface the historical setting out of which they were composed. These include: Psalm 3, 7, 18, 34, 51, 52, 54, 56, 57, 59, 60, 63, and 142. Psalm 3, for example, records that it was written by David when he fled from his son Absalom (2 Sam. 15-18). Psalm 51 was written by David as an expression of repentance after his adultery with Bathsheba. It is hazardous to attempt to reconstruct the historical setting of a psalm where none is clearly indicated.

Why was it written?

The book of Psalms is written as poetry, packed with theology, and designed for praise. The purpose of Psalms is to express the devotional sentiments of God's people and ultimately praise God.

What's the theme?

The theme of Psalms is the praise of God--the public acknowledgment of His greatness and goodness (Psa. 150:6).

What kinds are there?

Although the five-fold division of Psalms has been recognized (1-41, 42-72, 73-89, 90-106, 107-150), the book is a collection of independent poems and is not really suited for outlining. However, we recognize the varied types of psalms based on their theme and content. Ten of those categories are listed here.

Creation Psalms 19, 104, 148	Royal Psalms 47, 93, 96-99
Exodus Psalms 95, 114, 135	Didactic Psalms 14, 15, 24, 95
Imprecatory Psalms 35, 58, 59, 137	Wisdom Psalms 1, 37, 112, 133
Penitential Psalms 6, 32, 51	Torah Psalms 19, 119
Pilgrim Psalms 120-134	Messianic Psalms 2, 8, 22, 110

What does it teach?

The book of Psalms makes a great contribution to the biblical theology of praise. Psalm 100:4 reveals that God desires thankful worship and praise from His people. The word translated "praise" (*yadah*) in the Hebrew text literally means "to confess publicly or give public acknowledgment." This word is never used of people. It is used regularly in the Bible of giving public, verbal acknowledgment of God's character or activity.

While you can thank God or worship Him in private, praise has a forum and always occurs in a group where others can hear and grow in their awareness and appreciation of the greatness and goodness of God.

Praise occurs in speaking a sentence in which the one being praised is honored and elevated. There are basically two kinds of praise found in the Bible. Descriptive praise declares what God is like. It focuses on His attributes. Declarative praise recounts what God has done. It focuses on His actions. One of the greatest ways a believer can praise God is by sharing a personal testimony. "God has delivered me from my burden of sin." This is declarative praise. "God is so very gracious." This is descriptive praise. Praising God in the biblical pattern with freedom and spontaneity could certainly enliven our corporate worship!

The author of Hebrews encourages believers to praise God when he writes, "Through Him let us continually offer up a sacrifice of praise to God, that is, the fruit of lips that give thanks [literally "confess"]to His name" (Heb. 13:15).

Where's Jesus?

Jesus isn't hard to find in the Book of Psalms. In fact, there is a whole category of psalms that feature the person and work of Jesus–the Messianic Psalms. These include Psalm 2, 8, 22, 40, and 110. Many others, like Psalm 16, 41, 45, 68, 69. 72, 78, 89, 102, 109, 118 and 132 have verses which are Messianic.

Psalm 22, quoted 24 times in the New Testament, is one of the best known Messianic Psalms. Here David describes his personal struggle with language which looks ahead and anticipates the suffering Jesus experienced during His crucifixion (see Matthew 27:35, 39. 43, 46, and John 20:25).

Psalm 110, the most quoted in the New Testament, describes Jesus as sharing God the Father's kingly throne and ruling Israel's future kingdom (110:1-2). Reading a Messianic Psalm is a great way to start the day with Jesus!

PROVERBS

Have you ever received invitations to different events

scheduled for the same evening? You are forced to choose which to attend. The book of Proverbs is like that. Here we are presented with the rival invitations of Lady Wisdom (9:1-6) and Madam Folly (9:13-18). These two ladies personify the contrasting pathways of wisdom and folly in the book of Proverbs.

Lady Wisdom teaches and exemplifies godliness. She is honest, faithful and trustworthy. Guests in her home are served the finest of foods. They depart with appetites satisfied and souls nourished. They sense a deep pleasure in growing wise.

In contrast to Lady Wisdom is Madam Folly who also extends her invitation. Those who respond are attracted to her seductive attire and sensual propositions. Guests at her home usually come after dark. They are served cheap wine and spoiled food. They come seeking the sensual thrills of life. But they depart dissatisfied. In their search for life, they find darkness, disappointment and death.

You're faced with a choice. To which invitation will you respond? The book of Proverbs teaches that how you respond to the rival invitations of Lady Wisdom and Madam Folly will determine the course of your life.

What's the title?

The title, "Proverbs," is derived from a Hebrew verb (*mashal*) meaning "to be like or resemble." Proverbs are simply moral lessons presented through contrast and comparison.

Who wrote it?

Solomon is the most noteworthy author and contributor of the book (1:1, 10:1, 25:1). Two sections of Proverbs (22:17-23:14 and 24:23-34) are attributed to "the wise." Proverbs 30:1-30 was written by Agur the son of Jakeh, and Proverbs 31:1-9 is said to be the sayings of king Lemuel.

When was it written?

While most of the proverbs were written during the lifetime of Solomon, the final form of the book could not have appeared before the time of King Hezekiah (25:1). The book was probably in its completed and final form around 700 B.C.

What is the historical setting?

According to Jeremiah 18:18 the religious life of the Hebrews was molded by the prophets, the priests, and the sages. Although the wise were never as prominent in national life as the priests and prophets, they did exert a considerable influence as teachers of wisdom. Their sayings enshrined truths gleaned from Scripture and experience in life.

The instruction of the wise involved a practical knowledge and an ability to use knowledge effectively. Their great concern was for the application of divine truth to daily living. According to Proverbs, merely knowing information is not the same as having wisdom. Many theologians and philosophers know a great deal, but that doesn't necessarily make them wise. Wisdom involves *applying* what we know about God and living according to His revealed will.

Why was it written?

The proverbs are intended to serve as practical guidelines for successful living. The purpose of Proverbs is to know wisdom and to allow it to govern one's life (1:2-4).

What's the theme?

The theme of Proverbs is the distinctive motto of the wisdom teachers, "The fear of the Lord is the beginning of knowledge" (Prov. 1:7, Job 28:28, Ecc. 12:13). Reverence toward God and obedience to His will is the first step toward wisdom and successful living.

What's it about?

Introduction to Proverbs 1:1-7	More Proverbs of Solomon 25:1-29:27
Discourses on Wisdom 1:8-9:18	Words of Augur Ben Jakeh 30
Proverbs of Solomon 10:1-22:16	Words of King Lemuel 31:1-9
Words of the Wise 22:17-24:34	Description of a Worthy Woman 31:10-31

What does it teach?

The fundamental lesson in our study of Proverbs is the concept of "fear of the Lord." While not distinctive to Proverbs, this phrase encapsulates the theme of the book (1:7). But what exactly does it mean to "fear the Lord?"

Many associate the emotion of fear with dread, apprehension, trembling hands and knocking knees. While I would not deny a place for such fear in relationship to God's eternal judgment on unbelievers or His discipline on disobedient Christians, this is not the major thrust of "the fear of the Lord" as revealed in Proverbs.

Fearing God is equated in Proverbs 2:5 with knowing God. Those who truly know God and appreciate His divine attributes can't help having a heathy respect for His person. If you know that He is holy, just, sovereign, and omnipotent, you can't help but want to obey and please Him. Proverbs reveals that the "fear of the Lord" is not only an attitude, but an action. "By the fear of the LORD one keeps away from evil" (Proverbs 16:6, cf. Psa. 111:10). According to Proverbs 8:13, "The fear of the LORD is to hate evil."

Proverbs teaches that the "fear of the Lord" is an action oriented attitude that is derived from a knowledge of the will of God and involves a whole-hearted response to it. The fear of the Lord involves not only right thinking about God, but right action. The one who truly fears the Lord is seeking to obey Him and striving to do His will.

Where's Jesus?

Many scholars and commentators have found Jesus in Proverbs 8:22-31. But more careful study reveals that passage is really about "wisdom," a major focus of Proverbs. While Proverbs 8:22-31 is not a picture of Jesus, the wisdom of Proverbs certainly points to Jesus "in whom are hidden all the treasures of wisdom and knowledge" (Col. 2:3). Jesus is the ultimate "wise man" who presents the way of wisdom and successful living (Matt. 7:24-27).

ECCLESIASTES

Do the inevitable frustrations of daily life get you down? You probably experience them on a daily basis. You are about to sit down to breakfast and you hear a shout from upstairs, "Help! The toilet is over flowing." After turning off the water, you dash to the garage to get the plunger. But the automatic garage door opener suddenly jams and partially disconnects from the ceiling. You prop up the garage door with a ladder, find the plunger and fix the toilet. By this time, your shirt is dirty and you are late for work. You know it's going to be a tough day.

How do you cope with this kind of frustration? Is there any hope of maintaining your composure . . . and your sanity? The book of Ecclesiastes has a surprising message designed for people like you. To those who are weary of life's frustrations, Solomon says, "Don't let the bumps in the road take the joy from your journey."

What's the title?

The Hebrew title of the book is the Hebrew word *Qohelet*, which means "one who convenes and speaks at an assembly." The title "Ecclesiastes," is taken from the Greek title given to the book by the Septuagint.

Who wrote it?

The author identifies himself as the "son of David, king of Jerusalem." While Solomon is not specified as the author, he is the most likely candidate. References to the author's unrivaled wisdom (1:16), unequaled wealth (2:7), opportunities for pleasure (2:3), and extensive building activities (2:4-6) support the well-established tradition that Solomon authored the book.

When was it written?

If Solomon was indeed the author, then the book was probably composed late in his life (c. 935 B.C.). At the end of Solomon's life he would have been able to draw upon his great wisdom and unsurpassed experience to provide very helpful and wise instruction. The writer's consciousness of old age and death (2:18, 12:1-7) would indicate that the book was written as Solomon was nearing the end of his life.

What is the historical setting?

The book appears to be an address by Solomon to an assembly of the wise (cf. 1 Kings 4:31). Wise men and women in ancient Israel were a medium which God used to communicate His truth (Jer. 18:18). They gave people counsel and presented wisdom from life and by divine inspiration. This book may have been the record of Solomon's teaching at an assembly of the wise sometime late in Solomon's life.

Why was it written?

Ecclesiastes was written to demonstrate the utter futility of trying to assimilate all the riddles and paradoxes of life. God simply has not revealed all the answers. So, in light of the futility of trying to put all of life together, people must live by faith and use their one opportunity to enjoy life to the fullest (2:24, 3:12, 3:22, 5:18, 8:15, 9:7, 11:9).

What's the theme?

Enjoy God's gift of life to the fullest, living in obedience to God with an awareness of impending judgment (2:24, 12:13-14).

What's it about?

Solomon's Prologue 1:1-11	Wisdom and Folly 7:1-14
Paradoxes of Life 1:12-2:23	Enigma's of Wisdom 7:15-8:15
Solomon's Grand Solution 2:24-26	Summary of Solomon's Quest 8:16-9:10
The Sovereign Plan of God 3	Lessons on Wisdom 9:17-11:8
Futility Caused by Suffering 4:1-5:20	Instruction to a Young Man 11:9-12:7
Futility of Riches 6:1-12	Solomon's Epilogue 12:8-14

What does it teach?

Ecclesiastes presents us with a theology of joy. This is evidenced by the words "joy" and "rejoice" which appear 17 times in the book. Seven times Solomon repeats some form of the command, "Eat, drink, and enjoy life" (cf. 2:24, 3:12,22, 5:18, 8:15, 9:7-9, 11:9). The message is clear! God certainly intends for those who know and obey Him to enjoy His gift of life to the fullest.

Paul picks up this theme in Philippians where he writes, "Rejoice in the Lord always; again I will say, rejoice" (Phil. 4:4). It is significant that in later Judaism it became the custom to read Ecclesiastes on the third day of the Feast of Tabernacles, a harvest and thanksgiving festival--a season for rejoicing!

Sometimes the message of Ecclesiastes has been mistakenly interpreted as Epicurean or hedonistic. While the Epicureans said, "Avoid life and its pains by retiring from the world," the hedonists recommended, "Exploit life and its pleasures through sensual indulgence." In Ecclesiastes, Solomon rejects both extremes. He demonstrates in Ecclesiastes that there is no contradiction between enjoying life to its fullest and living in obedience to God.

Where's Jesus?

Those who regard Ecclesiastes as man's philosophy rather than God's wisdom might have a hard time finding Jesus in the book. But I believe Jesus can be found in Ecc. 12:11, "The words of wise men are like goads, and masters of these collections are like well-driven nails; they are given by one Shepherd." The term "shepherd" often refers to God (Psalm 23:1, Isa. 40:11) and points us to Jesus, "the good Shepherd" (John 10:11-15) who is both a source of wisdom and salvation for His people.

SONG OF SOLOMON

"Adults only!" That is the label given to this book by the early church leader, Jerome. He insisted that because of its erotic content, the Song of Solomon should not be studied by anyone under thirty years of age! Concerns about eroticism in the Song of Solomon were eventually resolved by giving it an allegorical interpretation.

Consider the words of the Shulamite maiden in 1:13, "My beloved is to me as the pouch of myrrh which lies all night between my breasts." Jewish rabbis interpreted this to refer to the *shekinah* glory between the two cherubim that stood over the ark in the Tabernacle. Christian allegorists understood the text to refer to Christ appearing between the Old and New Testaments!

The best approach in studying the Bible is to read it as we would any other book. When we interpret the Song of Solomon normally or literally as we do the rest of the Bible, we discover that it is a love song–a poem that exalts the beauty and purity of love in marriage. That's all. And that's enough!

What's the title?

The Hebrew title is "the Song of Songs." This is a Hebrew superlative (like "holy of holies" or "king of kings") and denotes the book as the best or most excellent of songs. Since the song is attributed to Solomon, many English translations recognize that in the title, "The Song of Solomon."

Who wrote it?

The book is attributed to Solomon (1:1). This is confirmed by the repeated references to royal luxury and costly imported products such as spikenard (1:12), myrrh (1:13), frankincense (3:6), silver, gold, purple, ivory, and beryl--items with which only royalty would be so familiar.

When was it written?

The mention of geographical localities found in both the Northern and Southern Kingdoms would suggest that the book was written before the division of the monarchy. The Song of Solomon was probably composed by Solomon sometime during his reign as king in Jerusalem (970-931 B.C).

What is the historical setting?

The Song of Songs is a lyric dialogue accompanied by a certain dramatic movement. A true story in the life of Solomon and a young lady lies at the background of the song.

King Solomon apparently had a vineyard in the mountains of Lebanon (4:8, 8:11) which he entrusted to caretakers consisting of a mother, two sons (1:6) and two daughters--the Shulammite (6:13) and a little sister (8:8). While traveling in the north, Solomon encountered the lovely Shulammite maiden. He spoke loving words to her (1:8-10) and won her affection (2:16).

Eventually, Solomon took the Shulammite to Jerusalem to become his bride (3:6-7). The two were married and their love was consummated (4:16-5:1). But all was not well with the royal couple.

The Shulammite dreams of being separated from Solomon (3:1-2, 5:2-6, 6:1) and expresses her desire to spend more time with her husband (7:11-12, 8:1-2). Eventually they go together to the country (8:5) where they talk of love (8:6-7) and give themselves to each other (7:12, 8:12,14).

Why was it written?

The purpose of the book is to set forth the purity and beauty of wedded love and its expression. The book also warns against arousing one's passions before there is a pleasing,

God-honoring relationship and a proper marriage union.

What's the theme?

The theme of this love poem is the purity and beauty of wedded love as a divine gift (5:1).

What's it about?

Mutual Affection of the Bride and Groom 1:1-2:7
The Shulammite Speaks & Dreams of Her Beloved 2:8-3:5
The Shulammite's Marriage to Solomon 3:6-5:1
The Shulammite Dreams of Solomon 5:2-6:3
The Shulammite and Solomon are Reunited 6:4-13
Solomon's Praise for his Beloved 7:1-8:4
A Visit to the Shulammite's Country Home 8:5-14

What does it teach?

Genesis 1:27 records that God created mankind "male and female." It is clear from Scripture that our sexuality was God's idea. And what God created is "very good" (Gen. 1:31). But sinful people sometimes take the best of God's good gifts and use them contrary to God's design. A misuse of our sexuality through immoral and illicit relationships certainly perverts the good gift of our sexuality and results God's chastening (Hebrews 13:5).

The Song of Solomon presents an important message to a world characterized by sexual obsession and confusion. The message is simply that God designed our sexuality to be expressed in the loving and intimate context of marriage. It is in that context that sex can be enjoyed fully as God intended without guilt or fear of negative consequences.

The Song of Solomon teaches that husbands and wives should delight in God's gift of the physical expression of their love in marriage. This message is captured in the poetic invitation of 5:1, "Eat, friends; drink and imbibe deeply, O lovers." In Proverbs Solomon counsels young men, "And rejoice in the wife of your youth. As a loving hind and a graceful doe, let her breasts satisfy you at all times; be exhilarated always with her love" (Prov. 5:18-19).

As the Song of Solomon has a message for the married, it also has a message for those who are single. Single people are warned not to arouse or awaken the sexual expression of love until its appropriate (2:7, 3:5, 8:4). Sexual immorality is not only sinful, it is foolish and self-destructive (Prov. 6:32-33). Sex is good, but not outside of marriage. It's a gift worth waiting for.

Where's Jesus

Where is Jesus in the Song of Solomon? Those who interpret the Song allegorically find Him everywhere! Taking a more cautious approach, I believe Jesus can be found in the institution of marriage which is elevated and extolled throughout the Song of Solomon (Song of Solomon 3:6-5:1). According to Paul, the institution of marriage was designed by God to illustrate the relationship between Christ and the church (Eph. 5:31-32). The love and sacrifice that is so essential to a happy and blessed marriage is ultimately demonstrated by Jesus in His relationship with His body, the church (Eph. 5:25-28).

CHAPTER FOUR

The Major Prophets

The next chapter in the story of the Bible is the writings of the prophets. The biblical term "prophet" refers to one who speaks for another. The term is used for Aaron who spoke for Moses (Exod. 7:1-2). Most frequently it is used in the Bible for those who speak for God. The prophets in ancient Israel interpreted and expounded the Mosaic Law. They also predicted God's judgment on those who broke their covenant agreement with God and proclaimed God's blessings on those who were faithful to the covenant obligations. As watchmen on the city wall, the prophets looked over the activities of the Israelites, warning them against political alliances, Canaanite worship, and religious formalism.

While the prophets functioned in various ways to communicate God's message to His people, there was one major role which they occupied in Israel. The prophets served as *prosecuting attorneys* representing God in bringing His case against a nation guilty of violating the covenant.

In order to understand and fully appreciate the role of the prophet in Israel, we have to go back to Mount Sinai where God met with His people and entered into a covenant relationship with them. This covenant was mediated by Moses who went up Mt. Sinai to meet with God receive the regulations governing the covenant relationship. The regulations of the covenant are recorded for us in Exodus 20-24 and Deuteronomy 5-30. The summary of Israel's obligations to God under the covenant relationship are found in the Ten Commandments (Exod. 20:1-17; Deut. 5:6-21).

The prophets came onto the scene during Israel's monarchy to remind the rulers and people of the covenant relationship between God and His people (Isa. 1:2-3, Jer. 2:13, Amos 2:4). They reminded the Israelites that obedience to the covenant would result in prosperity and blessing, and that disobedience would result in God's chastening and judgment (Amos 5:14-15). The prophets functioned as official representatives of the God of Israel (Micah 6:2). Like a prosecuting attorney bringing charges against the guilty, the prophets reminded the people of the regulations (God's law), called them to obedience, and confronted them with the consequences of continued disregard of their covenant obligations. These consequences were spelled out for Israel in Leviticus 26:14-39 and Deuteronomy 28:15-68.

The prophets didn't just pronounce God's judgment on the wayward and disobedient people. The Mount Sinai covenant made provision for the restoration of blessing and prosperity based upon repentance. God had promised Israel that if they confess their sins and turn back to God, He would remember His people and restore their land and blessing (Lev. 26:40-45; Deut. 30:1-5). And so the prophets continually preached that repentance is the prerequisite for restoration and blessing. In the words of Isaiah, "If you consent and obey, you will eat the best of the land!" (Isa. 1:19).

The books of the prophets have been traditionally divided into two sections–the Major Prophets and the Minor Prophets. The Major Prophets not necessarily more important, but they are longer. The Minor Prophets, also known as The Twelve, are not less important, but they are shorter. Isaiah is the longest book of the prophets with sixty-six chapters. Obadiah is the shortest prophet and is just *one* chapter or 21 verses in length.

The Major Prophets begin with Isaiah who prophesied around 700 B.C. He condemned the people of Judah and Jerusalem for breaking the covenant and warned of how God was going to use the Assyrians to chasten His people. But the tone of the prophet shifts in the second half of the book to offer comfort and encouragement to the exiles who have been taken captive to Babylon. Isaiah assures them that there is a future and a hope for God's repentant people.

The prophet Jeremiah ministered around 600 B.C., about a century after the time of Isaiah. Jeremiah realized that the people had gone so far in violating their covenant with God that judgment was inevitable. He warned the Judeans that God would use the Babylonians to discipline His disobedient people. The destruction of Jerusalem and Babylonian captivity came in fulfillment of Jeremiah's prophecies. Jeremiah's Lamentations record the prophet's grief over the destruction of Jerusalem and demonstrate how completely his predictions were fulfilled.

Ezekiel and Daniel were prophets who ministered during the Babylonian captivity (605-537 B.C.). Daniel was among the first of the Judeans to be taken to Babylon by Nebuchadnezzar. He served in Babylon as a court prophet, speaking God's word to the rulers of Babylon and Persia. His visions and their accompanying messages emphasize the theme of God's sovereignty over the affairs of Israel and the Gentile nations.

Although Ezekiel was trained as a priest, he became a prophet after being exiled to Babylon in 597 B.C. There he ministered to a community of the exiles, revealing the reasons for the captivity and the destruction of Jerusalem. But like the other prophets, Ezekiel gave the exiles a basis for hope as he announced the future restoration of Jerusalem and the temple.

ISAIAH

The book of Isaiah introduces us to the first of a series of Spirit inspired leaders who spoke and wrote for God. They are called "prophets," a Hebrew word (*nabi*) that refers to one who "speaks for another." The prophets were men who spoke and wrote for God.

Our first prophet, Isaiah, was a member of the tribe of Judah and, according to Jewish tradition, a prophet of royal descent. It is believed that he was the cousin of Judah's King Uzziah. His contemporaries in the prophetic ministry were Hosea, prophesying in the north, and Micah, prophesying in both Israel and Judah.

What kind of man was Isaiah? More than anything else, Isaiah was a man intimately acquainted with God. About twenty-five times Isaiah refers to God as "The Holy One of Israel." Isaiah was a man who had a view high view of God and His holiness. His view of God no doubt sustained him during the difficulties of His life. Jewish tradition records that Isaiah was martyred, sawn in half by wicked King Manasseh (2 Kings 21:16, Heb. 11:37).

What's the title?

The book of Isaiah is named for the prophet Isaiah whose name means, "Yahweh saves."

Who wrote it?

The book indicates the author to be "Isaiah the son of Amoz" (1:1). Some scholars, however, deny the unity of Isaiah and suggest that chapters 40-66 were written not by Isaiah, but by an unknown author or authors living near the close of the Babylonian exile.

In answer to this viewpoint, we should note that the New Testament quotes the prophet Isaiah 21 times and clearly indicates that *both* sections (1-39 and 40-66) were written by Isaiah. It is significant that the scroll of Isaiah discovered in the cave near Qumran has no break in the Hebrew text between chapters 39 and 40. The early Hebrew scribes clearly recognized Isaiah as a unified document written by a single author.

When was it written?

Isaiah 1:1 records that the prophet ministered in the days of Uzziah, Jotham, Ahaz, and Hezekiah, a period extending from 739 to 686 B.C. The book was probably written sometime after Sennacherib's 701 B.C. invasion and siege of

Jerusalem.

What is the historical setting?

The first half of Isaiah (chap. 1-39) is set against an Assyrian background and is principally concerned with rebuking and condemning the people and leaders of Judah and predicting the overthrow of the kingdom. Most of the prophecies against Jerusalem and Judea found in the first section of the book were fulfilled with Sennacherib's attack on Judah in 701 B.C. Isaiah 37-38 provides the dramatic details of this crisis. God graciously delivered Jerusalem and sent the Assyrians homeward after miraculously decimating Sennacherib's army.

The second half Isaiah (chap. 40-66) is written from the viewpoint of the Babylonian exile of 586 B.C. In these chapters Isaiah addresses prophetically the Jews of the Babylonian captivity providing encouragement and a promise of return to their homeland. Spiritually, Isaiah ministered during a period of degeneracy and apostasy, especially during the reigns of Ahaz and Manasseh.

Why was it written?

Isaiah had two purposes in mind when he recorded his prophecies. He wrote to condemn the wicked and comfort God's people. To accomplish this Isaiah announces inescapable judgment for the unbelieving world and promises God's comfort and deliverance to the righteous remnant of His people.

The book is sprinkled with prophecies about the Messiah and His coming kingdom, providing the Jews in Babylon a basis for hope (7:14, 9:1-7, 11:1-16, 52:13-53:12).

There are approximately 64 references to the prophecies of Isaiah in the New Testament which demonstrates the impact of Isaiah on the thought and theology of the early church.

What's the theme?

Isaiah reveals that God must judge sin and apostasy, but that He delights in deliverance and redemption (1:18-20).

What's it about?

The Condemnation of Judah and the Nations 1-35	King Hezekiah of Judah and the Assyrians 36-39	God's Comfort and Blessing for Israel 40-66

What does it teach?

Isaiah teaches the great doctrines of God (41), man (1:3-15), salvation (55) and last things (58-66). But more than anything else, Isaiah is remembered for his many messianic prophecies. Isaiah predicts the virgin birth of Christ (7:14), the ministry of Jesus in Galilee (9:1-2), the kingdom rule of the promised Messiah on the throne of David (9:6-7), the peace and righteousness of the future kingdom (11:1-9), the suffering of the Servant Jesus for the sins of humanity (53:4-6), his death (53:7-8), burial (53:9), resurrection (52:12), and exaltation (52:12). Isaiah presents a biblical study of the life and ministry of Jesus before He was even born! He was clearly a prophet with a message from God.

Where's Jesus?

You won't have a hard time finding Jesus in the Book of Isaiah. As noted in the previous paragraph ("What does it teach?"), Isaiah is the prophet who predicted many details about the person and work of Jesus which were literally fulfilled in the New Testament (7:14, 9:1-7, 52:13, 53:1-12). No wonder some have referred to this book as "the Gospel of Isaiah."

In Isaiah 9:6 the prophet announces, "A child will be born to us, a son will be given to us, and the government will rest on His shoulders." The child, Jesus, was born in Bethlehem (Micah 5:2); the Son of God took on humanity (John 1:18); but the government is *not yet* on his shoulders. That prophecy awaits fulfillment when Jesus returns to inaugurate and rule God's Kingdom (2 Sam. 7:12-16, Luke 1:32-33, Rev. 19:11-20:6).

JEREMIAH

As you cross over the Mount of Olives, traveling east from Jerusalem, you can look over your left shoulder and see a little village in the distance. It is the village of Anathoth, the home town of Jeremiah the prophet. Although born into a priestly family, Jeremiah was called to the prophetic ministry and served as God's spokesman for over forty years.

During his long lonely career, Jeremiah witnessed many of the troubles that God brought upon His people to challenge and correct them. He witnessed the Babylonian siege of Jerusalem and trials experienced by those who resided in the city. He preached an unpopular message concerning God's judgment on Judah and Jerusalem through the Babylonians. Because of this message, Jeremiah, more than most prophets, experienced the rejection and hostility of his own people.

Jeremiah is known as the "weeping" prophet because of his "Lamentations" over Jerusalem.

What's the title?

The book was named for the prophet Jeremiah, whose name means "Yahweh establishes."

Who wrote it?

While the book was authored by the prophet Jeremiah, the actual writing was done by Jeremiah's secretary Baruch

(36:4,32). If you would like to impress your friends, you can refer to Baruch as Jeremiah's "amanuensis," the technical word for one who copies a manuscript or takes dictation. Baruch may have edited Jeremiah's collection of prophecies and added the historical appendix (chap. 52).

Since Jeremiah's life was to be a symbol of the coming judgment on Judah, he was given some unusual instructions by Lord (Jeremiah 16:1-9). Jeremiah was to (1) take no wife, (2) not enter a house of mourning to comfort the people, and (3) not enter a house of feasting to enjoy a celebration.

When was it written?

Jeremiah began his ministry in the 13th year of the reign of Josiah or 627 B.C. and continued until after the fall of Jerusalem (586 B.C.). Since Jeremiah records the release of Jehoiachin in the 37th year of his exile (52:31-34), the book was probably completed after 560 BC.

What is the historical setting?

Jeremiah began his prophetic ministry as a young man (1:6) during the reign of King Josiah. He ministered in the kingdom of Judah during the reigns of the last five kings of Judah. Through the wise leadership of such kings as Hezekiah and Josiah, Judah was able to continue as a kingdom after the fall and exile of the Northern Kingdom. But eventually the kingdom of Judah also reaped the consequences of breaking the covenant (Deut. 28:15-68).

Jeremiah would have witnessed such events as the revival under Josiah, the captivity of Daniel, the deportation of Jehoiachin and ten thousand Judeans, the siege of Jerusalem, and the burning of the temple.

Prophets contemporary with Jeremiah include Zephaniah and Habakkuk in Judah, and Ezekiel and Daniel in Babylon.

Why was it written?

The book records the warnings, rebukes, and exhortations of Jeremiah to the unrepentant people of Judah. Jeremiah was written to show the exiles the reasons for their captivity and to encourage them with promises of restoration.

What's the theme?

The theme of Jeremiah is God's judgment on unrepentant Judah for unfaithfulness to God and His covenant (1:15-16).

What is it about?

The Call of Jeremiah 1
Prophecies Concerning Judah's Destruction and Exile 2-20
Prophecies Against the Leaders and People of Judah 21-29
Future Restoration and Messianic Kingdom 30-33
Disintegration of the Kingdom of Judah 34-36
Siege and Destruction of Jerusalem 37-39
History and Prophecies after the Fall of Jerusalem 40-45
Prophecies against the Foreign Nations 46-51
The Fall of Jerusalem Further Detailed 52

What does it teach?

Jeremiah makes a distinctive contribution to Old

Testament theology with his promise of the New Covenant (Jer. 31:31-34). The New Covenant replaces the Old Covenant which was established between God and Israel at Mt. Sinai. It amplifies and confirms the blessing promises of the Abrahamic Covenant (Gen. 12:1-3). Unlike the Old Covenant, the New Covenant is both eternal (32:40, 50:5) and unconditional (31:33).

The New Covenant promised by Jeremiah was inaugurated by the shedding of Christ's blood on the cross (Hebrews 8:6). The New Covenant promises for God's people redemption, the forgiveness of sin, the law written on the heart, the indwelling ministry of the Spirit and the privilege of being the people of God (Jer. 31:31-34, Ezek. 36:25-28). These blessings are made available to all believers–both Jewish and Gentile--through faith in Christ.

Where's Jesus?

You might expect to find Jesus in Jeremiah 31 where the prophet writes of a New Covenant, one which is inaugurated by the sacrifice of Jesus (Hebrews 8:6). But there is no direct reference to Jesus there. But I think you will find Him in Jeremiah 23:5-6 and 33:15-16, both of which refer to a "righteous Branch" who will reign on the throne of David administering judgment and righteousness on the earth. Like a "branch" from the stump of the fallen tree of Judah (Isa. 6:13, 11:1), Jesus will "spring forth" and prosper during His future, kingdom reign over the earth. In Jeremiah 23:6 He is called "The LORD our righteousness," a messianic title with an echo in 1 John 2:2.

LAMENTATIONS OF JEREMIAH

There is a period of transition between youth and manhood where our culture says that it is inappropriate for a fellow to cry. This was reinforced in my childhood by the often repeated statement, "Big boys don't cry." I am confident that many men of my generation are not as emotionally and psychologically healthy as they might be otherwise since as children they had to stifle their tears. The book we are now considering proves that this was not the case with the prophet Jeremiah. He was not a man who held back his tears. He must have recognized with Solomon that there is "a time to weep" (Ecc. 3:4).

Jeremiah is known as "the weeping prophet" because of his "lamentations" over Jerusalem. He did not hold back his emotions and sorrow when he saw what was happening to the people of Judah and Jerusalem. He wept. He wept for the people who were enduring a needless tragedy. And he wept for Jerusalem because it was under God's judgment because of sin.

What's the title?

The title "Lamentations," reflects Jeremiah sadness and tears over the destruction of Jerusalem by the Babylonians in 586 B.C.

Who wrote it?

Although the author is not named, the book has traditionally been attributed to Jeremiah. In matters of style and phraseology there are numerous and striking similarities between the words of Jeremiah and the book of Lamentations. The scenes described in the book require an eyewitness, and no other likely author besides Jeremiah.

When was it written?

Lamentations records Jeremiah's lament over the destruction of Jerusalem by the Babylonians in 586 B.C. The book was probably written shortly afterwards, probably no later than 570 B.C.

What is the historical setting?

The siege of Jerusalem by the Babylonians (588-586

B.C.) ended with the destruction of the city and burning of the temple. The citizens, except for the poorest of the land, were exiled to Babylon (2 Kings 25:11-12) and Gedaliah was appointed governor to administer the land under Babylonian authority. Mizpah, eight miles north of Jerusalem, was selected as the governor's residence. Jeremiah remained in Judah until Gedaliah's assassination when he was taken by the rebels to Egypt.

Why was it written?

It was customary in ancient times to commemorate the fall of a great city, and the author of Lamentations stood in this ancient literary tradition. The sight of a ruined and deserted Jerusalem compelled Jeremiah to write his lament over the city.

The purpose of Lamentations is to commemorate the destruction of Jerusalem. The book records how completely Jeremiah's prediction of the destruction of Jerusalem was fulfilled. Lamentations also presents God's faithfulness and compassion (3:19-39) as a basis for future hope.

What's the theme?

The theme of Lamentations is the prophet's grief over the destruction of Jerusalem (1:16, 2:11).

What does it teach?

Paul wrote the Thessalonians believers that although they may grieve, they do not do so as those who have no hope (1 Thess. 4:13). This point is reflected in the message of Lamentations. Yes, there was plenty to grieve for in the time of Jeremiah. The city of Jerusalem and Solomon's Temple lay in smoldering ruins. Yet as Jeremiah expresses his grief, he is not without hope. Notice the message of hope in Lamentations 3:22-23, "The LORD's lovingkindnesses indeed never cease, for His compassions never fail. They are new every morning; great is Thy faithfulness." And again, "For if He causes grief, then He will have compassion according to His abundant lovingkindness" (3:32). The good news of Lamentations is that there is hope in the Lord (Rom. 15:4,13)!

What's it about?

Lament for the City of Zion 1	Divine Source of Zion's Sorrows 2	Consolation in God's Faithfulness 3	Horrors of Zion's Great Calamity 4	Lament and Petition for Restoration 5

Where's Jesus?

Jeremiah was a prophet who entered into the griefs and sorrows of his people. While Ezekiel and Daniel were removed from the place of judgment by their exile to Babylon, for nearly fifty years Jeremiah stood with the people of Jerusalem as they went through their deepest trial. Jeremiah's willingness to identify with his people points to Jesus' identification with suffering humanity through His incarnation. And as Jeremiah wept over Jerusalem as he recalled the Babylonian destruction, so Jesus wept over the city in anticipation of its coming desolation by the Romans (Luke 19:41-43). Jeremiah's exclamation, "Great is Your faithfulness" (Lam. 3:23) reminds us of God's covenant faithfulness, blessing all nations through the promised Messiah (Gen. 12:3, Gal. 3:8,14).

EZEKIEL

Ezekiel might best be remembered as the prophet of pantomime. Many of the prophets used symbolic actions as a vehicle for divine revelation. But Ezekiel excelled them all in his use of symbolic actions.

For Ezekiel, everything had a message. His dramatic actions, later combined with words, were a powerful means of communicating God's revelation to the Judeans in captivity. Ezekiel's symbolic actions had an even greater impact because during the first seven-and-a-half years of his ministry, he was mute. The prophet Ezekiel could not speak unless God chose to speak through him. Ezekiel could never say, "Honey, please serve me some more of that unleavened bread," or "What's new in the Jerusalem Times?" He could only say, "Thus says the Lord…."

To carry on his ministry, Ezekiel would walk to the city center and begin his pantomime. The people would gather around and wonder, "What is the old man up to today?" They would question each other and debate the meaning. Finally, when the symbolic action was complete, Ezekiel would return home. Later, the city elders would come to his house saying, "Ok, Ezekiel, what is God saying?" Then the prophet of pantomime would explain the symbolic action and declare God's message to the people.

What's the title?

The book is named for the prophet Ezekiel whose name means "God strengthens."

Who wrote it?

The book was authored by the prophet Ezekiel who was a contemporary of Daniel in Babylon and Jeremiah who prophesied in Jerusalem. Ezekiel, the son of a Zadokite priest, was taken to Babylon with the group of 10,000 Judeans who were exiled in 597 B.C. by Nebuchadnezzar. He lived in Babylonia among a colony of Jews at a place called Tel-abib, located 50 miles south of Babylon.

At the age of 30 a priest would begin his ministry in the temple. But Ezekiel reached his thirtieth birthday in Babylon, hundreds of miles from Jerusalem and the temple. So instead of beginning his ministry as a priest, God called Ezekiel to become a prophet, a "spokesman" for God to the community of exiles.

When was it written?

Ezekiel began his ministry in the fifth year of Jehoiachin's exile or 593 B.C. The book was probably completed after Ezekiel's last dated prophecy which was given in 570 B.C.

What is the historical setting?

Through the prophet Jeremiah, God had announced that His people would be removed from their homeland to Babylon for seventy years, after which they would be brought back to their Promised Land (Jer. 25:11-12, 29:10).

The seventy years began in 605 B.C. with the captivity of Daniel (Dan. 1:1-4) and concluded in 536 B.C. when the returned exiles began to rebuild the Jerusalem temple (Ezra 3:1-6). Ezekiel was taken to Babylon as part of the second deportation when Nebuchadnezzar exiled Jehoiachin and 10,000 Judeans in 597 B.C. His prophetic ministry began in 593 and continued for about twenty-three years.

Ezekiel was contemporary with two other prophets, Jeremiah and Daniel. Jeremiah was ministering in Jerusalem at the beginning of this period. Ezekiel and Daniel were both ministering in Babylon, Ezekiel in the community of the exiles and Daniel in the royal court.

Ezekiel's ministry to the colony of exiles can be divided into two main periods. From 598 to 586 B.C., or up to the fall of Jerusalem, his ministry consisted primarily of preaching about the coming judgment on Judah. After the fall of Jerusalem and the destruction of the temple, Ezekiel ministered consolation, predicting the future restoration of the nation and the Jewish temple.

Why was it written?

The prophecy of Ezekiel was intended to show that Jerusalem's destruction was on account of the sins of the nation. This discipline was designed to bring them to the knowledge that "Yahweh is God" (6:7,10,13). The prophecy also intended to comfort the people through God's promise of future restoration and blessing.

What's the theme?

The theme of Ezekiel is the destruction and future restoration of Jerusalem and the temple (5:5-8).

What's it about?

Ezekiel's Call and Commission 1-3	Ezekiel's Symbolic Actions 4-24	Prophecies about the Nations 25-32	Prophecies about Israel 33-39	Vision of a Temple 40-48

What does it teach?

Ezekiel makes a distinctive contribution to theology by emphasizing the glory of Yahweh. The vision which introduces Ezekiel's call left him with an abiding sense of God's glory, a theme which he develops throughout his book (1:28, 3:23, 8:4, 10:4, 11:22).

The Hebrew word translated "glory" is derived from a word meaning "weight." God's "glory" refers to his "social weight" or weighty reputation. When God revealed His glory to Ezekiel, he revealed something of His attributes or glorious reputation. Although we cannot add to God's character or attributes, we can help draw attention to them. This is what it means to glorify God. We glorify God as we magnify through our lives and words the character and attributes of Almighty God. Paul said, "Whether, then, you eat or drink or whatever you do, do all to the glory of God" (1 Cor. 10:31).

Where's Jesus?

In John 10:11 and 11:14, Jesus says, "I am the good Shepherd," distinguishing himself from the wicked and abusive leaders--false shepherds of His time. You will find Jesus' shepherd ministry predicted in Ezekiel 34:23 where God says, "I will set over them one shepherd, My servant…, and he will feed them; he will feed them himself and be their shepherd." The ministry of Jesus, the Good Shepherd, is further described in Ezekiel 34:11-16. God Himself, the Good Shepherd, will search for His sheep, deliver them from danger, care for them, feed them, and lead them to rest. What a blessing to be in the care of the Good Shepherd!

DANIEL

Daniel was a young man in a foreign land. He had been taken from his home and family by Babylon's king Nebuchadnezzar. The king wanted to train him as a government administrator so that he could supervise the Jews Nebuchadnezzar planned to bring to Babylon. Daniel would have the privilege of studying at Babylon's most recognized university. He would be tutored in the Babylonian language, literature and religion.

But before his training program got under way, Daniel made a decision that marked his career. Arrangements had been made that Daniel and his fellow students to receive their daily food from the king's table–the best food in the land. The problem was that the food on the king's table had not been prepared according to Jewish law and would have included things which the Hebrews were prohibited from eating. What would Daniel do?

Daniel didn't wait to see what the others were going to do. Daniel just made up his mind. For him there would be no compromise of God's law. Daniel refused to "defile himself with the king's choice food" (Dan. 1:8). God blessed Daniel's decision. And the Book of Daniel tells the exciting story of how God used a young man who made the right choice.

What's the title?

The title of the book is taken from the name of the principle character, Daniel, whose name means "God is my judge."

Who wrote it?

The author's consistent use of the first person pronoun accompanied by the name "Daniel" (7:2,15,28; 8:1, 15, 27; 9:2,22; 10:2,7,11,12; 12:5) clearly indicates that Daniel wrote this book. The prophecies in the book have led some scholars to suggest that the book was written by someone who simply used Daniel's name. Since the book records intricate details of history, they must have been written after these events took place. Right? Well, not necessarily.

If you believe that God knows the future, then He could have *supernaturally* revealed the future to Daniel. But if you reject the possibility of predictive prophecy, then you must conclude that someone other than Daniel wrote the book. Daniel's authorship of the book is confirmed by Jesus in the Olivet Discourse (Matt. 24:15).

When was it written?

The date of writing is bound up with the question of authorship. If Daniel did indeed write the book, then it was probably completed by 530 B.C., about 75 years after he was taken to Babylon by Nebuchadnezzar.

What is the historical setting?

Daniel was taken into captivity in 605 B.C. He served as a court prophet under Nebuchadnezzar, Belshazzar and Cyrus [Darius]. Daniel was a contemporary of Ezekiel who ministered to a colony of exiles in Babylon (Ezek. 3:15).

Why was it written?

The book of Daniel was designed to encourage the Jews in Babylon who were spiritually weary from the exile and needed to be reminded that God was in control of their destiny. The book also provided the example of Daniel and his friends who remained faithful to God while living in a pagan culture.

What's the theme?

The theme of Daniel is the sovereignty of God over the affairs of the nations. The key verse is Daniel 4:17, "The Most High is the ruler over the realm of mankind, and bestows it on whom He wishes, and sets over it the lowliest of men."

What's it about?

Daniel's Ministry 1-6	Daniel's Visions 7-12
Daniel's Preparation 1 Nebuchadnezzar's Image Dream 2 Nebuchadnezzar's Golden Image 3 Nebuchadnezzar's Tree Vision 4 Belshazzar's Downfall 5 Daniel's Deliverance 6	Vision of Future World History 7 Vision of the Ram and Goat 8 Vision of the Seventy Weeks 9 Vision of Israel's Future 10:1-12:3 Sealing Daniel's Book 12:4-13

What does it teach?

The book of Daniel teaches a great deal about God's dealings with Israel in the past and in the future (2:36-45; 7:17-28; 9:24-27). Daniel reveals that God has not abandoned the people of Israel and has a future for the nation. Daniel 9:24-27 reveals many of the details concerning Israel's future including the rebuilding of Jerusalem, the coming of the Messiah, the rejection of the Messiah, and the cessation of temple sacrifice in Jerusalem. The book also reveals many practical lessons such as the blessings of obedience (1:8-21; 3:16-27; 6:10-23) and the divine judgment on pride (4:30-37; 5:17-23).

Where's Jesus?

You will find Jesus in Daniel's vision where "one like a Son of Man" approaches the Ancient of Days and is given "dominion, glory and a kingdom" (Daniel 7:13-14). The term, "Son of Man," reappears in the Gospels as the favorite self-designation used by Jesus. Drawing on Daniel's vision of the establishment of the Messiah's eternal kingdom, Jesus repeatedly identifies himself as "the Son of Man," the one who fulfills all that the vision promised. This messianic designation is used by Jesus 32 times in Matthew's gospel alone. Whenever Jesus referred to himself as "the Son of Man," both His friends and enemies knew that He was making a messianic claim. His followers acknowledged Jesus as Israel's Messiah. His enemies, on the other hand, accused Jesus of blasphemy and sought to put Him to death (Matt. 26:65-66).

Was Daniel a Prophet?

If you open a Hebrew Bible you will find that the Book of Daniel is not included among the Prophets (*Nevi'im*). Instead, this book is included among the Writings (*Ketivum*). You might wonder why. The answer is that the Book of Daniel does not contain proclamations in the "name of the Lord" as do the canonical prophets. Daniel receives and interprets visions, but you won't find the words, "Thus says the Lord" on the lips of Daniel. However, Daniel is spoken of as a "prophet" both in the writings of Qumran and in the New Testament (Matt. 24:15).

CHAPTER FIVE

The Minor Prophets

The fifth chapter in the story of the Bible continues the theme of chapter four, the ministry of the prophets. Christians customarily refer to these books as the "Minor Prophets." In Jewish tradition, they are called "The Twelve."

Although all the writing prophets were men, there were women who also represented and spoke for God. Recall the ministry of Deborah (Judg. 4:4) in the time of the judges and the prophetess Hulda in the time of Josiah (2 Kings 22:14). There was Anna who was among the first to announce the coming of the Messiah to Israel (Luke 2:36-38). And Philip the evangelist had four virgin daughters who were prophetesses (Acts 21:8-9). Joel announced that both "sons and daughters will prophesy" (Joel 2:28).

Readers of Scripture often find the prophets confusing because they don't understand the historical context in which they ministered. My students have found it helpful to study the prophets in the chronological order in which they ministered rather than the canonical order in which they appear in Scripture. The following chart may help you place the twelve Minor Prophets in their historical context:

Prophet	Date	Kings/Governors	Recipients
Obadiah	845 B.C.	Jehoram	Edom
Joel	835 B.C.	Joash	Judah
Jonah	760 B.C.	Jeroboam II	Nineveh
Amos	760 B.C.	Uzziah-Jereboam II	Israel
Hosea	725 B.C.	Uzziah-Hezekiah	Israel
Micah	735-700 B.C.	Jotham-Hezekiah	Israel & Judah
Nahum	650 B.C.	Manasseh	Nineveh

Zephaniah	640-621 B.C.	Josiah	Judah
Habakkuk	607-606 B.C.	Jehoiakim	Judah
Haggai	520 B.C.	Gov. Zerubbabel	Returned Exiles
Zechariah	520-500 B.C.	Gov. Zerubbabel	Returned Exiles
Malachi	432-431 B.C.	Gov. Nehemiah	Returned Exiles

The first of the writing prophets was probably Obadiah who announced God's judgment on Edom, the descendants of Esau, for their pride and sins against Judah. Obadiah is followed by Joel who had recently witnessed a devastating locust plague on Judah. He used imagery of the locust swarm to illustrate the coming Day of the Lord, a day of judgment on the wicked and deliverance for the righteous. Thirteen of the sixteen prophets highlight and elaborate on this Day of the Lord theme. Jonah was a reluctant prophet, but he eventually had a ministry beyond the borders of Israel. He carried a message of God's mercy and compassion to the people of Nineveh, fierce enemies of Israel! His ministry was intended to show that God's mercy extends even to the heathen nations on the condition of repentance.

Amos was a shepherd who tended a grove of sycamore figs before God called him to the prophetic ministry. He was called of God to go to the Northern Kingdom of Israel and announce God's righteous judgment on those who had broken the covenant.

Hosea, the next prophet to appear on the scene, is remembered for his tragic marriage and unhappy family circumstances. But God used Hosea and Gomer to demonstrate that God's love for His people was unceasing in spite of Israel's sin and apostasy. Isaiah, the major prophet, and Micah ministered during the same period. Micah has the distinction of being the only minor prophet who addressed his prophetic messages to both Israel and Judah. He announced coming divine judgment on both kingdoms and predicted Israel's ultimate deliverance through the coming of the Messiah.

Like Jonah, the prophet Nahum had a message for Nineveh. Sadly, the Ninevites had fallen back into their sinful ways and God spoke through Nahum to announce the judgment and destruction of Nineveh, the defiant capital of the Assyrian empire. Zephaniah appeared on the prophetic scene in Judah shortly before the time of Jeremiah to announce the coming Day of the Lord, a message of universal judgment and deliverance for a repentant remnant.

Habakkuk ministered alongside Jeremiah around 600 B.C. near the end of the Judean Monarchy. Habakkuk was perplexed as he wondered why the holy God had not undertaken more serious discipline against the people of Judah for breaking the covenant. God informed him that judgment was coming soon through the invading Chaldeans (Babylonians).

The ministry of Habakkuk was followed by Judah's exile to Babylon. There the people spent the next seventy years, hundreds of miles away from their Promised Land and beloved city of Jerusalem. Ezekiel and Daniel were God's spokesmen during the long and difficult years of exile. But God wasn't through with His people. In 539 B.C. the Babylonians were overthrown by the Persians. And in the first year of his reign king Cyrus announced that the Jews in Babylon could return to their homeland and rebuild the temple of the Lord.

The return to Judah was an exciting time for the exiles who returned. Most of those who returned were born in Babylon and had never seen Jerusalem. But they knew that the Promised Land was a land of blessing and they were anxious to raise their families in the homeland of their ancestors. But things didn't go quite as planned and the purpose for which they returned to Jerusalem was forgotten. Around 500 B.C. God raised up the prophet Haggai to remind the people of their spiritual priorities and call them to rise up and rebuild the temple. The prophet Zechariah joined him about two months later calling the people to repent and not be like their ancestors who were judged for breaking the covenant.

Malachi was the last of the prophets to speak God's word to the restoration community. He addressed certain the addressed such issues as divorce, intermarriage with unbelievers and the neglect of tithing, calling people to repentance as a prerequisite for blessing. After Malachi's final prophecy--the coming of Elijah--the Judeans entered into a period of 400 years without a prophetic voice.

While it is helpful to study the prophets in their historical context following their chronological order, we will consider each of the Twelve in their traditional, canonical order.

HOSEA

Is God's love conditioned on our love and faithfulness toward Him? Does our sin and failure turn God's love for us down a notch or two? Imagine the very worst sin that you could commit. Will that or any other sin cause God to love you less? What is God's attitude toward those of us who fall far short of His high and holy standard?

The book of Hosea is a classic love story in which true love is thwarted by the repeated adulteries of the prophet's wife, Gomer. This is a story of painful marital separation and sorrow due to sin. But in the end we discover that true love prevails! Following God's instructions, Hosea forgave and restored his unfaithful wife.

The story of Hosea and Gomer ultimately illustrates the unceasing love of God for His unfaithful people. Although they have sinned against Him, God remains faithful, extending compassion and forgiveness in spite of Israel's unfaithfulness.

What's the title?

The book is named for the author Hosea, whose name means "salvation" or "deliverance."

Who wrote it?

The book was written by the prophet Hosea. Although the author is not mentioned outside this book which bears his name, there is no prophet whose marriage and family life is known more fully than Hosea's. The tragedies this family experienced serve as a living illustration of God's relationship with his covenant-breaking people.

When was it written?

Hosea began his ministry in the reign of Israel's king Jeroboam II (793-753 B.C.) and continued into the reign of Hezekiah (728-686 B.C.). Since the fall of Samaria is not mentioned as an accomplished fact, the prophecy was probably recorded around 725 B.C., shortly before the Assyrian invasion of the Northern Kingdom.

What is the historical setting?

Hosea began his prophetic ministry in Israel during the prosperous reign of Jeroboam II. Internationally, Assyria was in the ascendency and moving west. The Assyrian kings were soon nibbling away at the northern territories of Israel. Samaria fell to the Assyrians in 722 B.C.

Spiritually, the kingdom of Israel was at an all-time low during Hosea's ministry. The priests were corrupt. Idolatry and temple prostitution was rampant. Amos, Isaiah and Micah were contemporaries of the prophet Hosea.

Why was it written?

Hosea wrote to convince the inhabitants of Israel that

they needed to repent and return to God so that judgment might be averted.

What's the theme?

The theme of Hosea is "Israel's apostasy and God's unceasing love for the nation" (3:1).

What's it about?

Israel's Unfaithfulness Illustrated 1-3	Prosecution Against the Unfaithful Nation 4-13	The Pardoning Power of Loyal Love 14

What does it teach?

Hosea teaches a great lesson concerning the nature of God's loyal-love (*hesed*). This term denotes the love and loyalty operative within the covenant relationship into which Yahweh and Israel entered at Mt. Sinai. Loyal-love was Yahweh's delight (6:6), yet this was seriously lacking in Hosea's day (4:1, 6:7).

God's loyal-love for His unfaithful people is beautifully illustrated in 3:1 where Hosea is commanded to take Gomer back as a wife and love her again "even as the Lord loves the sons of Israel, though they turn to other gods...." God keeps loving His people even when they are unfaithful. Our sin and failure does not decrease God's love for His people, although sin often results in unpleasant consequences.

Where's Jesus?

Our search for Jesus gets some help from Matthew who quotes a prophecy from Hosea and announces its' fulfillment in

Jesus. According to Matthew 2:15, Jesus' return from Egypt after the death of King Herod took place in order to fulfill the prophecy of Hosea 11:1, "Out of Egypt did I call my son." While Hosea was referring to the experience of the nation of Israel, divine inspiration led Matthew to see an analogy between Jesus and the nation of Israel. Both were persecuted by kings. Both were protected by God in Egypt. And the return of both to the land of Israel was providential in the history of God's people. But there is a difference. God's "son" Israel was redeemed out of Egypt. By contrast, the Son of God (Jesus) came forth from Egypt as Israel's Redeemer.

JOEL

The book of Joel is set against the background of a devastating locust plague which had recently ravaged the crops and denuded the land of Judah. Few westerners realize the tremendous damage caused by locust swarms. In some years the desert locust is just a "stay-at-home" grasshopper. But they can rapidly change their character, gather into a swarm, and begun a gluttonous migratory spree.

Strong winds and powerful wings carry the swarming locust from Africa to India. Breeding along the way repopulates and invigorates the swarm. With serrated jaws rasping from side to side, adult locusts consume the equivalent of their body weight daily. A locust swarm can cover more than a square mile with some fifty million insects. It is estimated that such a swarm could devour in one day what 40,000 people eat in one year! Such was the tragedy that the people of Judah recently witnessed. But the prophet Joel warns them that when it comes to God's judgment, they haven't seen anything yet! An even greater judgment–the Day of the Lord–is on the horizon.

What's the title?

The title of the book is taken from the name of the author, Joel, whose name means "Yahweh is God."

Who wrote it?

The prophet Joel, the son of Pethuel, lived and ministered in Judah and Jerusalem (1:9, 2:15-17,23,32, 3:1). He witnessed a disastrous locust plague which came upon Judah and used it as an illustration and warning of the coming judgment on God's disobedient people.

When was it written?

The book does not mention any reigning king or otherwise datable event. The allusion to the neighboring nations as Judah's foes, rather than Assyria, Babylon, or Persia, points to an early date for the book. Its position in the Hebrew Bible between Hosea and Amos suggest a date before the exile. And the evidence of Amos' borrowing from Joel (compare Joel 3:18 with Amos 9:13, Joel 3:16 with Amos 1:2) indicates that Joel must have been written before 760 B.C. These considerations suggest that the book was written early in the reign of Joash (835-796 B.C.), most likely in the time of Jehoiada the high priest, around 835 B.C.

What is the historical setting?

Joash (835-796 B.C.) came to the throne of Judah as a boy, having been hidden and protected when his mother Athaliah usurped the throne and killed the royal offspring (2 Kings 11:1-3). He was crowned as king at the age of seven by Jehoiada the high priest who enlisted the aid of the royal guard to depose Athaliah. The young king needed an advisor and Jehoiada filled this role, instructing the king in ruling wisely (2 Kings 12:2).

Sometime during the early reign of young king Joash, a series of unprecedented and devastating locust swarms invaded Judah. The land was ravaged and crops were destroyed. This great catastrophe sounded the alarm for a call to repentance in view of the greater judgment to come, the "Day of the Lord."

Why was it written?

The book of Joel was designed to call the nation to repentance on the basis of the calamity of the locust plague. Joel emphasized that future judgment may be averted by humble repentance (Joel 2:12). The prophecy also served to comfort the nation with promises of future salvation and blessings in the coming Day of the Lord when Israel would be delivered and her enemies destroyed.

What's the theme?

In Joel, history, poetry, and prophecy unite to focus on a common theme, "the Day of the Lord," a day of judgment on the wicked (1:15) and salvation for the righteous (3:18).

What's it about?

Devastation by the Locust Plague 1	The Coming Day of the Lord 2	The Judgment on the Nations 3:1-17	The Promise of Kingdom Blessing 3:18-21

What does it teach?

The Day of the Lord, a major theme of the Old Testament prophets, is brought into sharp focus in the book of Joel. The Day of the Lord can be defined as a time of God's intervention to judge the wicked and deliver God's people. Many of the references to the Day of the Lord in the prophets refer to past historical events (Lam. 1-2, Ezek. 13:1-9, Jer. 46:2-12, and Isa. 22:1-14). These texts reflect such things as military defeat, national tragedy and divine judgment. But the Day of the Lord is not seen only in past history. The prophets anticipate a future, eschatological "Day of the Lord" which God will once again intervene into human history to judge and deliver.

The eschatological Day of the Lord can be defined as that time during which God will deal with Israel and the nations through judgment and deliverance. In that day the disobedient will be confronted with God's wrath and judgment while the righteous will be blessed with experience deliverance and restoration (Isa. 4:2-6, Hosea 2:18-23, Joel 3:18-21, Amos 9:11-15, Micah 4:6-8).

New Testament references (1 Thess. 5:2, 2 Pet. 3:10-13) suggest that the eschatological Day of the Lord will include the prophesied events of the Tribulation period, the Second Coming, the Messianic Kingdom, the final revolt of Satan, the Great White Throne Judgment, and the purging of the earth in preparation of the New Heavens and Earth. It is both a day of destruction and salvation, a day of wrath and grace.

Joel uses the disaster of the locust plague as a warning of an even greater future disaster which the people of Judah will encounter if they do not repent. Joel predicts that in the future Day of the Lord God will first judge the nations (3:1-17) and then bless His people during the future Messianic age (3:18-21).

Where's Jesus?

Joel predicts that when God restores His blessing on Israel during the Messianic kingdom, the nations will be gathered and judged for their past persecution of His people (Joel 3:1-3). Jesus refers this same event in his Olivet Discourse where He describes the nations being gathered and judged following His second coming (Matt. 25:31 ff.).

Jesus is the Judge of the nations announced in Joel's prophecy! Joel also predicts that the Messiah's kingdom will be characterized by an abundance of sweet wine (Joel 3:18), a prophecy anticipated by Jesus' first miracle when He created a profusion of wine (about 120 gallons!) at the wedding in Cana (John 2:1-11).

AMOS

What responsibility do Christians have in relationship to the oppressed, the poor, and the defenseless? What are the social implications of Christianity? Should evangelicals give greater attention and energy to meeting the physical needs of lost people? Or should we maintain our focus on presenting the gospel and avoiding social activism?

The book of Amos helps us find a balanced and biblical answer to these questions. Amos was a prophet who was uncompromising in his proclamation of God's Word. At the same time, he was actively involved in promoting social justice. He rebuked oppressors and defended the rights of the defenseless.

The prophet Amos serves as a prophetic model for Christians who are looking for a balanced approach to social responsibility. According to Amos, Christians shouldn't choose between presenting the gospel and offering hurting people a helping hand. God's people should do *both!*

What's the title?

The title of the book comes from the name of the author, whose name means "burden" or "burden-bearer."

Who wrote it?

The book was written by the prophet Amos, a native of the village of Tekoa, about five miles SE of Bethlehem. Before being called to the prophetic ministry, Amos was a sheepherder and a grower of sycamore figs (1:1, 7:14). The sycamore fig is unusual in that it is necessary to make a small incision in the fruit about three or four days before harvest to insure that it ripens properly.

Although Amos was from Judah, he was sent by God with a message for the Northern Kingdom of Israel.

When was it written?

The prophecy is dated to the reigns of king Uzziah (791-739 B.C.) and king Jeroboam II (793-753 B.C.). The reigns of the two kings as sole regents overlap between 767 and 753. The book was probably written around 760 B.C.

What is the historical setting?

Amos prophesied at a time when both kingdoms were at the height of their prosperity. Religiously, the period was marked by moral and spiritual corruption. Jeroboam did evil in the sight of the Lord and continued in the idolatrous ways of his ancestor, Jeroboam I (2 Kings 14:23). Although Uzziah was a good king, he failed to remove the high places and the people of Judah continued their pagan sacrifices (2 Kings 15:4). Amos denounced Israel and Judah for their sinful self-security, violence, wanton luxury, and injustice.

Why was it written?

Amos records prophetic judgment on the Northern Kingdom for their social injustices, moral degeneracy, and spiritual apostasy.

The prophet Amos writes to remind God's people of their accountability to the covenant obligations, both in letter and spirit. According to Amos, external religion apart from righteous ethical conduct is unacceptable to God!

What's the theme?

The theme of Amos is the righteous judgment of God on His disobedient people (2:4).

What's it about?

Prophecies against the Nations 1-2	Sermons against Israel 3-6	Visions of Judgment 7:1-9:10	Promises of Restoration 9:11-15

What does it teach?

The book of Amos makes an important contribution to our understanding of the doctrine of election. Amos teaches that Israel's privileged position as an elect nation (2:9-11, 3:2) did not give the people impunity from divine judgment on sin and apostasy (5:18-20). Great privilege is always accompanied by corresponding responsibility.

The people of Israel were highly privileged. Not only did they have the light of nature to guide them in right living (Psa. 19:1-6), but they also had the light of God's direct revelation (Psa. 147:19-20; Amos 2:4). Israel's great privilege as the people of God carried with it the consequence of a weightier and more certain judgment (3:2).

Where's Jesus?

Where do you find Jesus in the book of Amos? I suggest that you look at the end of the last chapter. Amos concludes his prophecy with God's promise of restoration and blessing for His people (Amos 9:11-15). These promises anticipate the blessings of the messianic kingdom. The people of Israel will be restored to their land where they will be prosperous and blessed. In verse 11 God promises to "raise up the fallen booth of David." This is a promise to restore the throne and dominion of David's dynasty. According to the words of the angel Gabriel to Mary, Jesus is the Davidic descendant who will rule God's kingdom forever (Luke 1:32-33). David's dynasty ("the fallen booth") will be restored when Jesus ascends His throne!

OBADIAH

Have you ever known a very proud person–someone who is brilliant, knows it, and wants you to know it too? Pride may be a positive virtue. We want our children to take pride in their work. We are proud of them for their accomplishments. But through a perverse twist, pride may take on a spirit of independence, presumption, and disobedience.

A proud person forgets that their gifts and accomplishments must ultimately be traced to God. The proud person believes that his or her achievements have come by the exercise of their own might and ability. The proud person forgets the importance of accountability to God. Proud people assert their own desires and authority over God's will and His commands.

The book of Obadiah presents a case study in pride. Here we find the truth of Proverbs 16:18 graphically illustrated, "Pride goes before destruction, and a haughty spirit before stumbling."

What's the title?

The book is named after the little known prophet, Obadiah.

Who wrote it?

This shortest of the prophetic books was authored by Obadiah, whose name means "servant of the Lord." I really wish we knew more about him!

When was it written?

The date of Obadiah can be determined only by relating

vv. 11-14 to a specific occasion in Israelite history. The two possibilities are (1) 845 B.C. during the reign of Jehoram, and (2) 586 B.C. after the destruction of Jerusalem by the Babylonians which the Edomites applauded (Psa. 137:7, Lam. 4:21, Ezek. 25:12, 35:10). The 586 B.C. date seems to be excluded by the fact that there is no mention in Obadiah of King Nebuchadnezzar, the destruction of the temple or the deportation to Babylon.

What is the historical setting?

Obadiah records another chapter in the long story of strife which existed between the descendants of Esau and Jacob (Gen. 25:29-34, Num. 20:14-21, 1 Sam. 14:47, Psa. 137:7). Although the brothers were eventually reconciled, their descendants remained enemies. This strife was evidenced during the reign of King Jehoram of Judah (853-841 B.C.).

After Edom revolted against Judah and set up their own king (2 Chron. 21:8-10), Judah was invaded by the Philistines and Arabs who pillaged the king's house and captured his family except for his youngest son (2 Chron. 21:16-17). The Edomites applauded this invasion, persecuting their Israelite kinsmen instead of protecting them. The prophet Obadiah condemned this hostility against brothers and promised divine recompense for Edom's attitude and actions against Judah.

Why was it written?

The book of Obadiah is designed to show God's faithfulness to Israel and illustrate His sovereignty over the nations. Obadiah also intends his prophecy to comfort Judah through God's promise of future restoration and blessing.

What's the theme?

The theme of Obadiah is divine judgment and destruction of Edom…and all nations which rage against Israel (v. 10,15, also Gen.12:3).

What's it about?

| The Prediction of Edom's Destruction 1-9 | The Reason for Edom's Destruction 10-14 | Judgment and Restoration in the Day of the Lord 15-21 |

What does it teach?

Although Obadiah is the shortest of the Hebrew prophets, it makes a significant contribution to Old Testament theology. Obadiah teaches a lesson concerning divine retribution on those who do wrong to others. Verse 15 states this concisely, "As you have done, it will be done to you." God holds people accountable for their actions. How we treat others will affect how we will be treated. God is a righteous Judge "who will render to every man according to his deeds" (Rom. 2:6).

The book of Obadiah also teaches that God hates pride and will punish the proud. Pride is sinful presumption, a dependence on self rather than upon God. Edom's self-confidence was in her secure and well protected city (3-4), her treasures (6), her allies (7), her wisdom (8), and her strength (9). But God shows us that none of these things are a source of real security. In spite of her position of power, God brought proud Edom low. And He continues to follow this pattern in dealing with the proud today (Prov. 16:18).

Where's Jesus?

You can find Jesus in the last line of the last verse of Obadiah. After announcing Edom's thorough destruction, the prophet declares, "And the kingdom will be the LORD's" (verse 21). The kingdom Obadiah is referring to is the coming Davidic kingdom to be ruled by King Jesus (Luke 1:32-33). In spite of Edom's best attempts at destroying the people of Israel, Esau's descendants will disappear and Jacob's will flourish in Messiah's future kingdom. Edom's last great attempt to sabotage God's plan for the descendants of Jacob was when king Herod (an Edomite) tried to kill Jesus shortly after his birth in Bethlehem (Matthew 2:16-18). But the plan failed. Jesus was protected by God and wicked King Herod died a few months later.

JONAH

In the spring of the year, after the opening day of trout season, you begin hear fishing stories—usually about the "big one that got away." The book we are about to explore contains the greatest fish story of all! The book of Jonah tells the story of a man who was swallowed by a great fish and lived to tell about it!

Many scholars have questioned the historicity and reliability of Jonah because of the fish story. Could a person survive being swallowed by a great fish? In his book, *The Harmony of Science and Scripture*, Harry Rimmer tells of an English sailor who fell overboard and was swallowed by a Rhinodon shark. The fish was later caught and killed. When the body cavity of the shark was opened, the fishermen reportedly found the lost sailor unconscious but alive! Francis Fox, in his book *Sixty-three Years of Engineering*, tells a similar story about James Bartley, a man who was swallowed by a sperm whale and later rescued from the animal's stomach when the whale was caught and killed.

Whether or not these stories are reliable, the historicity of Jonah and his experience in the great fish is confirmed by Jesus (Matt. 12:40-41; Lk. 11:29-32). It is good to be reminded that what appears to be impossible from man's perspective is but a simple matter for God. People often don't realize that the story of the great fish in Jonah is really the story of a *great*

God–a God who is sovereign over nature and all creation. He can even use wild sea creatures to accomplish His purposes!

What's the title?

The book of Jonah was named for the principle character of the narrative. The name, "Jonah," means "dove."

Who wrote it?

While the book is anonymous, it is traditionally ascribed to Jonah. The use of the first person in chapter 2 would indicate that Jonah at least authored the prayer.

When was it written?

Jonah lived and ministered during the reign of Jeroboam II (793-753 B.C.) who ruled the Northern Kingdom of Israel (2 Kings 14:25). His experience as a missionary to Nineveh was probably recorded in the latter part of his career, around 760 B.C.

What is the historical setting?

The site of Nineveh is located just east of the Tigris River in northern Mesopotamia. According to ancient mythology, Nineveh was founded by a fish. Hence, the name "Nineveh" means "fish" or "fish town." Although Nineveh was the largest Assyrian city in the time of Jonah, it was not the capital city. At the time of Jonah's visit, the capital of Assyria was at Calah, about 25 miles SE of Nineveh. Nineveh was a magnificent city and served as the last capital of the Assyrian empire. At the time of its greatest prosperity, Nineveh was surrounded by a wall nearly eight miles in length. The moral corruptness of the city is attested by the prophet Nahum.

Why was it written?

The book is intended to demonstrate that Yahweh is a

God of universal judgment and universal grace. While He must judge the wicked, His grace and mercy extends to the repentant, even when they are as wicked as the cruel and idolatrous Assyrians.

What's the theme?

God's mercy and compassion extend even to the heathen nations on the condition of repentance (4:11).

What's it about?

Jonah's First Commissioning 1-2	Jonah's Second Commissioning 3-4

What does it teach?

The book of Jonah offers some tremendous insights into the person and character of God. Jonah teaches that God is sovereign over the unbelieving nations even though they do not recognize Him as God. He still holds them accountable and He will judge. But as a reflection of His grace, God provides an opportunity for wicked unbelievers to repent and be delivered. As Peter acknowledges, God is "not wishing that any to perish but for all should come to repentance" (2 Pet. 3:9).

In Jonah 4:2, the prophet quotes God's self-revelation to Moses (Exod. 34:6-7), declaring the attributes of God. Jonah acknowledges that God is "gracious and compassionate…, slow to anger and abundant in loving-kindness, and one who relents concerning calamity." The incredible thing here is that Jonah had a sound theology but not a heart for lost sinners. Jonah had compassion for the plant which died from the worm and the heat of the sun, but Jonah did not have compassion on spiritually ignorant people who were made in the image of God. Those who embrace Jonah's good theology must also share

God's love and compassion for the lost.

Where's Jesus?

Jesus Himself provides the clue as to where we can find Him in Jonah. In response to a request for another miracle by the religious leaders who were rejecting Him, Jesus said there would be no other sign given to Israel "except the sign of Jonah" (Matt. 12:39). And what sign is that?

Quoting from Jonah 1:17 Jesus explains, "For just as Jonah was three days and three nights in the belly of the sea-monster, so shall the Son of Man be three days and three nights in the heart of the earth" (Matt. 12:40). In both cases there is a similar time period followed by a surprise ending. Jonah was delivered from the belly of the fish and Jesus was resurrected from the grave!

MICAH

Long ago in ancient Israel there lived a Hebrew couple who longed to have a son. Every day they prayed together that Yahweh, the God of Israel, would hear their prayer and give them a child. Other Israelites in their village suggested that they might approach the priests of Baal with this request. Perhaps they could stir this god to send them a son. Others suggested that a visit to the grove of Asherah may be the answer. It was even suggested by one idolatrous Israelite that Molech would send a son if they promised to dedicate the infant to the fiery god.

Refusing to turn to vain idols, they kept on praying that their God, Yahweh, would grant them a child. Then one spring day word spread through the village that the once barren wife was expecting a child. And when a son was born late that fall, the neighbors said to one another, "Mika-Yahweh?" ("Who is like Yahweh?") in answering prayer. And so the child was called "Micah," an abbreviated form of the Hebrew question,

"Who is like Yahweh?"

It may have been circumstances like this that led to the naming of the prophet Micah. Whatever the case, his name serves as a reminder to the people of Israel that there is no god who is so great, so good, and so faithful as the Yahweh, the God of Israel.

What's the title?

The book is named after the prophet Micah of Moresheth. The name "Micah" is an abbreviated form of Mika-Yahweh which means, "Who is like Yahweh?"

Who wrote it?

The book was written by the prophet Micah. Micah was a native of Moresheth, a city located on the Philistine coastal plain in the vicinity of Gath. Micah was the only prophet whose writing ministry was directed to both the Northern and Southern kingdoms (1:1). Micah apparently enjoyed and used them frequently to communicate his prophetic message (Micah 1:10-15). During much of his ministry he went "barefoot and naked" to symbolize the coming judgment and exile of the people of both kingdoms.

When was it written?

Micah carried out his ministry during the reigns of Jotham (750-731 B.C.), Ahaz (743-715 B.C.), and Hezekiah (728-686 B.C.). His writing ministry can be dated between 735 and 700 B.C.

What is the historical setting?

Micah ministered in the days of the Assyrian menace, a time of unrest, insecurity, and hardship, especially for the common people. The moral and spiritual situation in both kingdoms was at a low point. Religion was a matter of mere form (6:6-8) and the religious establishment was corrupt (3:11). Idolatry (1:3,7), injustice (3:1) and avarice (3:2-3) was widespread throughout the land. Micah addressed himself to these wrongs, championing the cause of the weak and the oppressed (2:9). Micah's contemporaries in ministry include the prophets Hosea, Amos, and Isaiah.

Why was it written?

Micah was written to encourage repentance by threats of judgment and assurances that God's purposes for His people will finally prevail.

What's the theme?

The theme of Micah is the approaching judgment on both kingdoms and the ultimate deliverance through the coming Messiah (4:10, 5:2).

What's it about?

Micah contains three prophetic addresses, each of which is introduced by the Hebrew word, "hear" (1:2, 2:1, 6:1). In each message Micah condemns sin, announces judgment, and promises restoration and blessing for the repentant.

Rebellion Punished 1-2	Leadership Corrected 3-5	Israel Delivered 6-7

What does it teach?

While Micah addresses the social, moral, and religious issues of His day, his theology focuses on reinstating a high view of God. According to Micah, Yahweh is no less than the "Lord of the whole earth" (4:13). He is the covenant keeping God who is intimately related to "His people" (6:2). And although He must punish sin and rebellion (1:2-5, 3:8-12), He also delivers His own (2:12-13, 4:1-8, 7:14-17).

At the end of his book, Micah raises the rhetorical question, "Who is a God like You, who pardons iniquity, and passes over the rebellious act of the remnant of His possession? He does not retain His anger forever, because He delights in unchanging love" (7:18). Tucked away in this obscure text of the Old Testament is a strong affirmation of God's grace. There is no God like Yahweh who is so ready to forgive the sin and rebellion of His people because mercy and forgiveness are His delight!

Two poetic images are used to picture how God deals with sin (v. 18). He subdues our sins as His enemies and then casts them into the depths of the sea! Little wonder that these verses are part of the Scripture reading in the Jewish synagogue on *Yom Kippur*, the Day of Atonement!

Where's Jesus?

Where do we find Jesus in the prophet Micah? The religious leaders of Jerusalem had the answer when King Herod asked them where the Messiah was to be born (Matthew 2:4). They promptly answered, "Bethlehem of Judea," and then quoted Micah 5:2 to validate their response, "But as for you, Bethlehem Ephrathah, too little to be among the clans of Judah, from you One will go forth for Me to be ruler in Israel. His goings forth are from long ago, from the days of eternity" (see Matthew 2:7).

The promised Messiah would be born in the little known city of Bethlehem, a place not even mentioned among the list of the cities of Judah (Joshua 15). The uniqueness of this individual is seen in the fact that although He is born in time, He actually exists from eternity. Thousands of children were born in Bethlehem during the biblical period, but only Jesus fulfills this description.

NAHUM

Nahum contains the message of God's judgment and destruction of Nineveh. That's right, Nineveh! The city had been spared in the time of Jonah because the people had genuinely repented and turned to the Lord. Unfortunately, the spiritual revival which took place in Nineveh was not passed on to the next generation. And when the people of Nineveh fell back into their cruel and wicked ways, God said "Enough!" and called another prophet to address the situation.

It has been suggested by some preacher with a sense of humor that Nahum is Jonah's favorite book since it contains the message he really wanted to deliver! God's patience with the people of Nineveh had reached its limit. When His grace is refused, His wrathful judgments must fall.

If you like fast-action and adventure films, you are going to love Nahum. He has some of the most vivid battle scenes in all of Ancient Near Eastern literature. The book serves to comfort those who had experienced firsthand the Assyrian war machine. Never again would they face the savagery of the Assyrian warriors cutting their way through the land.

What's the title?

The title of the book is taken from the name of the prophet Nahum, whose name means "comfort" or "consolation."

Who wrote it?

The book was written by Nahum. Unfortunately, we know little about this prophet except that he was a native of Elkosh, a city of uncertain location.

When was it written?

Internal evidence indicates that the earliest possible date

would be the capture of the Egyptian city of Thebes or "No-amon" (3:8) by Assyria in 663 B.C. The mention of the capture of Thebes indicates that the event was in the recent past. The latest possible date would be the destruction of Nineveh, 612 B.C., which Nahum predicts.

The book of Nahum was probably written while Nineveh was still in its glory around 650 B.C.

What is the historical setting?

Nahum prophesied during the long reign of wicked king Manasseh (697-642 B.C.). Manasseh introduced many pagan practices in Jerusalem and was severely disciplined by the Lord. He underwent a personal captivity to Assyria and eventually returned to the Lord. Upon his return to Judah, he sought to institute religious reform (2 Chron. 33:10-13).

Assyria was at its apex of power at the time of Nahum's ministry. Judah had witnessed a succession of cruel Assyrian invaders. Nineveh, the proud capital of Assyria, seemed invulnerable. Her rulers boasted for their atrocities against their hapless victims. The Assyrians flayed captured soldiers alive and cut off their noses, ears and fingers.

It was Nineveh's prideful attitude and cruel aggression others that God condemned and judged. The prophesied judgment on Nineveh, "the bloody city" (Nahum 3:1), was fulfilled in 612 B.C. when the city fell to the Median and Babylonian armies.

Why was it written?

Nahum was written to comfort and console Judah by its announcement of judgment on wicked Nineveh. The book demonstrates that the God of Israel is sovereign over the destinies of all nations. Even the greatest of world powers must submit to His court of justice.

What's the theme?

The theme of Nahum is the divine judgment and destruction of Nineveh (3:7), the defiant capital of the Assyrian empire.

What's it about?

Prediction of Nineveh's Destruction	Description of Nineveh's Destruction	Reasons for Nineveh's Destruction
1	2	3

What does it teach?

The prophecy of Nahum begins with a poem which emphasizes the certainty and severity of God's vengeance upon the wicked (1:2-8). This is not a popular message with the diversity embracing culture of today. Many people who love to sing of God's goodness want to set aside the hard teachings of the Bible about God's justice and judgment. Nahum's theology provides us with a biblical balance.

Although Yahweh is long-suffering (1:3) and good (1:7), Nahum points out that there comes a point where God must execute justice in a manner consistent with His holy character. Persistent wickedness will be judged by divine wrath (1:2). God is good, but don't miss the flip side. He will execute judgment on those who raise their fists against His righteous rule.

Where's Jesus?

You will have to dig pretty deep to find Jesus in the book of Nahum since there is no direct reference to the Messiah. However, Nahum does refer to "the feet of him who brings good news" (Nahum 1:15), a text nearly identical to one in Isaiah

52:7 which is used by Paul in Romans 10:15. Nahum was writing about the messenger who announced the good news of God's judgment on Nineveh. Isaiah was referring to the messenger who announced the good news of the Judean's return from exile. These announcements are all surpassed by the good news that Jesus delivers us from our ultimate enemy– sin and death! The "good news" in Nahum 1:15 points believers ahead toward the "best news," the Gospel (literally, "good news") of Jesus Christ.

HABAKKUK

Have you ever wondered if God really exists and if your prayers are really being heard? Have you ever had doubts about your faith and wondered if life would be any different if you were a Hindu instead of a Christian? Have you ever wondered if heaven really exists or if death is the end of our existence?

If you have struggled with these or similar issues, you will be able to identify with Habakkuk, the perplexed prophet. The book of Habakkuk appeal to the honest doubter because Habakkuk struggled with doubt. Rather than merely announcing future judgments on Israel or Israel's enemies, this book contains the record of Habakkuk's personal struggle with theological issues that just didn't make sense to him. In studying this book we can learn how to face our doubts honestly and seek God's answers.

What's the title?

The book of Habakkuk is named for the author, Habakkuk, whose name means "embrace" or "embracer."

Who wrote it?

The book was written by the prophet Habakkuk whose name may tell us something of his relationship with people. I imagine this prophet as a big, friendly fellow who liked to give people hugs. And so he gained the nickname, Habakkuk, which may be rendered, "the hugger." Habakkuk was a contemporary of the prophets Zephaniah and Jeremiah. Little is known of his life or circumstances.

When was it written?

The book is not dated by any reference to a king or ruler. The only clear historical reference in the book is in 1:6, probably referring to the Babylonian threat to Judah which was realized after the battle of Carchemish in 605 B.C. The wickedness and corruption mentioned in Habakkuk 1:2-4 corresponds to the description in Jeremiah 22:13-23 of the reign of Jehoiakim. The book may be dated to the reign of Jehoiakim (609-597 B.C.), probably around 607-606 B.C.

What's the historical setting?

After the death of Josiah king (609 B.C.), the spiritual conditions of the people in Judah rapidly degenerated. Wickedness, injustice, and disregard of the law (1:3-4) came to characterize the moral attitudes and actions of the Judeans. Jehoiakim, king of Judah, is known for his grave disrespect for the written Word of God which he destroyed (Jer. 36:23,28). The sins of the rulers and the people left the nation ripe for divine judgment.

Although Egypt's Pharaoh Neco challenged the ascendancy of the Babylonians, he was defeated at Carchemish in 605 B.C. Nebuchadnezzar then advanced south to secure the newly won territory of Judah. His destruction of Jerusalem in 586 B.C. and exile of the people fulfilled the predictions of Jeremiah and Habakkuk.

Why was it written?

Habakkuk is intended to provide comfort and hope during one of the darkest periods of Israel's history. Although

God would judge, He would "remember mercy" (3:2). The book also deals with the moral dilemma of how a holy God could allow a wicked enemy nation to punish a people more righteous than itself (1:13).

What's the theme?

The theme of Habakkuk is the holiness of God in judging Judah (1:12) through the instrumentality of the Chaldeans (Babylonians).

What's it about?

| Habakkuk's Perplexity 1-2 | Habakkuk's Prayer 3 |

What does it teach us?

Habakkuk makes an important contribution to Old Testament theology concerning the subject of God. Yahweh, the God of Israel and of Habakkuk, is the Holy One (1:12, 3:3). He is a rock (1:12) and the sovereignty ruler of the nations (1:51, 3:6,12). He is a God who answers prayer (2:2), delivers His people (3:13,19), and controls the course of history (2:3).

Habakkuk sets forth the principle of faith righteousness, a theme further developed in the New Testament (Rom. 1:17, Gal. 3:11, Heb. 10:38). The righteousness man is one who exercises a continuous and abiding confidence in God in the face of adversity. According to Habakkuk 2:4, that person shall be preserved through the hard times and live to enjoy God's blessing–both now and forever!

Where's Jesus?

The prophet Habakkuk makes a startling announcement in 2:14, "For the earth will be filled with the knowledge of the glory of the LORD, as the waters cover the sea." This prophetic text is restated four other times in Scripture (Numbers 14:21, Psalm 72:19, Isaiah 6:3 and 11:9. Each of these announcements anticipate that future day when God's glorious character and attributes will be publicly and universally acknowledged. When will that become reality? When Jesus returns to earth, assumes His throne in Jerusalem, and rules over all the earth. Then the knowledge of God's glory, which gets little press today, will be the front page story in God's future kingdom!

ZEPHANIAH

Malinta Tunnel is located on the Island of Corregidor in Manila Bay. The tunnel was completed in 1922 and served as an arsenal before World War II. When the Japanese Imperial Army invaded the Philippines in 1941, the Malinta Tunnel became an army hospital and the headquarters of General Douglas MacArthur. It was Malinta Tunnel which protected MacArthur, his family, and President Manuel Quezon from the bombing raids which devastated the island. The tunnel provided protection until General Wainwright surrendered the troops to the Japanese. Malinta Tunnel remains today a mute witness to the protection it offered American and Filipino forces in the face of deadly bombardment.

Have you ever experienced the need for safety and refuge? I hope you never face a bombardment by war planes. But we will experience the hostilities that come with living in an unbelieving world. The book of Zephaniah announces a judgment worse than any military bombardment. But the prophet also offers a message of grace. He tells how believers may be "hidden in the Lord" and protected in the day of God's judgment.

What's the title?

The title of the book is taken from the name of the

author, the prophet, Zephaniah, whose name means "Yahweh hides," signifying that God protects His people.

Who wrote it?

The ancestry of Zephaniah is traced by four generations to show the prophet's relationship with Hezekiah, king of Judah (Zeph. 1:1). This means that Zephaniah was a prophet with royal blood and was a distant relative of Josiah, under whose reign he prophesied. Zephaniah apparently lived in Jerusalem (Zeph. 1:4,10-11) and may have been influential in stirring Josiah to his reforms (2 Chron. 34:1-7). His contemporaries in ministry were Nahum and Jeremiah.

When was it written?

Zephaniah ministered in the days of Josiah king of Judah (640-609 B.C.). The moral and religious conditions described by the prophet (1:3-12, 3:1-7) suggest that the book was written before Josiah's reforms of 621 B.C. The book should be dated between 640 and 621 B.C.

What's the historical setting?

The spiritual condition of the kingdom of Judah progressively worsened from the death of Hezekiah (728-686 B.C.) until the reform of Josiah (621 B.C.). Josiah, the greatest of the reformers of Judah, inherited a kingdom plagued with ruinous spiritual and moral problems. He instituted vast religious reform in Judah and Jerusalem, a movement no doubt influence by Zephaniah and his contemporaries. During the period in which Zephaniah ministered, Judah was free from foreign intervention, but facing a growing Babylonian threat.

The prophecy of Zephaniah is an announcement of judgment on Judah in particular and the world in general. Whereas Isaiah, Habakkuk, and Jeremiah specified that the Babylonians would be God's instrument of judgment, Zephaniah presents Yahweh as the One instigating the judgment without specifying the instrument.

What's the purpose?

Zephaniah is intended to warn of the impending universal judgment of the Day of the Lord and to call the remnant of God's people to repentance (2:3) and be protected from the coming calamity.

What's the theme?

The theme of the book is the coming Day of the Lord and judgment on Judah (1:7,14).

What's it about?

Announcement of Judgment 1	Judah Called to Repentance 2	Destruction and Deliverance 3

What does it teach us?

Like Joel, Zephaniah makes a major contribution regarding the Day of the Lord--a day of wrath on sin and deliverance for God's people as they are purified through chastisement. According to Zephaniah, the Babylonian threat was simply a foretaste of the judgments of the great and terrible Day of the Lord. This day of wrath will fall upon Judah and Jerusalem (1:4, 3:1-7) and on the foreign nations as well (2:4-15). The severity of the judgment is evidenced by the fact that only a remnant will survive (3:9-12).

But the prophet Zephaniah offers the prospect of preservation through judgment for the humble who seek the Lord (2:3). As Malinta Tunnel offered protection to the American and Filipino soldiers, so God's people are encouraged to seek the Lord and be preserved from His judgment. Those who do so may be "hidden in the Lord," for it is God's nature to hide and protect His own.

Where's Jesus?

The prophecy of Zephaniah closes with a picture of the future blessings God's people are to experience in the Kingdom. First and foremost, the King of Israel will be in their midst (Zephaniah 3:15). This prophecy anticipates the return of Jesus who will judge Israel's enemies and establish an eternal kingdom characterized by justice, prosperity and peace.

Zephaniah assures us that there will be no reason for fear in the kingdom because the Messiah, Jesus, will be there with His people as a protective warrior (Zeph. 3:17). All can be assured of safety and security in His presence.

HAGGAI

The Jewish exiles who returned from the Babylonian captivity came home with a good deal of excitement and enthusiasm for worshiping God in the land of Israel. But the newness of it all soon wore off as the people faced the realities of repairing Jerusalem, rebuilding their homes, and planting their crops. Soon, the duties of daily living sapped their energy and attention. As a result, the people became preoccupied with their personal lives. Houses needed to be rebuilt. City walls needed repair. Gardens needed to be planted. As life became busier, the people began to lose sight of the reason for their return to Jerusalem–to rebuild the holy temple!

It happens today as it did then. Good things often crowd out the best and most important things in life. Many of us experience this when the demands of the temporal press hard against the priorities of things eternal. The prophet Haggai shows us the need to establish and maintain priorities so that the good things won't crowd out God's best.

What's the title?

The title of the book is taken from the name of the prophet Haggai and means "festal" or "my feast." Possibly the prophet was given the name because he was born on some important feast day.

Who wrote it?

Haggai is the first of three prophets who ministered in Judah after the return from the Babylonian captivity. Haggai was probably born in Babylon and returned to Judah with the first group of returning exiles under Sheshbazzar (Ezra 5:14) in 537 B.C. Haggai and his contemporary, Zechariah, were influential in encouraging the people of Judah to rise up and rebuild their temple.

When was it written?

The oracles of Haggai are precisely dated in the second year of the reign of Darius (522-486 B.C.). All four messages of the book were given within a four-month period during the second year of Darius, or 520 B.C.

What's the historical setting?

After Babylon fell to the armies of Persia in 539 B.C., Cyrus gave permission for the Jews to return to their homeland in Judah (Ezra 1:1-4). The first group returned in 537 B.C. under the leadership of Sheshbazzar. The foundation of the temple was laid, but the builders soon met with opposition. Work on the temple stopped and did not begin again until the time of Haggai.

It was Haggai and his fellow prophet, Zechariah, who reminded the people that if they were to enjoy God's blessing, they must recognize their spiritual priorities.

Why was it written?

The purpose of Haggai is to stimulate the lethargic leaders and people of Judah to recognize their spiritual priorities and rise up and rebuild the temple. Neglecting their obligations had brought drought and economic depression. Haggai told the people that if they would recognize their spiritual priorities, then their present poverty and failure would give way to God's blessing and spiritual prosperity.

What's the theme?

The theme of Haggai is a call to the leaders and people of Judah to "Rise up and rebuild" the temple (1:8)!

What's it about?

Exhortation to Rebuild 1:1-15	A Word of Encouragement 2:1-9	A Promise of Blessing 2:10-19	Messianic Prophecy 2:20-23

What does it teach us?

Haggai teaches a great truth concerning God's presence among His people. In the midst of their spiritual discouragement, God told the people, "I am with you" (1:13, 2:4). This message was particularly relevant for the returned exiles. According to Jewish tradition there were five things missing from the Second Temple: the Ark of the Covenant, the Urim and Thummim (Exod. 28:30), the holy fire, the Shekinah glory, and the Holy Spirit (Talmud *Yoma* 21b).

The returned exiles certainly needed to be reminded that God was with them. He had not forgotten them. The truth of God's perpetual presence among His people has its ultimate fulfillment in Christ, our Immanuel ("God with us," cf. Matt.

28:20). When you are discouraged, your spirit can be lifted by remembering and recognizing God's presence (Heb. 13:5).

Where's Jesus?

If you look carefully, I believe you will find Jesus in the last verse of Haggai where God declares to Zerubbabel, "I will make you like a signet ring, for I have chosen you" (Haggai 2:23). While Zerubbabel is promised a place in God's future kingdom, this divine promise extends beyond Zerubbabel to the Davidic line which he represents. God is speaking to Zerubbabel as a Davidic descendant announcing that his family line will be like a signet ring (kept and preserved) for the fulfillment of the promises God made to David (2 Sam. 7:12-16).

Matthew's genealogy records that Zerubbabel's line was preserved. And Jesus, the Messiah, is Zerubbabel's most notable descendant (Matt. 1:12, also Luke 3:27). God's promise to Zerubbabel guarantees the preservation of the Davidic line until the coming of Jesus!

ZECHARIAH

The prophet Zechariah lived in an exciting and challenging period of Judah's history. The Jews had recently returned from Babylon after seventy years of captivity. The Temple and the city walls of Jerusalem needed rebuilding; the worship institutions needed refurbishing; and the people, still weary from long years of exile, needed encouraging. In the face of those challenges were threats from the Arabs and Samaritans who wanted to prevent the reestablishment of Judah.

It was during this tempestuous period of rebuilding Judah and the Jewish faith that Zechariah declared his challenging and encouraging message. He called for repentance, announced the coming of the Messiah, and presented a detailed portrayal of God's future dealings with His chosen people, Israel.

What's the title?

The title of the book is taken from the name of the author, Zechariah. His Hebrew name, *Zekar-Yah*, means "Yahweh remembers," a reminder that God is faithful to His promises and will not forget His people.

Who wrote it?

Zechariah a descendant of one of the priestly families that returned to Judah after the exile (Neh. 12:4). He was a contemporary of the prophet Haggai who ministered with him encouraging the people of Judah to rise up and rebuild the Jerusalem temple (Ezra 5:1-2, 6:14). Zechariah began his prophetic ministry two months after Haggai concluded his first oracle. Jesus apparently refers to Zechariah's martyrdom on the temple grounds in Matthew 23:35.

When was it written?

The text states that Zechariah commenced his prophetic ministry in the second year of Darius (522-486 B.C.) or 520 B.C. (1:1). His last dated prophecy (7:1) was two years later (518 B.C.). The last chapters of the book (9-14) were probably completed around 500 B.C.

What's the historical setting?

Zechariah lived and ministered in Jerusalem during the restoration period that followed the Babylonian Exile. He began his prophetic ministry just two months after Haggai's first message (Hag. 1:1, Zech. 1:1). Conditions in Judah were rather discouraging. The temple was still unbuilt and the walls of Jerusalem were in ruins. The people were experiencing drought and adversity because of their sinful neglect of spiritual priorities. It was to such a despairing people that Zechariah offered a message of Messianic hope and promise.

Why was it written?

Zechariah was intended to challenge the exiles to turn from their sins and to the Lord for cleansing and blessing (1:3). The book also provides encouragement by revealing future glories, the overthrow of Israel's enemies, and the universal reign of the Messiah.

What's the theme?

The theme of Zechariah is the cleansing of God's people through the redeeming and delivering work of Messiah (13:1).

What's it about?

Zechariah's call to Repentance 1:1-16	Zechariah's Eight Night Visions 1:17-6:15	A Question about Fasting 7:1-8:23	Oracles about the Future 9:1-14:21

What does it teach us?

Zechariah teaches a great deal concerning the first and second advents of Israel's Promised One, the Messiah. Concerning the first coming of Jesus, Zechariah prophecies His entrance into Jerusalem on a colt (9:9), His rejection by Israel (11), His betrayal for thirty pieces of silver (11:12-13), the piercing of His hands and feet (12:10) and His work on the cross (13:1). You would think that Zechariah had been reading the Gospels! But if that were not enough, he goes on to foretell of Messiah's second coming.

Zechariah prophecies the future repentance of Israel (13), the destruction of Israel's enemies by the Messiah

(14:3,12-15), the restoration of Jerusalem (14:8-11,16-21) and the reign of the Messiah from Jerusalem (14:9). One could almost write a book about Jesus simply from the predictions made by the prophet Zechariah!

Where's Jesus?

It is *not* hard to find Jesus in Zechariah. In this prophet it seems that He is everywhere! Zechariah predicts Jesus' coming into Jerusalem riding on the colt of a donkey (9:9). His betrayal for thirty pieces of silver is announced in 11:12-13. Zechariah prophecies that the Messiah's hands and feet will be pierced (12:10) and that his sacrifice will provide a spiritual cleansing for God's repentant people (13:1).

According to the prophet Zechariah 12:10-13:1 Jesus will one day be accepted by the people of Israel who rejected Him. The prophet Zechariah foretells of Jesus' return to the Mount of Olives and His glorious reign over God's people from Jerusalem (14:9).

With all these astonishing predictions someone might suspect that Zechariah had a pre-release copy of Matthew's Gospel! But we know that these prophecies were given around four-hundred years before the birth of Jesus by an all-knowing and sovereign God.

MALACHI

The last words of a leader or loved one are often very special and memorable. We tend to cling to those words as an expression of the life that has departed. Jesus' last words were *tetelestai*, "it is finished" (John 19:30), signifying that His redemptive work had been accomplished.

In the book of Malachi, we have God's last words in the Old Testament. These would be His final words to His people for a period of four hundred years–until the coming of John the

Baptizer. In this book, Malachi points the people back to the past, reminding them to obey the law which was given to them by God at Mt. Sinai. And he points the people ahead, announcing the coming of a prophet who would minister in the spirit and power of Elijah.

Malachi is known as the syllogistic prophet. A syllogist is one who argues in a very logical way. Following that pattern, Malachi uses questions and answers as a literary device to communicate his message. He begins by making an assertion or statement. Next, he anticipates an objection in the form of a question or challenge. Finally, he refutes the objecting, defending the original statement.

What's the title?

The title of the book is taken from the name of the prophet, Malachi, whose name means "My messenger," indicating that the prophet is God's messenger to the people of Judah.

Who wrote it?

The book was authored by the prophet Malachi who lived in Jerusalem late in the Restoration Period. Nothing is recorded in Scripture about his background or circumstances. Jewish tradition includes him as a member of the Great Synagogue with Haggai and Zechariah.

When was it written?

The book is not dated, yet internal evidence indicates a postexilic date. Close agreement between the sins which Malachi denounced and those which Nehemiah sought to correct (priestly laxity, neglect of tithes, and intermarriage with idolatrous women) suggests that Malachi ministered in Jerusalem between the first and second governorships of Nehemiah. In the thirty-second year of Artaxerxes (464-424 B.C.) or 431 B.C., Nehemiah left Jerusalem to visit the king in

Babylon (Neh. 13:6). It was probably during Nehemiah's absence from Jerusalem that the corruption and abuses developed. It is reasonable to assume that Malachi protested these abuses prior to Nehemiah's return and reform around 430 B.C. A probable date for the book is around 432-431 B.C.

What's the historical setting?

Malachi prophesied about seventy-five years after the temple had been completed (515 B.C.). The Jews had been home from Babylon for about one hundred years. Although cured of idolatry, they had lost their enthusiasm over God and worship. They had succumbed to religious indifference and moral laxity.

After suffering under God's discipline (3:11), the Judeans had begun to doubt God's love (1:2). They questioned His justice (2:17) and the benefit of obeying His commandments (3:14-15). The priesthood was corrupt (1:6, 2:1-9) and the Levitical offerings were unacceptable for sacrifice (1:8-10). The people were neglecting their responsibility of tithing (3:7-9) and were wearying God with their hypocrisy (2:17). They were even involved in a scandal of mixed marriage and divorce (2:10-16). It was such a wayward people that the Lord called to repentance and obedience through the prophet Malachi.

Why was it written?

Malachi presents God's case against Israel and calls His people to repentance. The prophecy of Malachi was intended to restore the Jewish people to a right relationship with God by exposing the causes of their spiritual declension and setting forth the steps for renewal.

What's the theme?

The theme of Malachi is the necessity of genuine repentance to assure God's blessing and avert His coming judgment (4:1-2).

What's it about?

God's Love for Israel 1:1-5	Corruption of Priests and People 1:6-2:16	Coming of Divine Judgment 2:17-4:3	Concluding Exhortation and Promise 4:4-6

What does it teach us?

Malachi makes an important contribution to the Old Testament theology in his statements regarding the Lord's love for Israel as demonstrated by His sovereign choice of Jacob over Esau (1:2-5). The book is also instructive concerning the Day of the Lord (3:2,17, 4:1,3,5), a day characterized both by judgment and deliverance.

Malachi's most unique contribution to Old Testament theology is his promise of the coming of Elijah as Messiah's forerunner (4:5-6) before the "great and terrible day of the Lord." According to Malachi, this Messianic forerunner would turn many Israelites back to God, effect a reconciliation between generations, and persuade the disobedient to embrace righteousness.

Although Jewish tradition still anticipates the return of Elijah himself, this prophecy was apparently fulfilled by John the baptizer who came preaching in the "spirit and power of Elijah" (Luke 1:17, Matt. 17:12-13, Mark 9:11-13).

Where's Jesus?

You will find Jesus in Malachi 3:1 where the Lord declares, "Behold, I am going to send My messenger, and he will clear the way before Me." Jesus makes it clear in Matthew

11:10 that the "messenger" is none other than John the Baptizer who prepared the way for Messiah's coming. Malachi goes on to write, "And the Lord whom you seek, will suddenly come to His temple." Although Jesus cleansed the Jerusalem temple at His first coming (John 2:14-16, Matt. 21:12), the context here indicates that Malachi is writing prophetically about Messiah's second coming when Jesus returns to cleanse His people in preparation for the establishment of His future kingdom. The Jerusalem temple will be the location of the Messiah's earthly throne (Ezek. 43:7)!

Malachi brings us to the end of what is often called the Old Testament, although I prefer to use the term "Hebrew Bible." The words "Old Testament" imply something that is antiquated and no longer of much good use. But we have discovered that the Hebrew Bible is a great treasury of truth, revealing who God is and what He has accomplished for His people. The Hebrew Bible reveals God's love, grace, sovereignty, holiness and plan to redeem fallen humanity, reestablish His kingdom authority and judge sin and sinners.

But now we turn to what is called the New Testament. This name for the second half of the Bible comes from the words of Jeremiah where God promises that He will "make a new covenant" with His people to replace the Mosaic covenant (Exodus 19-20) which they broke by their disobedience. The second half of our Bible explains, applies and celebrates this New Covenant which was inaugurated by Jesus through His sacrifice on the cross (Luke 22:20).

Four hundred years of Jewish history passes between the last chapter of Malachi and the first chapter of Matthew. A good deal of that history is recorded for us in the Books of Maccabees. Some of the key events of that period are listed in Appendix 4, "Important Dates to Remember" (p. 302).

But now we turn to the pages of the New Testament to continue our study of God's divinely revealed truth.

CHAPTER SIX

The Gospels

The next chapter in the story of the Bible brings us to the New Testament. The word "testament" refers to the disposition of one's personal property, as in someone's "last will or testament." This term appears several times in the Bible referring to what Jesus accomplished and left His people through His death (Lk. 22:20, 1 Cor. 11:25, Heb. 8:8).

The more contemporary designation for the second half of the Bible is the "New Covenant." This title is derived from God's promise through the prophet Jeremiah that He would make a "new covenant" with His people to replace the covenant which they had broken (Jer. 31:31). Speaking to His disciples in the Upper Room, Jesus presented the Passover cup saying, "This cup which is poured out for you is the new covenant in my blood" (Luke 22:20).

The writer of Hebrews tells us that this New Covenant was inaugurated through the sacrificial death of Jesus (Hebrews 8:6) and is now in force. The 27 books in the Christian Scriptures are called the New Testament (or "New Covenant") because they focus on the life and work of the preeminent New Covenant figure–Jesus.

The Gospels are the ancient record the life and ministry of Jesus. The Greek word "gospel" means "good news." Good news is worth sharing. You read a good book and you want to tell others. You watch a thrilling movie, and you can't keep the story to yourself. You're going to be a parent (or a grandparent!) and just have to share your joy. Mark's gospel begins with the words, "The beginning of the *gospel* of Jesus Christ, the Son of God." Mark is writing to announce to his readers the "good news" about Jesus, the divine Messiah and world Savior.

Each of the gospel writers tell the story of the life and teachings of Jesus. But each tell it from their own vantage point and perspective. Just as two witnesses to an accident may report different details as they recount the same event, so each gospel is similar to the others, yet distinctive and unique.

The first three Gospels are called "Synoptic Gospels." The Greek word *synoptic* means "to see together." The Synoptic Gospels see the life of Jesus in much the same way and report many of Jesus' travels and teachings in nearly parallel presentations. The fourth gospel, the Gospel of John, is different from the others in that it omits much of the biographical details of Jesus' life and focuses on His miracles and discourses.

The first of the four gospels was written by Matthew Levi, one of Jesus' apostles and an eyewitness of the events he records. As a Jewish believer in *Yeshua* (Messiah), Matthew was anxious to tell his Jewish kinsman about the life and teachings of Jesus. He appeals frequently to Old Testament prophecies to demonstrate that Jesus, the descendant of Abraham and David, has fulfilled the messianic expectations of the people of Israel. Matthew's style is methodical and massive. He records Jesus' great discourses including the Sermon on the Mount and the Olivet Discourse.

The Gospel of Mark wasn't written by an apostle. Mark was the nephew of Barnabas who was so influential in the early life and ministry of Paul. According to early church tradition, the Gospel of Mark contains the teaching of Peter which Mark was asked to record for the benefit of Roman readers. Mark's Gospel is more concise than Matthew's. He is less interested in showing how Jesus fulfilled prophecy and focuses instead on Jesus' mighty miracles.

The Third Gospel was written by Luke, the Greek physician and traveling companion of Paul. Luke didn't have firsthand experience with Jesus, but as a careful researcher and historian he presents an accurate record of the life of Jesus based on the reports of others. Like Matthew, Luke's gospel is more thorough and complete. Luke is fond of Jesus' parables and includes 19 which do not appear in another other gospel.

The Fourth Gospel and probably the last written was authored by the Apostle John. He states very clearly that his purpose in writing is to record selected miracles performed by Jesus to inspire faith and life in Him (John 20:30-31). John's gospel is more theological and reflective than the Synoptic gospels. He features several unique discourses and memorable interviews, such as the interview with Nicodemus and His conversation with the Samaritan woman at Jacob's well. John wants his readers to come to "believe" or *trust* in the saving work of Jesus, the divine Son of God.

Each of the four Gospels contribute uniquely to our understanding of the life and ministry of Christ. While each Gospel is complete in itself, each has a different perspective and is written for a different purpose with different readers in mind. It is only by reading all four gospels that we learn how all the details fit together and see the complete picture of Christ's life. The following chart presents a brief overview of the distinctive characteristics of the four gospels:

DISTINCTIVES OF THE GOSPELS

Distinctives	Matthew	Mark	Luke	John
Addresses	Jews	Romans	Greeks	Mankind
Date of Writing	A.D. 50	A.D. 65-70	A.D. 60	A.D. 85-90
Christ Presented As	King Zech. 9:9	Servant Isa. 42:1	Son of Man Dan. 7:13	Son of God Isa. 40:9
Purpose	To demonstrate that Jesus is the Messiah of OT prophecy	To present Christ as God's Servant, attested by His mighty works	To present the events of the life of the Son of Man who came to save lost humanity	To present the truth about Jesus, the Son of God, inspiring faith and life in Him
Theme	"This is Jesus, the King of the Jews" (27:37)	"The Son of Man came not to be served, but to serve, and to give His life a ransom for many" (10:45)	"The Son of Man came to seek and to save that which was lost" (19:10)	"Belief in Jesus, Messiah and Son of God" (20:31)
Design	Dispensational	Chronological	Historical	Theological
Style	Methodical & Massive	Colloquial & Concise	Artistic & Classical	Abstract & Profound
Emphasis	Discourses Sermon on Mt. Olivet Discourse	Miracles 18 of the 35 in the gospels	Parables 35 total 19 unique	Interviews Nicodemus & the Samaritan Woman
OT References	129	63	67	43
Prominent Words	"fulfilled" 12x	"immediately" 40x	"Son of Man" 26x	"believe" 98x

MATTHEW

Dr. Bill Bright, founder of Campus Crusade for Christ, used to ask Christians on the college campus, "What is the most important thing anyone has ever done for you?" The answer: "Someone told me about Jesus." Dr. Bright's follow-up question was, "What is the most important thing you can do for someone else?" The answer: "Tell them about Jesus."

The concept of sharing good news was not unfamiliar to this gospel writer. Someone had told Matthew, a Jewish tax collector, about Jesus. And Matthew wrote his gospel to make sure that all his Jewish friends and relatives heard about Him too.

What's the title?

The title, "The Gospel According to Matthew," indicates that this account is the story of Jesus as remembered and recorded by Matthew.

Who wrote it?

The gospel is anonymous, but from a very early period the author has been identified as Matthew (Levi) the Galilean tax collector who became one of Jesus' disciples. Matthew, originally named "Levi," was the son of Alpheus (Mark 2:14). He worked at a tax collection station in Capernaum, a city located on the northwest shore of the Sea of Galilee. While sitting at his tax office in Capernaum one day, Jesus said to him, "Follow me!" Matthew immediately responded to the invitation and eventually became one of the Twelve Apostles.

To whom was it written?

Matthew appears to have been written primarily for Jewish people who had not yet accepted Jesus as Israel's Messiah. This is evidenced by the Jewish genealogy in chapter one, the emphasis upon the fulfillment of prophecy throughout the book, and Matthew's use of Jewish terminology such as "Son of David."

When was it written?

Scholars have debated whether Matthew or Mark wrote first. Early tradition, however, indicates that Matthew's gospel was the first gospel. Eusebius, the early church historian, quotes Clement of Alexandria (A.D. 144-200) as saying that the gospels with the genealogies (Matthew and Luke) were written first. Matthew was written for the benefit of the Jewish people, probably around A.D. 50.

What's the historical setting?

Matthew begins his gospel with an account of Jesus birth in the winter of 5/4 B.C. He reports on the life and ministry of Jesus, including His crucifixion, April 3, A.D. 33, and events of his forty-day post resurrection ministry. Like Mark and Luke, Matthew focuses on the ministry of Jesus in Galilee.

Why was it written?

Matthew writes to share the good news about Jesus. The purpose of his gospel is to demonstrate and convince Jews everywhere that Jesus of Nazareth is the promised Messiah of Old Testament prophecy.

What's the theme?

The theme of Matthew is found in the inscription placed on Jesus' cross, "This is Jesus the king of the Jews" (27:37).

What's it about?

Matthew focuses on the message that Jesus came to establish God's Kingdom and reign as Israel's promised Messiah. Matthew wanted all his friends and readers to know that Jesus truly is "the King of the Jews."

Introduction of the King 1:1-4:11	Presentation of the King 21-23
Proclamation of the King 4:12-7:29	Predictions of the King 24-25
Authentication of the King 8-10	Rejection of the King 26
Controversy over the King 11:11-14:12	Crucifixion of the King 27
Instruction by the King 14:13-20:34	Resurrection of the King 28

What does it teach us?

Matthew teaches us about the messiahship of Jesus. The word "Messiah" is the Greek transliteration of the Hebrew term *mashiach* which means "anointed" or "anointed one." The word was used in the Hebrew Bible to designate those who had been set apart for religious purposes, such as the priest, prophets and kings of Israel. God had promised His people that there would be a very special Anointed One who would be a descendant of Abraham and David, who would be born of a virgin in the town of Bethlehem. This special person would come to deliver His people and establish God's kingdom rule on earth.

Matthew writes his gospel to show that Jesus of Nazareth fulfills all the qualifications for being Israel's promised

Messiah. He is a descendant of Abraham and David (Matt. 1:1-16); He was born of a virgin (Matt. 1:23); He was born in Bethlehem (Matt. 2:5-6); and He came out of Egypt (Matt. 2:15). When the angel of the Lord told Joseph that Mary was to bear a Son, it was announced, "You shall call His name Jesus ("salvation") for it is He who will save His people from their sins" (Matt. 1:21). Matthew devotes his gospel to proving that Jesus is indeed the long-awaited Deliverer, the Promised One–the Messiah of Israel.

Where's Jesus?

This is an easy one! You will find Jesus *everywhere* in the Gospel of Matthew. Look especially at the many places where Matthew writes something like, "Now this took place that what was spoken by the prophet might be fulfilled…." Matthew uses 129 quotations from the Hebrew Bible, many of which demonstrate how Jesus has fulfilled messianic prophecy. But Jesus isn't just in the Gospel of Matthew. As His name Immanuel ("God with us") reveals that He is with each believer today. Jesus' promise in the last verse of the Gospel confirms this. "I am with you always, even to the end of the age" (Matt. 28:20).

MARK

The Gospel of Mark would not be in our Bibles if the Lord was not a God of grace and forgiveness. Mark, the cousin of Barnabas, joined Paul on his first missionary journey. But after reaching Perga, on the southern coast of modern Turkey, Mark abandoned the missionary team and returned to Jerusalem. In light of his unfaithfulness, Paul refused to take him on his second journey. But in spite of his early failure, Paul later acknowledged that Mark had become "useful" for the ministry (2 Tim. 4:11). Mark's usefulness is evident by the existence of this gospel–a reminder that God doesn't give up on people He has called. We serve the God of the second chance.

What's the title?

The title of this book is "the Gospel According to Mark," indicating that this book is the record of the good news about Jesus Christ as recounted by Mark.

Who wrote it?

Mark's Gospel is anonymous, but the testimony of the early church fathers (including Irenaeus, Clement of Alexandria, Origen, and Jerome) indicates that John Mark was the author of the work. Papias, the bishop of Hierapolis (AD 60-130), reports that Mark recorded in his gospel what Peter taught about Jesus.

John Mark was the son of a certain Mary in Jerusalem (Acts 12:12) and the cousin of Barnabas (Col. 4:10). His home was Jerusalem and he may have witnessed some of the events of the life of Christ, possibly being the young man referred to in Mark 14:51.

Mark accompanied Paul and Barnabas from Jerusalem to Antioch (Acts 12:25) and set out on their first missionary journey but upon reaching Perga, returned home to Jerusalem (Acts 13:5,13). He later accompanied Barnabas on a missionary journey to Cyprus (Acts 15:37-39). Mark was with Paul at Rome during his first imprisonment (Col. 4:10; Philemon 23,24). Paul requested Mark's presence in Rome during the days of his second imprisonment (2 Tim. 4:11). According to tradition, Mark founded the church in Alexandria and became its first bishop.

To whom was it written?

Both internal evidence and external testimony suggests that Mark wrote his gospel for Roman readers. According to Clement of Alexandria, Mark recorded Peter's words for the benefit of Roman inquirers.

Other evidence for Roman readership includes: (1) the explanation of Greek terms with Latin words; 12:42, 13:16, (2) the explanation of Jewish customs; 7:2, 7:11, 14:12, (3) the explanation of Palestinian geography; 13:3, and (4) the use of Latin words; 6:27, 7:4,8, 12:42, 15:39,44,45.

When was it written?

Those who believe that Mark was the first of the New Testament writings suggest that it was written around AD 50. However, the historical evidence for such an early date is lacking. Since the book contains no reference to the destruction of Jerusalem, it may be concluded that it was probably written before AD 70.

Clement of Alexandria indicates that the Gospel was written during Peter's lifetime and authorized by him (Eusebius *Historia Ecclesiastica* 2.15, 3.39). Since Peter died in AD 64, it is probable that Mark was written during the 60's, perhaps around AD 64 or 65.

What's the historical setting?

The Gospel of Mark makes no reference to the birth of Jesus or His early ministry in Judea. The record begins with the commencement of Jesus' public ministry at His baptism which was sometime during the summer or autumn of AD 29.

The Gospel records the life of Christ including His death (April 3, AD 33) and resurrection. Mark records the ministry of Jesus in Galilee (1:14-9:50), Perea (10), and Judea (11-13).

Why was it written?

The purpose of Mark is to present the person and work of Christ as God's Servant and Son as demonstrated by His mighty works. Mark presents to his Roman readers the dynamic Son of Man as Servant, eliciting faith in Him.

What's the theme?

The theme of the Gospel is expressed in Mark 10:45, "For even the Son of Man did not come to be served, but to serve, and to give his life a ransom for many."

What's it about?

Mark knew that his Roman readers would be more impressed with the mighty works of Jesus than His fulfilling prophecy. So the outline reflects his focus on Christ the Servant, attested by His mighty works.

Introduction of the Servant 1:1-13	Presentation of the Servant 11-12
Proclamation of the Servant 1:14-20	Predictions of the Servant 13
Authentication of the Servant 1:21-3:5	Rejection of the Servant 14
Controversy over the Servant 3:6-6:29	Crucifixion of the Servant 15
Instruction of the Servant 6:30-10:52	Resurrection of the Servant 16

What does it teach us?

The Gospel of Mark presents a theology of servanthood.

This is highlighted in Mark 10:45 where it is recorded that "the Son of Man did not come to be served, but to serve, and to give his life a ransom for many." Although Jesus is the Son of God, the Creator of the universe, he did not come to earth to be served by others. Rather, he took on a physical body in order that He might *serve* humanity.

The particular service of Jesus in our behalf is captured in the phrase, "to give his life a ransom for many." In ancient times a "ransom" was the price paid for the release of a slave. A slave could actually buy his own release or the price of release could be paid by family or friends. We were once slaves in bondage to sin and death, but Jesus paid our ransom and set us free! The ransom was paid by the shedding of His blood on the cross. Jesus stood in our place, receiving the just condemnation for our sin.

But this is not just ivory tower theology. The point of the passage (Mark 10:35-45) is that Jesus' willingness to humble Himself in sacrificial service for others is intended as a pattern for the lives of His followers. If the Master serves, how much more ought His followers serve one another (Gal. 5:13).

Where's Jesus?

Where is Jesus in the Gospel of Mark? You will find Him in the miracles. Mark records 18 of the 35 specifically detailed miracles of the Gospels. There are more miracles per page in Mark's gospel than in Matthew, Luke or John. What does this heavy concentration of miracles suggest? Mark wants his readers to know that Jesus is all powerful! He is not limited by the natural laws of the universe. Jesus can heal the sick, still the storm, cast out demons, raise the dead, feed the multitude and walk on water. Jesus reminds us that what seems impossible from a human point of view is always possible with God (10:27). What an encouragement to know that Jesus specializes in making things considered impossible a living reality (Mark 10:27).

LUKE

Unlike the other gospel writers, Luke wasn't Jewish. Nor was he born and raised in the land of Israel. And he wasn't an apostle! But as a Greek Gentile believer in Jesus, Luke was anxious to tell the story of Jesus to the world, showing his fellow Greek Gentiles that Jesus–the Jewish Messiah--had provided salvation for them too!

What's the title?

The title, "The Gospel According to Luke," indicates that this book records the good news about Jesus as researched and recounted by Luke.

Who wrote it?

Although the Gospel of Luke is anonymous, both internal and external evidence point to Luke, the Gentile physician (Col. 4:14) and companion of the Apostle Paul as the author. Internal confirmation of Lukan authorship is seen by the close relationship between the Gospel and Acts. Both books were addressed to the same man, Theophilus (Lk. 1:3, Acts 1:1) and both use medical terminology. The writings of the early church fathers (Irenaeus, Tertullian, Clement, Origen, Jerome, and Eusebius) confirm that Luke wrote the Third Gospel.

Luke was a Gentile convert (Col. 4:10-14), possibly from Syrian Antioch, as stated by the early church leaders, Jerome and Eusebius. Luke joined Paul at Troas (Acts 16:10) during his second missionary journey and accompanied him to Philippi. Luke later traveled with Paul to Jerusalem (Acts 20:5-21:15) and finally to Rome (Acts 27:1-28:15). Luke was affectionately referred to by Paul as "the beloved physician" (Col. 4:14, Philemon 24), and was Paul's last friend to remain with him during his final imprisonment (2 Tim. 4:11). Luke was an able historian, physician, writer and missionary.

To whom was it written?

The Gospel of Luke was written for a certain prominent individual named "Theophilus" (1:3). This reference is really a dedication to Theophilus who may have financed the publication and distribution of the Luke's book. The work was clearly written for the benefit of Gentiles in general and for Greeks in particular.

As a result of Paul's travels, the good news about Jesus spread through the Greek world. Soon there arose a need for a record of the life and teachings of Jesus that would speak to the Greek mind. The Greek nature of the book is seen in the fact that the genealogy is traced to Adam, the father of the human race, rather than Abraham, the father of the Hebrew nation.

Luke also avoids the use of Jewish terminology like "rabbi" and instead uses "master" or "teacher." Luke places less emphasis on the fulfillment of prophecy and substitutes Greek names for Hebrew names (Mark 3:18/Luke 6:16, and Luke 23:33). This evidence suggests that Luke had Greek Gentiles in mind as he wrote his gospel.

When was it written?

The Gospel was written before Acts (see Acts 1:1) and after Christianity had developed to the point where it would attract the attention of a Gentile inquirer like Theophilus. The abrupt ending of Acts indicates that Luke concluded his writing at the end of Paul's imprisonment in Rome in A.D. 62. The Gospel was composed prior to that, probably about A.D. 60.

What's the historical setting?

The historical setting of the Gospel is the period of the life of Christ, 5/4 B.C. to April 3, A.D. 33, and the forty-day period of His post-resurrection ministry.

Why was it written?

The purpose of the Gospel is clearly stated by the author (Lk. 1:1-4). Luke intends to present an accurate record of the events of the life of Christ in order that Theophilus and other Greek Gentiles might receive careful instruction. In his gospel Luke presents Christ as the perfect Son of Man who came to save lost humanity.

What's the theme?

The doctrine of salvation is central to Luke. He uses the word "to save" 18 times, more than any other gospel writer. The theme of the Gospel is captured in Luke 19:10, "for the Son of Man came to seek and to save that which was lost."

What's it about?

Luke is particularly fond of the expression "Son of Man," which he uses in his gospel to emphasize Jesus' association with humanity. Our outline of Luke recognizes that emphasis.

Arrival of the Son of Man 1-2	Presentation of the Son of Man 19:28-21:4
Introduction of the Son of Man 3:1-4:13	Predictions of the Son of Man 21:5-28
Ministry of the Son of Man 14:14-9:50	Rejection of the Son of Man 22-23
Mission of the Son of Man 9:51-19:27	Resurrection of the Son of Man 24

What does it teach us?

The ministry of the Holy Spirit is prominent in Luke's Gospel. He records the prophecy that John (the Baptizer) would be filled with the Spirit from his mother's womb (1:5). Elizabeth and Zacharias are said to be filled with the Spirit (1:41,67). The Holy Spirit, the Second Person of the Trinity, is repeatedly mentioned throughout the book.

Luke also stresses the importance of doctrine of prayer. He does this by recording the prayers of Jesus (3:21, 5:16, 6:12, 9:18,28f, 10:21, 11:1, 22:41f, 23:46) and recording certain parables which have lessons about prayer (11:5, 18:1, 19:10).

Where's Jesus?

The life and ministry of Jesus is featured throughout Luke's gospel, but I believe He is particularly featured in the parables. Luke records 35 parables of Jesus, 19 of which are unique to his gospel. It is here in Luke's gospel that we find such memorable parables as the Good Samaritan (10:30-37), the Great Supper (14:16-24), the Lost Coin (15:8-19), the Prodigal Son (15:11-32), and the Rich Man and Lazarus (16:19-31). If you are looking for Jesus in the Gospel of Luke, you will find Him teaching the parables!

JOHN

To get to know God better I suggest reading Deuteronomy and the Gospel of John–in that order. What these books share in common is the theme of God's love (Deut. 7:7-8, John 3:16). God has a sacrificial love for His people that is evidenced not only by His words, but also His actions. God declares His love, and then demonstrates it through His work of redemption. And as God loves His people, so they are to love Him. Such love is best displayed through loyalty, service and obedience. As Jesus said, "If you love me, you will keep my commandments" (John 14:15).

Who wrote it?

Although the Fourth Gospel is anonymous, both internal and external evidence point to John the Apostle, the son of Zebedee, as the author. John 21:10,24 indicates that the author is the "disciple whom Jesus loved, the one who "leaned" on Jesus' breast at the last supper (13:23).

The biblical evidence and writings of the church fathers (Irenaeus, Clement, Origen, and Tertullian) confirm that John the apostle authored the Fourth Gospel.

John, an early disciple of John the Baptizer, followed Jesus after meeting Him at Bethany beyond the Jordan (Jn. 1:35-42). Along with his brother James, John later quit the fishing business to become "fishers of men" (Matt. 4:19-21). John and his brother James were both present at Jesus' transfiguration (Matt. 17:1). He occupied a place of privilege at the Last Supper (Jn. 13:23). He witnessed the trial and crucifixion of Jesus and assumed responsibility for Jesus' mother after He committed her to his care (Jn. 19:26-27).

John not only wrote the Fourth Gospel, but authored First, Second and Third John and the Book of Revelation. After the assassination of Domitian (A.D. 96) John was released from exile on Patmos and took up residence in Ephesus. According to Polycrates, an early bishop at Ephesus, John died and was buried in Ephesus.

To whom was it written?

While the Jewish terms and background of the gospel may indicate that John wrote for the benefit of Jewish readers, the universal tone (3:16, 10:16, 12:32) suggests that the circle of readers should not be too narrowly restricted. It seems that John wrote his gospel from his own Jewish background but with the whole world in mind.

When was it written?

Most conservative scholars argue for a date of around A.D. 85-90 since John appears to supplement the other gospels which were written earlier. But some scholars believe that the gospel should be dated before A.D. 70. John writes in 5:2 "there is" a pool, but in 18:1 he says, "there was" a garden. This may indicate that John wrote when Jerusalem was under siege by the Romans after the gardens around the city had been destroyed, but before the walls had been breached. This would fit the conditions in Jerusalem around A.D. 68-69.

What is the historical setting?

According to an early church leader named Irenaeus (A.D. 130-202), the gospel was written at Ephesus, John's residence and place of burial (Against Heresies 3.1.1). John had been ministering in Ephesus for 20-25 years, and the elders of the Asian churches may have requested a written record of his teaching before he died.

Ephesus was ranked with Alexandria and Syrian Antioch as one of the three greatest cities of the east. It was the political center for Roman administration of the province of Asia and the guardian of the temple of Artemis and her sacred image.

The Gospel of John emphasizes the ministry of Jesus in Judea and Jerusalem (5, 7-20) while the Synoptic Gospels present more about His Galilean ministry. John also records some significant events in Jesus' ministry in Galilee (2, 4:3, 6, 21) and Samaria (4).

Why was it written?

The evangelistic purpose of John's Gospel is set forth in 20:30-31, "Many other signs therefore Jesus also performed in the presence of the disciples, which are not written in this book but these have been written that you may believe that Jesus is the Christ, the Son of God; and that believing you may have life in His name." John has presented a record of the miraculous signs performed by Jesus in order to inspire faith and life in Him. The Fourth Gospel supplements the Synoptic Gospels, presenting the truth of the Person and work of Christ.

What's the theme?

John's gospel is the "Gospel of Belief." The theme is "belief in Jesus, the Messiah and Son of God" (John 20:30-31).

What's it about?

John's outline centers on the two responses to the Person of Christ–belief and unbelief–acceptance of Jesus as Savior and the rejection of His person and work.

The Prologue 1:1-18	Prayer for the Believers 17
Beginnings of Belief 1:19-4:54	Consummation of Unbelief 18-19
Development of Unbelief 5-12	Confirmation of Belief 20
Strengthening of Belief 13-16	Responsibilities of Belief 21

What does it teach us?

The frequent repetition of the word "believe" (*pisteuo*) suggests the book's great theological emphasis. The word "believe" is used 98 times in John and essentially means "to trust." It never means mere intellectual assent to a proposition, but involves a personal response and commitment. Belief is equated with "receiving" Jesus (1:12), "obeying" the Son (3:36), and "abiding" in Him (15:1-10).

When Ann Seward was asked to co-star with high-wire artist Philippe Petite at the opening of the Portland Center for the Performing Arts, she knew that her stage would be high above the streets of Portland on an 80 ft. wire strung between two buildings. Yet she willingly placed her life in the hands of Philippe Petite as he walked the high-wire. She commented later that her performance took "a lot of trust–absolute trust." And that is what biblical belief is all about. It is not merely believing that someone could be carried safely on the wire.

Biblical belief is the act of putting yourself in hands of the high-wire artist--trusting Him to carry you safely from this life to your heavenly home.

Where's Jesus?

While Jesus can be found in every chapter of the Gospel of John, He is especially prominent in the seven "I Am" statements which are unique to the Fourth Gospel. Jesus declares, "I am the bread of life" (6:35), the "light of the world" (8:12, 9:5), the "door of the sheep" (10:7), the good shepherd" (10:14), and the "resurrection and the life" (11:25), "the way, the truth, and the life (14:6), "the true vine" (15:1). These seven declarations give great insight into the person of Jesus and His messianic mission.

CHAPTER SEVEN

Acts of the Apostles

The Acts of the Apostles is the seventh great chapter in the story of the Bible. This chapter is extremely important because it tells how the followers of Jesus carried on after His ascension back to heaven. Did they lose their faith and give up their confidence in the messiahship of Jesus when He was no longer with them on earth? Or were they so convinced by his teachings and miracles that they continued sharing the good news even at great personal cost?

The book of Acts is the story of the expansion and growth of God's kingdom through the faithful witness of the apostles who were empowered by the indwelling presence of the Holy Spirit.

Acts begins with the ascension of Jesus. But before His return to the Father, Jesus promised that He would send the Holy Spirit to be personally present with His followers as they told others about His redemptive work. Acts 2 records the events of the Day of Pentecost and how the believers in Jesus were filled with the Spirit and empowered for their work. Their mission, as given by Jesus, was to be "witnesses" of His person and work.

The word "witness" is the Greek word *martures* and is used of those who give testimony of certain truths by their deaths. Many gave witness by their words. Some did so by their deaths. Stephen was the first to give his life as a witness for Christ by his martyrdom in Jerusalem (Acts 7).

But persecution did not silence the early believers! Acts records how the early church grew in Jerusalem and then spread into the surrounding district of Judea. Philip, the evangelist, carried the good news of Jesus' death and resurrection to the people of Samaria. Although there was some hesitance about welcoming Samaritans into the church

(John 4:9), no one could deny that they had received the same Holy Spirit as had the believers in Jerusalem.

The next stage in the advance of the gospel is recorded in Chapter 10 where God led Peter to preach the gospel to a Roman soldier named Cornelius. As a god-fearing Gentile, Cornelius prayed to the God of the Jews but knew nothing about God's provision of salvation through Jesus, the Jewish Messiah. While Peter was preaching to Cornelius and his family, the Holy Spirit was poured out on these new believers. Peter understood this to mean that the gospel was not just for Jewish people, but that salvation was available to all who would receive it!

The Apostle Paul is the witness that carried the gospel on its third great advance to the Gentile nations of the Roman world. As an observant Jew, a Pharisee, and a persecutor of the early Christians, we would least expect for someone like Paul to become a witness for Christ. But we serve a God who delights in wonderful surprises! Saul the persecutor was brought to faith on the road to Damascus and immediately became a proclaimer of the gospel.

Commissioned by the church at Antioch, Paul and his missionary associates were sent out to preach the gospel and establish churches. The rest of the book of Acts records Paul's travels to Cyprus, Galatia, Macedonia, Greece, Asia Minor, and Rome. God worked mightily through Paul's labors and churches were established at such significant cities as Philippi, Thessalonica, Corinth, and Ephesus.

Upon his return to Jerusalem after a three-year ministry in Ephesus, Paul was arrested and accused of bringing Gentiles into the temple area. Threats against his life resulted in him being transferred to Caesarea where Paul remained for two long years awaiting formal charges against him. Finally, Paul exercised his right as a Roman citizen and appealed to Caesar.

The book of Acts ends with the Apostle Paul in Rome awaiting a hearing before the Roman emperor Nero. But even during this imprisonment the Holy Spirit was at work providing Paul with countless opportunities to witness to Jews, Gentiles and Roman soldiers. In addition, the imprisonment gave Paul a much needed respite from travel to write letters to the churches where he had ministered.

The Book of Acts begins with Jesus in Jerusalem teaching the things concerning the kingdom of God (Acts 1:3). It ends with Paul in Rome, preaching the kingdom of God and teaching about the Lord Jesus (Acts 28:31). The good news about Jesus had been faithfully announced from Jerusalem to Rome. And this was just the beginning.

ACTS

I enjoy reading about the experiences of Christian leaders who have been on the cutting edge of world outreach. And that is precisely what we discover in the book of Acts! Here Dr. Luke, a historian and fellow-traveler with Paul, tells the story of the beginnings and outreach of the first Christian church. He tells of acts of bravery, bold witness, martyrdoms, travel adventure, ship wrecks, miracles, mass conversions and more. The book of Acts is my kind of book--a true Christian adventure story! As you begin studying its pages, I'm sure you discover that it is *your* kind of book too.

What's the title?

The title, "Acts of the Apostles," first appeared around the middle of the 2nd century. The abbreviation "Acts" also dates from ancient times.

Who wrote it?

Although the author of Acts is not named, the evidence points to Luke, the historian, physician, writer and missionary.

The medical vocabulary used in Acts supports the view that the book was authored by "Luke, the beloved physician" (Col. 4:14). Luke joined Paul at Troas (16:11) and includes himself in the "we" sections (16:10-17, 20:5-21:18, 27:1-28:16). The church fathers (Irenaeus, Clement of Alexandria, Tertullian, and Origen) all support the view the Lukan authorship of Acts.

Luke was a Gentile convert (Col. 4:10-14), possibly of the church at Antioch as stated by Jerome and Eusebius. Luke joined Paul at Troas (Acts 16:10) during his second missionary journey and accompanied Him to Philippi. Luke later accompanied Paul to Jerusalem (20:5-21:15), and finally to Rome (27:1-28:15). He was Paul's last friend to remain with him during his second imprisonment (2 Tim. 4:11).

To whom was it written?

Like Luke's gospel, Acts was written for a prominent individual named Theophilus (1:1). The reference to Theophilus is really a dedication characteristic of Graeco-Roman literature. The universal scope of Acts indicates that it was written for the church in general.

When was it written?

The Book of Acts was probably written in Rome during or after Paul's first imprisonment (A.D. 60-62). Luke wrote his gospel around A.D. 60 and Acts shortly after that. The absence of any reference to the fall of Jerusalem (A.D. 70) or the anti-Christian policies of Nero (A.D. 64) serve to confirm the view that the book was written in the early sixties toward the end of Paul's imprisonment, around A.D. 63.

What's the historical setting?

Acts covers the period from the ascension of Jesus (May 14, A.D. 33) through Paul's first imprisonment in Rome (A.D. 60-62). The book describes the expansion of the church in Jerusalem, Judea, Samaria, and the Mediterranean world.

Noteworthy events in Paul's life and ministry include the following:

Paul's Conversion	A.D. 35
Paul's 1st Journey	Spring A.D. 48 – Fall 49
Paul's 2nd Journey	Spring A.D. 50 – Fall 52
Paul's 3rd Journey	Spring A.D. 53 – Spring 57
Paul Imprisoned at Caesarea	Summer A.D. 57 - Summer 59
Paul Imprisoned at Rome	Winter A.D. 60 – Spring 62
Paul's Death	Spring A.D. 68

Why was it written?

Luke intends his books (Luke and Acts) to present an accurate and orderly account of the origins and development of the Christian faith. His first volume presents the record of Jesus' Person and work. The Book of Acts traces the advance and development of the kingdom of God (1:3, 28:31) through the ministry of the Holy Spirit.

What's the theme?

The theme of Acts is the advance of the church and expansion of God's kingdom (Acts 1:8).

What's it about?

Ascension & Pentecost 1:1-2:4	Witness in Jerusalem 2:5-8:3	Witness in Palestine 8:4-12:25	Witness in the World 13:1-28:31

What does it teach us?

The "kingdom of God" is a prominent theological emphasis in the Book of Acts. It appears at the beginning of the book as the message Christ preached during his forty-day post resurrection ministry (Acts 1:3). It is the message Paul preached during his two-year imprisonment in Rome (Acts 28:23,31). This message was preached by Philip the evangelist in Samaria (Acts 8:12) and by Paul in the churches he planted (Acts 14:22, 19:8, 20:25). This must be an important message! But many Christians have only a vague idea of what God's kingdom is all about.

From the time when God's sovereign rule over the universe was challenged by Satan, God has been working to reassert His sovereignty in the place of where it was challenged. God's kingdom involves a king who rules, a people who are ruled, and a place where this rule is recognized. We could say that God's kingdom involves God's people, in God's place, under God's rule.

The development of God's kingdom is a central theme of Scripture. The people and place of the kingdom was announced by God to Abraham in Gen. 12:1-3. God promised that the descendants of Abraham (the people) would be given a land (the place). In 2 Samuel 7:12-16 God promises that the Ruler of the land and its people would be a royal descendant of David. Later on in the New Testament we read of Jesus, a descendant of David, who announces that the King has come and His kingdom is ready to be inaugurated (Matt. 4:17)!

Sadly, both the King and His kingdom offer were rejected by the people of Israel. Instead of welcoming their King, Jesus was arrested and crucified. But since God's promise to Abraham was unconditional, His kingdom couldn't be simply canceled. Instead, the kingdom would be delayed (Lk. 19:11-27) until a generation of Abraham's descendants arose who would welcome Jesus as their Messiah. This will take place at the Second Coming of Christ when the Jewish people embrace Jesus as their Messiah (Zech. 12:10-13:1).

Throughout the Book of Acts, the message of the Kingdom of God is being proclaimed. It is the simple message that God is not through with His Jewish people! Although they rejected Jesus at His first advent, the unconditional promise of the Kingdom will be fulfilled when Israel repents and welcomes their promised Messiah. And so as Jesus preached, the apostles also proclaimed in Acts, "Repent, the kingdom is at hand!"

Although the full inauguration of God's kingdom awaits the return of Christ, God is at work today calling a people to come under His authority and accept His rule over their lives. This spiritual dimension of God's kingdom is evident today in the growth and expansion of the church. The church is not the sum total of the kingdom of God, yet it is the most visible manifestation of God's kingdom as it is developing in the world today. One day when Christ returns the Kingdom of God will be established in all its fullness (Revelation 20:1-6) as Jesus (the King) rules His people (believing Jews and Gentiles) in the place promised (the land of Israel).

Where's Jesus?

You will find Jesus in Acts chapter one which records Jesus forty-day post-resurrection ministry leading up to His ascension to heaven (1:1-11). What was Jesus doing during this forty-day period? Luke records that Jesus was teaching the disciples "things concerning the kingdom of God" (1:3). It must have been an important truth if Jesus spent the last forty days of His earthly ministry teaching about it! Jesus was teaching that He had come to offer Israel the promised kingdom, but His rejection as Messiah meant that the kingdom would be postponed until a future day when Israel was ready to receive Him as their King (Zechariah 12:10, 13:1).

CHAPTER EIGHT

Paul's Epistles

The Apostle Paul was not only a zealous missionary, a successful church planter, and a strong preacher. He was also a prolific writer! During the course of his missionary travels Paul wrote 13 of the 27 New Testament books. The writings of Paul are the next great chapter in the story of the Bible.

Paul's writings are called "epistles" because they are actually letters which he sent to the churches. The Greek word "epistle" is based on the verb "to send." These letters follow the literary pattern of Greek letters which were written in the first century. The basic elements include the following:

The Salutation	"Paul, an apostle to the churches…"
The Health Wish	"Grace to you and peace."
Prayer for the Readers	"I pray that your love may abound…."
Body of the Letter	"Now concerning…."
Closing Greetings	"Greet the saints; the saints greet you."

The Book of Acts provides the historical context and background for most of Paul's letters. In teaching Paul's letters, my students find it helpful when I present the letters in the chronological order in which they were written, setting the historical context for each. You may find this to be a helpful approach as well.

Paul was accompanied on his first missionary journey by

Barnabas. Leaving Syrian Antioch in the spring of A.D. 47, they sailed for Cyprus, the homeland of Barnabas. After ministering in the major cities of Cyprus, they took a ship to a region known today as Turkey. There they had a successful church planting ministry, returning to Antioch in the fall of A.D. 49. But their rejoicing over the success of their mission soon changed to serious concern. Paul learned that the believers in the churches which had so recently been established were being taught that circumcision and keeping Jewish traditions was necessary for their complete salvation. Paul wrote his first letter, the Epistle to the Galatians, to refute this error and convince these new believers that people were justified by faith alone and not by works of the law (Galatians 2:16).

Paul set out from Antioch on his second journey in the spring of A.D. 50. Silas accompanied Paul on this journey, and they were later joined by Timothy and Luke. After visiting the churches which Paul and Barnabas had established on their first journey, the missionary team crossed the Aegean Sea and ministered for about six months in Macedonia. Luke records that during this period thriving churches were planted in Philippi, Thessalonica and Berea.

Paul then traveled south for a brief ministry in Athens before traveling on to Corinth where he spent the next year and a half. It was during this time that Paul joined with Aquila and Priscilla in a tent making business while he evangelized the city and established the church at Corinth. It was also during this period that Paul wrote his next two epistles–First and Second Thessalonians. Paul wrote the first letter to the believers at Thessalonica to commend their faithfulness in the face of conflicts and to correct certain errors which had been reported to him. His second letter, written about three months later, was primarily written to correct their misconception that the Day of the Lord had arrived.

Paul left Corinth in the fall of A.D. 51 and crossed the Aegean for a brief stay in Ephesus. There he left Aquila and Priscilla with plans to return if it was the Lord's will. After visiting the church in Jerusalem, Paul returned to Antioch where he had begun his mission two and a half years earlier. Paul reported to his supporters the wonderful things God had accomplished and took a well-deserved furlough before starting out on his third journey the next spring.

Paul third missionary journey began in the spring of A.D. 53. He traveled once again through the region of Galatia and then passed through the Lycus Valley to Ephesus where he spent the next three years. After speaking in the synagogue for three months in Ephesus, Paul established a school where he taught daily for two years. It was probably during these years that the churches in the Lycus valley (Colossae, Hierapolis and Laodicea) were founded. Around A.D. 56 Paul received some troubling news regarding the church at Corinth. Paul responded with the letter we know as First Corinthians addressing the matter of division within the body and replying to questions raised by the believers.

Leaving Ephesus in the spring of A.D. 56, Paul crossed the Aegean to Macedonia. While ministering among the churches in Macedonia, Titus reported to Paul that the situation in Corinth had improved. The Apostle sat down and wrote his second canonical epistle to the Corinthians (Second Corinthians) preparing them for his forthcoming visit.

Departing from Macedonia in the fall of A.D. 56, Paul traveled south to Greece where he spent the winter. Most of that time was probably spent at Corinth where he sought to encourage the believers and strengthen the church. It was during his winter in Corinth that Paul wrote his letter to the believers at Rome, preparing them for his forthcoming visit and enlisting their support for his anticipated travels to Spain. Paul also used this letter to expound the good news of justification by faith for all who believe in Jesus.

Bidding farewell to his friends at Corinth in late winter or early spring of A.D. 57, Paul returned to Jerusalem where he was arrested under suspicion of bringing Gentiles into the temple area. Paul spent his next two years in the custody of civil authorities in Caesarea awaiting formal charges against him. He eventually asserted his right as a Roman citizen and appealed to Caesar. Luke records Paul's perilous journey and ship wreck, but he was brought safely to Rome. There under house arrest, Paul had considerable freedom for witness and ministry. It was during these two years in Rome that Paul wrote his "prison epistles," Ephesians, Philippians, Colossians and Philemon.

Paul appears to have been released after his two years of house arrest in Rome. Perhaps formal charges were never brought against him and the statute of limitations expired. After his release in the spring of A.D. 62 Paul enjoyed further opportunities for travel and ministry. He was able to visit the believers in Ephesus, Colossae, and Philippi.

It was probably from Philippi that he wrote his first letter to young Timothy who was serving as Paul's representative in Ephesus. Paul wrote First Timothy to help Timothy exercise the leadership which had been entrusted to him. Later Paul journeyed to Crete where he left Titus in a similar capacity as Timothy. Paul wrote a letter to Titus from Asia Minor providing direction on matters on leadership and church order.

Paul's final epistle, Second Timothy, was written shortly before his death in Rome. He was once again in prison, but this time as a criminal. His death was imminent. Paul wrote Timothy, who was still in Ephesus, to bring Mark and join him in Rome before winter (A.D. 67/68). Second Timothy was written to encourage Timothy in his ministry. Paul urged him to endure hardship, do the work of an evangelist, and fulfill his ministry.

According to early Christian tradition, Paul was executed in early A.D. 68 outside the gates of Rome and buried in the catacombs south of the city. But the death of Paul was not the end of his ministry and influence, for he left us with thirteen New Testament epistles which continue to instruct and encourage Jesus' followers.

ROMANS

It is hard to imagine another New Testament book that has had a greater impact on the church than Paul's letter to the Romans. In the fall of 1515 a good monk in the pursuit of holiness through chastity, poverty, fasting, vigils and mortifications of the flesh began his study of Paul's epistle to the Romans. These studies proved to be for Martin Luther his "Damascus road."

Luther was perplexed by the concept of the "justice of God." He pondered the expression night and day until he understood that "the justice of God is that righteousness by which through grace and sheer mercy God justifies us through faith." With this understanding, Luther felt himself to be "reborn" and the whole of Scripture took on new meaning.

Luther's new understanding of the connection between God's justice and His grace kindled the fires of the Protestant Reformation. And it all began right here in the book of Romans!

What's the title?

The book is named for the city of Rome, the residence of the readers being addressed. Although the title is found in the oldest Greek manuscripts, it is not known for certain that the letter had a title originally.

Who wrote it?

The Pauline authorship of Romans is almost universally accepted on the basis of internal evidence (1:1, 15:25, 16:3) and the testimony of the church fathers. The actual writing was done by Tertius, Paul's scribe (16:22).

To whom was it written?

The letter is addressed to the believers in Rome (1:7).

The church at Rome was predominately Gentile with a sizable Jewish minority. This is a church that was not founded by Paul. Perhaps some Jews and proselytes from Rome who were in Jerusalem on the day of Pentecost became believers and carried the gospel back to their city (Acts 2:10).

When was it written?

The letter was written by Paul toward the end of this third missionary journey. Paul had received a collection from the churches in Greece (15:26) and was carrying it to Jerusalem. Romans was probably written in the winter of A.D. 56/57 before Paul's departure from Corinth.

What is the historical setting?

After Paul's three-year ministry in Ephesus (A.D. 53-57), he departed for Greece where he spent the next three months (Acts 20:3). Paul spent a good part of that time in Corinth and wrote Romans from that city (cf. Romans 16:23, 1 Cor. 1:14). Phoebe, from Cenchrea (Romans 16:1), the eastern seaport of Corinth, probably carried Paul's letter to Rome.

Why was it written?

Paul wrote the church at Rome to pave the way for his anticipated visit (1:11-13) and to enlist their support for his projected mission to Spain (15:24). But most importantly, Paul wanted to present the main truths of the gospel as he understood and proclaimed it (1:15,16). His goal was to show the implications of the gospel and preserve harmony between Jewish and Gentile Christians.

What's the theme?

The message of Romans is the good news of deliverance from sin by God's gracious bestowal of righteousness on all those who believe in Jesus (1:16,17). The great theme of the letter is "justification by faith."

What's it about?

Doctrine of Salvation 1-8	Unbelief of Israel 9-11	Conduct of Believers 12-16
Righteousness ...	Israel's ...	Christian ...
Needed 1:18-3:30	Past Election 9	Duties 12-13
Imputed 3:21-5:21	Present Rejection 10	Liberties 14:1-15:13
Imparted 6-8	Future Salvation 11	Greetings 15:14-16:27

What does it teach us?

Romans contains Paul's most thorough exposition of the doctrine of justification by faith apart from the works of the law (3:28). The Greek word translated "justification" is a judicial term which indicates that a verdict of acquittal has been announced. Someone has said that being justified is like "just as if I'd never sinned." But in reality, it means a whole lot more. To be justified means to be "declared righteous."

Justification means that the believing sinner has not only been acquitted from all past unrighteousness, but also that the positive righteousness of Christ has been applied to their otherwise bankrupt account. If my daughter overdraws her checking account to the tune of $200, and I graciously provide the $200 to cover the overdraft, then she is not in debt, but her account is still empty. What God has done in the act of justification is to place the positive righteousness of the Lord Jesus Christ in our personal account! So instead of seeing believers as bankrupt due to sin, God sees us as righteous on account of Jesus Christ.

Paul points out that justification by faith is really nothing new since both Abraham and David were justified the same way (4:1-8). And since Abraham was declared righteous before he was circumcised, he provides the pattern for Gentiles to be justified apart from the ceremonial requirements of Judaism. This was the great truth that changed the heart of Martin Luther and finally assured him that through faith in Jesus he could be righteous, finally enjoying peace with God.

Where's Jesus?

It would be hard *not* to find Jesus in the Book of Romans. But I believe He is particularly highlighted in chapter 5 where Paul compares and contrasts the impact of both Adam and Christ on the human condition. Through Adam's one transgression, all humanity became subject to sin, condemnation and death (5:16-18). But by contrast, those who accept Jesus' free gift of grace receive righteousness, justification and eternal life (5:16-18). Paul uses the expression "much more" (5:15,17) to indicate that the damage done by Adam's sin has been more than rectified by Jesus' sacrifice.

FIRST CORINTHIANS

Have you ever wondered what it was like to worship and fellowship in a first century church? Well, this book allows you to get up close and personal with a newly formed New Testament congregation. In this very practical letter Paul takes the roof off the church at Corinth to examine and address issues which still trouble God's people today– issues of divisions, lawsuits, sexual morality, divorce and remarriage, principles of decision making, spiritual gifts, gender based roles in church ministry and much more!

Although our culture is different, people's needs have not changed, and Paul's letter to the Corinthians provides much needed direction for God's people today.

What's the title?

The book is named for the "Corinthians," the addressees of the letter. It is called "First" Corinthians to distinguish it from Paul's second canonical letter to the same group of believers. Since Paul had already written a letter to the Corinthians (5:9), this letter is actually *Second* Corinthians! But to avoid confusion, let's leave the title as it is.

Who wrote it?

The Pauline authorship of the epistle is clear from 1:1 and 16:21 and is practically uncontested.

To whom was it written?

Paul wrote this letter to believers at Corinth (1:2). Corinth was a great commercial center strategically situated on the isthmus which links the Peloponnesus with mainland Greece. The city had two fine ports: Cenchreae on the Aegean Sea to the east, and Lechaeum on the Adriatic Sea to the west. In ancient times mariners avoided the treacherous 200-mile trip around the Peloponnesus by moving their ships on rollers across the narrow isthmus on a stone-paved road. As a commercial center, Corinth was known for its wealth, indulgence, and immorality.

The city was also a worship center for Aphrodite, the goddess of love. Strabo, a first century geographer, records that there were 1,000 temple prostitutes who served in the temple of Aphrodite on the high place, the Acrocorinth. Corinth was quite a testing ground for the Christian gospel of grace.

When was it written?

Paul wrote his letter to the Corinthians from Ephesus (16:8) towards the end of his ministry there during his third missionary journey (Spring 53 to May 57), probably around the spring of A.D. 56.

What is the historical setting?

Paul first visited Corinth in A.D. 51 on his second missionary journey after his ministry in Athens (Acts 18:1). There he met Aquila and Priscilla and joined them in a tent-making business to provide financial support while he evangelized the city. Paul was later joined by Silas and Timothy (Acts 18:5) and the team engaged in a very successful ministry for a year and a half (Acts 18:8,11).

The young church at Corinth was plagued with problems. The church was divided into factions. Some favored Peter, others Apollos, and some gave their allegiance only to Christ (1:12). Many of the believers at Corinth had been converted out of gross paganism and still participated in immoral practices (5:1). Some of the Corinthians were involved in lawsuits against other church members (6:1). There were also some doctrinal issues regarding spiritual gifts (12:4) and the resurrection (15:12).

A report of these problems had reached Paul through some members of Chloe's family (1:11). Paul had written an earlier letter (5:9) regarding some of these issues, but the problems had not been resolved.

The immediate occasion of Paul's writing was that he had received a letter (16:17) from the church inquiring concerning certain problem issues (7:1,25, 8:1, 12:1, 16:1). First Corinthians Paul constitutes Paul's reply to the questions and issues which had been brought to his attention.

Why was it written?

Paul wrote the epistle to correct the disorders within the church and answer to certain questions raised by the Corinthians. Paul's goal is to instruct the Corinthian believers in proper conduct and Christian doctrine.

What's the theme?

First Corinthians is intensely practical. The central theme of the letter is the life and conduct of believers in the church (10:31).

What's it about?

Reproofs of the Corinthians 1-6	Replies Concerning… 7-16
Introduction 1:1-9	Marriage 7
Concerning Divisions 1:10-3:23	Things Sacrificed to Idols 8-11:1
Concerning Pride 4	Spiritual Gifts 12-14
Concerning Discipline 5	The Resurrection 15
Concerning Lawsuits 6:1-11	The Collection 16:1-4
Concerning Immorality 6:12-20	Plans and Greetings 16:5-24

What does it teach us?

While Paul addresses many important issues in First

Corinthians, this letter contains his most thorough defense of the doctrine of the resurrection. There were those at Corinth who were denying this truth so important to the Christian faith. Paul responds by demonstrating that the resurrection of Jesus is an essential element of the gospel he and the other apostles preached (15:3-4). He goes on to show that if Christ has not been raised, then the Christian faith is built on a fallacy and the apostles would be false witnesses of an event which never happened. Beyond that, the Corinthians would still be unsaved, and those who have died as believers in Christ have perished tragically deceived (15:12-19).

Having demonstrated the serious consequences of denying the resurrection, Paul triumphantly affirms the resurrection of Christ and its implications for believers. Because of the union between Christ and believers, His resurrection must result in our own! Paul explains that Christ is the "first fruits" of a resurrection in which all believers have a part (15:20-22). The "first fruits" of the harvest were offered to God as an expression of faith that a full harvest would follow (Lev. 23:10-11). Christ is the first fruit of the resurrection, implying that there is more to come!

Paul goes on in 1 Corinthians 15 to explain the nature of the resurrection body. The resurrection body will differ from our earthly body. Believers will experience eternity in a very real, imperishable, glorified body—one that is perfectly suited for life in the age to come (15:35-44). Paul concludes his defense of the resurrection showing the practical application of the doctrine. Confident in their future hope of resurrection, believers are exhorted to be steadfast in their commitment to Christ and diligent in their tireless service for Him (15:58).

Where's Jesus?

Where should we look for Jesus in First Corinthians? I believe we will find him as we look at the life and character of Paul. The Apostle writes to the Corinthians, "Be imitators of me, just as I also am of Christ" (1 Cor. 11:1). Paul is confident enough in his relationship with the Savior that he can say, "follow my example, just as I'm following the example of Jesus." This means that when we look at Paul, we can expect to see Jesus! Can that be said of you? Paul's words challenge us to live our lives in such a way that people will see Jesus in what we do and say.

SECOND CORINTHIANS

Second Corinthians is the Paul's most personal letter. Here we discover just how human and problem prone was the Apostle Paul–the one led the advance of Christianity throughout the first century world! It seems from his letter that his relationship with the Corinthians was not all that he wanted it to be. His change of travel plans had offended the Corinthians and Paul has to spend the first seven chapters of the book explaining what happened and attempting to reconcile with his readers.

There were also those at Corinth who were questioning whether Paul was an authentic apostle. He knew that if his apostolic authority was rejected, his teaching would be as well. So Paul must spend the last four chapters of the book defending his apostleship.

Interwoven with his explanations and defense Paul reveals something of his own heart, character and motivation for ministry. You will get to know Paul better as you read this book!

What's the title?

The book is named for the addresses of the letter. It is called "Second Corinthians" to distinguish it from Paul's first letter to the same group of believers. In fact, it is Paul's *third* letter since he wrote an earlier letter (see 1 Cor. 5:9, 2 Cor. 7:8,12, 2:3-4) to the church which was apparently lost and did not end up in the Bible.

Who wrote it?

The Pauline authorship of Second Corinthians is clearly evidenced in the salutation (1:1) and throughout the letter. The authorship and authenticity of the epistle are practically uncontested.

To whom was it written?

The letter is addressed to the believers at Corinth and those scattered throughout Achaia, the Roman province which included all of the Peloponnesus and much of central Greece. These would have included the believers at Athens (Acts 17:34) and Cenchrea (Romans 16:1).

When was it written?

Second Corinthians was written during Paul's third missionary journey (spring A.D. 53 - May A.D. 57). After his lengthy ministry at Ephesus, Paul headed north to Macedonia in route to Corinth. The epistle must have been written in the fall of A.D. 56, a few months before Paul's anticipated visit to Corinth (2 Cor. 12:14, 13:1).

What is the historical setting?

Paul wrote First Corinthians from Ephesus in the spring of A.D. 56, toward the end of his three-year ministry there. A riot in the city forced him to leave Asia for Macedonia (2 Cor. 7:5). While laboring there he was met by Titus who brought a favorable report concerning the Corinthian church (2 Cor. 7:6-7,13-15). With this encouragement Paul penned his second canonical epistle to the believers at Corinth.

The situation in Corinth had greatly improved as a result of the ministry of Titus. But things were still not what they could or should be. Some had accused Paul of vacillating in his plans to visit Corinth. Perhaps this led to the neglect of their commitment to complete the collection for the poor believers in Jerusalem. In addition, Paul's apostleship was under attack by certain false apostles and false teachers who had the ear of the Corinthian believers. Paul knew that these issues could not be neglected. While the church at Corinth had made significant progress under the ministry of Titus, Paul wrote to encourage further corrections before his forthcoming visit.

Why was it written?

The primary purpose of Second Corinthians was to prepare the believers at Corinth for Paul's third visit (2 Cor. 12:14, 13:1). Specifically, the letter was designed to cement Paul's bond of love with the Corinthians, encourage the collection for the poor in Jerusalem, and to defend his authority against those who doubted his apostleship.

What's the theme?

Second Corinthians offers a unique glimpse into the life and ministry of Paul. The theme of the letter is Paul's ministry (4:1, 5:18, 6:3) under the New Covenant.

What's it about?

Reconciliation with the Corinthians 1-7	Grace Giving from the Heart 8-9	Defending Paul's Apostleship 10-13

What does it teach?

If the theme of this letter is Paul's ministry, certainly the special contribution of 2nd Corinthians is a theology of ministry. In describing the ministry in 2 Cor. 2:14-17, Paul uses the image of the Roman triumph. Polybius wrote that the Senate could add glory to the success of their generals by bringing their achievements before the eyes of the Roman citizens through *triumphs*. A triumph was the highest honor that could be conferred on a Roman citizen. In a triumph, the victorious general entered the city on his chariot and led a procession to Capitoline Hill where an offering was presented to Jupiter. Incense would be offered up in the streets as the general, followed by captured slaves and booty, led the procession through the city.

With that image in mind, read again Paul's words to the Corinthians in 1 Cor. 2:14, "But thanks be to God, who always leads us in His triumph in Christ, and manifests through us the sweet aroma of the knowledge of Him in every place." In the next verse, Paul likens believers to the fragrant incense that burned in the streets during a triumph. To the unsaved, believers are an aroma of death, suggesting the spiritual consequences of rejecting God's provision of salvation. To the saved, we are an aroma of life, suggesting the sweet blessings of those who receive God's gift of eternal life. In verse 17, Paul emphasizes that Christians are not like peddlers, trying to sell an inferior product to an unsuspecting customer. Instead we speak the truth and freely offer God's gift of salvation.

"Who is adequate for such an awesome responsibility of ministry?" Paul muses in verse 16. The answer comes in the next chapter. "Not that we are adequate in ourselves to consider anything as coming from ourselves, but our adequacy is from God" (2 Cor. 3:5). Christian ministry is not something we do on our own. It is something Christ does through us. While we may feel unprepared and inadequate, God is the all-powerful resource and energizer for the ministry to which He calls us (Phi. 4:13).

Where is Jesus?

Where do we find Jesus in 2nd Corinthians? According 2 Corinthians 4:7-11, you will find Jesus being displayed in Paul's life through his suffering. Paul suggests that suffering is an opportunity for the life of Jesus to be manifested. It seems that the experience of suffering has the potential to bring into focus the ministry of Christ in the life of a believer. Paul was afflicted, but not crushed; perplexed, but not forsaken; persecuted, but not forsaken; stuck down, but not destroyed (4:8-9). Paul knew that the experience of suffering was just another opportunity to let others see Jesus magnified in his life. And what was true for Paul can be true for us as well when we encounter suffering.

GALATIANS

Have you ever heard a television or radio preacher whose message didn't seem to line up with the truth you have been taught? Sensing some discrepancy, you got out your Bible to compare what you heard with God's revealed Word. That kind of spiritual discernment and sensitivity is crucial in a world where truth and error are often mingled. It is true today, and it was true in Paul's time. Like the Bereans (Acts 17:10-11), we must examine the Scriptures carefully to see if what we are being taught is really so.

Paul's letter to the Galatians is written to a group of relatively new Christians who had not yet learned to be spiritually discerning. In fact, they had been duped into thinking that merely trusting in the work of Christ was not sufficient for one's salvation. Other duties were required, including many traditions which had long been followed by observant Jews.

In this letter Paul reminds the Galatians of the simplicity of the gospel message. Faith in Christ alone is sufficient, Paul insists. And so in Galatians, Paul exhorts his readers to stand firm in their freedom and not encumber themselves with Jewish regulations and traditions.

What's the title?

The book is named for the region of Galatia where the readers resided. In Paul's day, Galatia was a Roman province located in the highlands of Asia Minor (central Turkey).

Who wrote it?

The fact that Paul wrote the book is confirmed both by internal evidence and testimony of the early church. The writer calls himself "Paul and apostle" (1:1, 5:2). The early church fathers from Clement of Rome onward assert the Pauline authorship of Galatians.

To whom was it written?

Was Galatians written to the churches in the southern region of the province which Paul and Barnabas evangelized on their first journey (Acts 13-14)? Or was the epistle written to a group of churches in north Galatia which were founded on the second and third journeys (Acts 16:6, 19:1)? Which of these regions did Paul have in mind when he wrote the Galatians? This is a question that has been long debated by biblical scholars.

According to the North Galatian theory, Paul addressed the epistle to a region of Galatia which he did not visit until his second journey on his way to Troas (Acts 16:1-8). It is argued that the similarity of Galatians and Romans favors the view that Paul wrote Galatians about the same time that he wrote Romans (A.D. 56/57) to Christians in northern Galatia.

Advocates of the South Galatian view believe that Paul addressed Galatians to the churches which he established on his first missionary journey. The letter would have been written after returning to Antioch before the Jerusalem Council met.

The omission of any reference to the decision of the Jerusalem Council in favor of Gentile freedom from the exacting requirements of the Mosaic Law (Acts 15:28-29) would suggest that Galatians was written *before* the Council met, when Paul had visited only the churches of South Galatia.

The controversy over the North and South Galatian

viewpoints relates to the historical background of the book, but the life-changing message of Galatians is not dependent on either of these viewpoints.

When was it written?

Paul completed his first missionary journey in September of A.D. 49 and probably wrote Galatians from Antioch in the autumn of that year, just before attending the Jerusalem Council.

What's the historical setting?

After returning to Antioch following his first journey, Paul received some disheartening news. Among the Galatian believers were those who insisted on a Jewish model for Christianity (1:7, 4:17, 5:10). They argued that full justification for believing Gentiles could not be experienced apart from obeying the Mosaic Law and observing Jewish traditions.

In his response by letter, Paul sets forth the position he expected to debate at the Jerusalem Council. Forged out of heated controversy, Paul's letter to the Galatians stands as the great charter for Christian freedom from bondage to the law and works based salvation.

Why was it written?

Paul's purpose in writing is to refute the teachings of those who insisted that believing Gentiles follow Jewish traditions and to defend the gospel of justification by faith. Faith alone–not faith plus works–is the basis for a person's salvation.

What's the theme?

Paul insists that the works of the law are not necessary for a believer's salvation (2:16). The theme is "Christian freedom from the law" (5:1).

What's it about?

Paul's Concern 1:1-10	Revelation of the Gospel 1:10-2:21	Vindication of the Gospel 3-4	Application of the Gospel 5:1-6:20	Paul's Rule 6:11-18

What does it teach us?

Galatians emphasizes the same theology which Paul presents in Romans–justification by faith apart from the works of the law (Rom. 3:28). Galatians is Paul's first letter to underscore this point (Gal. 2:16). It is a letter penned in the heat of controversy in a situation that imperiled the spiritual health of newly established churches. Romans, written later during Paul's third journey, presents a more systematic and thorough exposition of this doctrine.

Both Romans and Galatians were significant in Martin Luther's formulation of the pinnacle of Reformation theology–justification by faith.

At the end of Galatians, Paul drives the final peg into his argument when he declares, "For neither is circumcision anything, nor uncircumcision, but a new creation" (6:15). Then he slams the door on those advocating Jewish traditions with the words, "And those who will walk by this rule, peace and mercy be upon them, and upon the Israel of God" (6:16).

The last "and" (Greek *kai*) in verse 16 could be translated "even." If so, the last phrase might better read, "even upon the Israel of God," thus equating both circumcised and uncircumcised believers as the "Israel of God." In this case, Paul is saying to his readers, "You don't need circumcision and Jewish ritual to share in the blessings God has for His people. Even Gentile believers become part of God's family--the 'Israel of God'--through faith!"

Where's Jesus?

Where do we find Jesus in Galatians? You will find him living in Paul. The apostle writes, "I have been crucified with Christ; and it is no longer I who live, but Christ lives in me; and the life which I now live in the flesh I live by faith in the Son of God, who loved me, and delivered Himself up for me" (Galatians 2:20). Paul is saying here that he has so completely identified with Christ and His death that the resurrected Christ now lives in Him, empowering him to live his life by faith rather than by legalistic self-efforts. And the Jesus who lives in Paul also lives in us as well.

EPHESIANS

As part of my duties as a pastor, I have had occasion to visit prisoners in the county jail and Oregon State Penitentiary. And I never leave a jail or prison without thinking to myself that I never want to do anything that would send me to such a place!

The Apostle Paul was in prison when he wrote the next four letters we are going to study. He had been arrested in Jerusalem because of a riot in the temple area instigated by Jews who charged Paul with preaching against the law and bringing Gentiles into the holy temple (Acts 21:28). After his arrest he was kept in Roman custody in Caesarea for two years (A.D. 57-59) as he waited the outcome his case. When he realized that the Roman governors where doing nothing to resolve his situation, Paul exercised his right as a Roman citizen and appealed to Caesar. His case was then transferred to Rome for a hearing before the emperor.

Paul reached Rome, the capital of the Roman Empire, in the spring of A.D. 60. There he was placed under "house arrest" in rented quarters (Acts 28:23, 30) with a Roman soldier assigned to guard him. He could receive visitors and continue his preaching and writing ministry, but Paul spent the next two years in confinement as he awaited the outcome of his case. It was during this time that he wrote four letters known as his "prison epistles." Ephesians is the first of Paul's letters from prison.

What's the title?

Although this letter is known by the name "Ephesians," the words "at Ephesus" are absent from the oldest Greek manuscripts. One second century Christian writer refers to it as "the Epistle to the Laodiceans." It is possible that the letter had no title originally, but became associated with several different Christian communities.

Who wrote it?

There is strong evidence for the Pauline authorship of Ephesians. Paul identifies himself as the author twice in the epistle (1:1, 3:1). The writings of the early church fathers confirm that Paul wrote the letter known as "Ephesians."

To whom was it written?

It is hard to be certain as to the identity of the original readers since the words "at Ephesus" are absent from the oldest Greek manuscripts. The letter may have been addressed to a single church, but was later adapted for wider circulation by dropping the original name. Others suggest that "Ephesians" was intended to be read by a circle of Christian communities and the copy we know ended up at the church at Ephesus. Without the words "at Ephesus" in 1:1, the address might be rendered, "To the saints who are also faithful in Christ Jesus."

When was it written?

Ephesians is the first of Paul's "prison epistles." He refers to himself as prisoner twice in this letter (3:1, 4:1). Since

Paul was imprisoned at Philippi (Acts 16:33), Jerusalem (Acts 23:18), Caesarea (Acts 23:35) and in Rome (Acts 28:20), one might wonder, "During which imprisonment did Paul write his prison epistles?"

Only during the imprisonments at Rome and Caesarea were there sufficient time for correspondence. Since Paul anticipates his forthcoming release in Philippians 1:19 and Philemon 22, it is probable that Paul wrote his prison epistles from Rome since no such release was anticipated at Caesarea. Paul's imprisonment in Rome lasted from February, A.D. 60 to March, A.D. 62. Ephesians was probably the first of the prison epistles and was written in Rome during the autumn of A.D. 60

What is the historical setting?

Since the title "Ephesians" is in question, we cannot be certain regarding the circumstances of the original readers. But assuming an Ephesian background, we are reminded that Paul visited Ephesus at least twice during his missionary journeys. He first visited Ephesus at the end of his second missionary journey (Acts 18:19) on his way back to Antioch. Paul returned to Ephesus on his third journey and spent about three years ministering there. For two of those three years Paul taught His disciples in the school of Tyrannus (Acts 19:8-10, 20:31).

Ephesus ranked with Alexandria and Antioch of Syria as one of the most important cities of the eastern Mediterranean Roman world. It was not only an important commercially, but was the worship center for the Greek goddess Artemis (Diana) whose image was housed in a temple, the Artemsion, four times the size of the Parthenon.

Paul's ministry at Ephesus was opposed by the silver craftsmen who felt both their pagan religion and trade being threatened by Paul's preaching. As a result of a riot instigated by the silver craftsmen of the city, Paul had to flee the city (Acts 20:1). He later ministered to the Ephesian elders at Miletus (Acts 20:17-38) on his last journey to Jerusalem.

Why was it written?

Ephesians sets forth the kind of conduct which is consistent with the believer's position in Christ. Paul wrote this letter to clarify the blessings of salvation and the obligations of the Christian life.

What's the theme?

The theme of the letter is captured in the words of 4:1, "I therefore, the prisoner of the Lord, entreat you to walk in a manner worthy of the calling with which you have been called" (4:1). In brief, the theme of Ephesians is "Christian conduct."

What's it about?

Sit: Seated with Christ 1-3	*Walk:* Walking Worthily 4:1-6:9	*Stand:* Standing against the Devil 6:10-24

What does it teach us?

While the second half of Ephesians deals with Christian conduct, the first half provides the theological basis for conduct that is truly Christian. Can you imagine what would happen if Prince Charles came to town, checked into a Motel 6, rented a car from "Rent-A-Wreck," and ate his meals at McDonalds. The British tabloids would print scathing headlines, "Royal heir lives like a commoner!" Paul is saying a similar thing in Ephesians. In light of the Christian's position as a son or daughter of the High King of Heaven, they should not live out of keeping with their royal position and eternal destiny!

Paul emphasizes the believer's spiritual position in Christ through the first three chapters of Ephesians telling us that we are blessed in Christ (1:3), chosen in Christ (1:4), predestined to sonship (1:5), graced in Christ (1:6), redeemed by Christ's blood (1:7-8), sealed by the Holy Spirit (1:13-14), and made members of God's family (2:19). Because of all that Jesus has done for us, Paul declares that believers are "seated with Him in the heavenly places" (2:6). Although our life now is earthly, we must live each day in light of our heavenly destiny.

Where's Jesus?

If you are looking for Jesus in Paul's letter to the church at Ephesus, you'll find him in Ephesians 5:31-33. Paul begins this section by quoting Genesis 2:24 which outlines God's plan for marriage. Then he announces, "This mystery is great; but I am speaking with reference to Christ and the church." Paul is saying that marriage was divinely designed by God to illustrate the loving relationship between Jesus and His followers. Paul instructs husbands to love their wives just as Christ loved and sacrificed Himself for the church. And wives are to be subject to their husbands just as the church is under the authority and leadership of Christ. A good marriage is not only a blessing to our families; it can be an amazing visual aid depicting the relationship of Christ and His church.

PHILIPPIANS

In ancient times, Philippi was inhabited by people who worked the gold mines in the nearby mountains. Later when the mines were depleted, Philippi became a Roman colony, established by Caesar for discharged Roman soldiers who were given fertile farmland and settled in the city. Being a Roman colony (Acts 16:22), Philippi had a form of government what was independent of the provincial administration. The people who lived at Philippi were recognized as Roman citizens. They had the same legal position and privileges of those living in Rome itself!

But as Roman citizens, they also had certain obligations and responsibilities including loyalty to the emperor and obedience to the law. Likewise, Paul explains to the church at Philippi, while believers are citizens of heaven (3:20), they have obligations on earth. As they have accepted the gospel privileges, they must also accept the gospel responsibilities.

Paul reminds the Philippians that their responsibility as citizens of heaven is to conduct themselves in a manner worthy of their privileged position (Philippians 1:27).

What's the title?

The name of this short book is taken from the addressees of the letter, the believers at Philippi. The city was named after Philip of Macedon, who assumed the throne of Macedonia at age 21 and through skillful diplomacy and military prowess led his people to victory over the threats of neighboring nations, giving him control of most of Greece.

Who wrote it?

The fact that Paul wrote Philippians is attested by internal evidence (1:1) and the testimony of church fathers. The biographical references are distinctively Pauline (3:4-11, 4:10-16).

To whom was it written?

The church at Philippi may have been largely Gentile for there was apparently no synagogue there when Paul first visited the city (Acts 16:13,20-21). The city, named after Philip of Macedon, was strategically located as the gateway to Europe. It was situated ten miles north of Neapolis, its port and terminus of the Egnatian Way. Philippi commanded the fertile plain through which the Egnatian way passed.

When was it written?

Philippians was written during Paul's imprisonment at Rome (1:7,13,17). Since Paul is evidently anticipating his release (1:19, 2:24), the letter was probably written late in his imprisonment, around early spring of AD 62.

What is the historical setting?

Paul first visited Philippi on his second missionary journey (Acts 16:11-40). Philippi was the first European city in which Paul preached, and Lydia was the first convert. During their first visit, Paul and Silas had been imprisoned in Philippi, but were miraculously released.

The church at Philippi was about 12 years old at the time Paul wrote this letter. Epaphroditus had recently come to Rome to bring Paul some aid (2:5, 4:18), but had fallen ill.

The immediate occasion of this letter was the return of Epaphroditus to Philippi following his illness in Rome (2:25-30). Paul took the opportunity to commend his fellow-worker and to write the Philippians about a variety of matters.

Why was it written?

Paul wrote to the Philippians to give news of his own circumstances (1:12-26), and to tell of his plans to send Timothy and subsequently visit Philippi himself (2:19-24).

In addition, Paul took the opportunity to warn the church against placing their confidence in anything but Christ (3:2-11); and to expressed appreciation for the Philippians' generous gift (4:10-20).

What's the theme?

The theme of "rejoicing" permeates this letter. Sixteen times the noun or verb is used. Paul knew that a heart filled with joy was better able to endure through difficult times (Neh. 8:10, James 1:2). The theme of the Philippians is "Rejoicing in the Lord in all circumstances" (4:4).

What's it about?

Progress of the Gospel 1:1-26	Conduct of the Christian 1:27-2:30	Testimony of the Apostle 3:1-21	Admonitions to the Philippians 4:1-9	Appreciation for the Gift 4:10-23

What does it teach us?

Philippians presents us with a theology of humility. He writes, "Do nothing from selfishness or empty conceit, but with humility of mind, let each of you regard one another as more important than himself" (2:3). Paul then presents his readers with the classic example of humility, the person of Christ. As the Son of God, Jesus had the highest possible position by divine right. He was equal with God (2:6). But in spite of His exalted status He humbled Himself, taking the role of a servant, accepting the physical limitations and discomforts of humanity, even submitting to a painful and humiliating death on a cross (2:7-8).

Instead of selfishly looking out for themselves with little or no regard for others, Paul exhorts his readers to "have this attitude in yourselves which was also in Christ Jesus" (2:5). Most of us don't mind serving others when people respond with appreciation and respect. Jesus demonstrates that true humility extends itself in serving others even when it is painful and costly (1 Pet. 2:21-23).

Where's Jesus?

You will find Jesus in each chapter of Paul's short letter to the Philippians. Paul wants his readers to know that Jesus is his life (1:21), his example (2:5), his goal (3:8,10), and his sufficiency (4:13,19). For Paul, life is wrapped up in Jesus–

knowing Him, imitating Him, pursuing Him, and trusting Him. Just as Jesus permeated every aspect of Paul's life, we find Jesus featured in every chapter of Philippians.

COLOSSIANS

I'll probably never admit to being *lost* in the woods, but there have been times when I have been somewhat confused about directions. During one back packing trip I found myself at the same lake I had started out from when I had intended to go in a completely different direction! I still haven't figured out how that happened!

Getting "confused" (not *lost*!) in the woods usually happens when hikers neglect the guidance available through the map and compass. Knowing where you are on the map will help you get where you need to go. And using a compass will keep you from inadvertently veering off course.

For the believer, there is no better map and compass than the Word of God. And when we drift into doctrinal error it is usually because we have neglected the resource that God has provided to enable us stay on the right path. Colossians was written to remind us of the truth about Christ and to keep us from getting lost in a world of humanistic relativism and speculative philosophy.

What's the title?

The title is taken from the location of the readers of the letter. Colossae was a city in the Roman province of Asia and is located today in modern Turkey.

Who wrote it?

The Pauline authorship of Colossians is clearly indicated by the first and last verse of the letter (Col. 1:1, 4:18). The authenticity of the letter was not challenged until the 19th century when some scholars claimed that the letter reflected 2nd century Gnosticism, a blending of Christianity with Greek philosophy. More conservative scholars view Colossians as reflecting a background of the beginning stages of Gnostic thought rather than the full-blown heresy which developed a century later.

To whom was it written?

Paul wrote Colossians to believers at Colossae (1:2), but he intended that the Laodiceans also read the epistle (4:16). Colossae was located about 10 miles up the Lycus Valley from Laodicea on the main road to Ephesus, 120 miles to the east. The city may have originally been a military base and benefitted commercially from its location along an east-west caravan route.

When was it written?

The close connection of Philemon with Colossians indicates that they belong to the same period. It is probable that Tychicus accompanied by Onesimus carried the letters to Colossae at the same time. Both letters were probably written in the early spring of AD 62, shortly before Paul's release from prison.

What is the historical setting?

The gospel was introduced to Colossae during Paul's long ministry at Ephesus (Acts 19:10,26), but Paul had apparently not visited the church (1:4, 2:1). The occasion of writing was the arrival of Epaphras from Colossae (1:7-9, 4:12) who brought news of theological error circulating in the church. The primary problem was a deficient view of Christ and His work. Paul immediately sent Tychicus back to Colossae with a letter for the church and a letter for Philemon, the master of Onesimus, a runaway slave who had been converted under Paul's ministry (4:7-9, Philemon 10).

Considerable discussion has been given over to the identification of the Colossian error which the letter was intended to refute. The error combined an emphasis on Mosaic ordinances (2:8,11,16) with man-made traditions (2:8) and the worship of angels (2:18). Paul is clearly aware of the potential danger to the doctrine of Christ and writes to stress the preeminence of Christ (1:15-19) stressing that believers can be complete in Him without mystical enlightenment, philosophy, or tradition (1:28).

Why was it written?

Paul wanted the Colossians to grow into maturity rather than be taken captive by philosophy and empty deception. He wrote the church to extinguish the Colossian error by presenting the truth of Christ and His work.

What's the theme?

The theme of Colossians is the preeminence of Christ and the believer's completeness in Him (2:9-15).

What's it about?

The Person of Christ 1:1-23	The Ministry of Paul 1:24-2:7	The Problem at Colossae 2:8-3:4	Conduct of the Christian 3:5-4:6	A Personal Note 4:7-18

What does it teach us?

Colossians sets forth a theology of the absolute sufficiency of Christ. Since Christ has completed the work of our salvation there is no reason for believers attempt to add anything to it. Paul is telling his readers, "Christ is all–and all you need!" You don't need Christ plus philosophy. You don't need Christ plus Yoga. You don't need Christ plus transcendental meditation. So beware of any philosophy, deception or tradition that suggests you need more than Him.

In Colossians 2:9-15 Paul refutes the Colossian's mistaken thinking making a series of statements of about what Christ has accomplished for believers. Note the repeated use of the phrase "in Him" and "with Him." In Christ you have been made complete so that there is nothing that human efforts can contribute to your salvation and standing before God. With Christ you have been "buried" in baptism and "raised" to new life by faith. Through Christ we have been "made alive" spiritually when through the cross He *canceled* "the certificate of debt" held against us (2:13-14). Since Christ has done it all, there's nothing left to do but to rejoice and thank Him for it!

Where's Jesus?

There are three classic discussions about Jesus in the New Testament and Colossians 1:15-23 is one of them. Here Paul presents Jesus as Lord of creation, head of the church, and reconciler of believers to God. Paul explains that Jesus is the visible "image" of the invisible God.

Although the Colossians had never seen the emperor, they had seen his "image" (*eikon*) on Roman coins. And those who had seen Jesus during His life and ministry had seen God! Paul goes on to say that Jesus is the Creator and Sustainer of the physical universe! This is the Jesus that believers serve!

FIRST THESSALONIANS

In 1981, Bill Maupin, the leader of a small Tucson, Arizona church preached that the rapture of the church would take place on June 28th and that Christians would be "spirited aloft like helium balloons." Some 50 people quit their jobs and gathered in anticipation of this prophetic event. When his June 28th prediction failed, Maupin explained that he had miscalculated and predicted that the event would occur forty days later. Once again the faithful gathered, only to have their hopes dashed a second time.

Failed predictions of prophetic events have caused many Christians to be rather skeptical regarding biblical prophecy. Is there a biblical and balanced approach to the doctrine of eschatology ("last things")? We find such balance in 1 Thessalonians where Paul corrects the thinking of those who were convinced they were witnessing prophetic fulfillment.

What's the title?

The title of this letter is taken from the name of the addressees, the church at Thessalonica. The city is known today as Thessaloniki or Salonika.

Who wrote it?

The Pauline authorship of the 1 Thessalonians is attested by internal evidence (1:1) and confirmed by the early church. The companions mentioned in the letter were known to have been with Paul on his second missionary journey (Acts 15:40, 16:1-3, 17:4, 18:5).

To whom was it written?

The letter was written to the believers at Thessalonica. Located on an excellent harbor at the northeastern corner of the Thermaic Gulf, Thessalonica was an important commercial center. The city was also strategically situated on the *Via Egnatia*, a paved roadway which stretched across Macedonia to the west. Little wonder the city had the reputation of being "the key to the whole of Macedonia."

In Paul's day, Thessalonica was the largest city of Macedonia, a teeming metropolis with a population estimate as high as 200,000. Because of its strategic location and sizable Jewish population, Paul recognized it as a strategic place to begin a church planting ministry.

When was it written?

Paul visited Thessalonica on his second missionary journey (April 50 - Sept. 52). The epistle was written about six months after Paul left Thessalonica, in the early summer of A.D. 51.

What is the historical setting?

Paul ministered in the synagogue at Thessalonica for three Sabbaths during his second missionary journey (Acts 17:1-10), preaching about Jesus and identifying Him as the promised Messiah. After a reasonably successful ministry, a plot against his life forced him to flee. The missionary team journeyed by night to Berea. Later the Jews of Thessalonica brought opposition to Berea forcing Paul to make another hasty departure. Silas and Timothy stayed to finish the work in Berea while Paul went on to Athens where the missionary team was reunited (3:1-2). Paul wanted to return to Thessalonica, but his plans were thwarted by Satan and he finally decided to send Timothy instead.

Timothy eventually caught up with Paul in Corinth and gave a good report about the young church. Encouraged by this news, Paul wrote the Thessalonians, commending their progress and encouraging them to go on in the faith.

Why was it written?

Paul seems to have had several purposes in mind when he wrote this letter. First, he wanted to commend the Thessalonians for their steadfastness in the face of conflicts (2:14) and encourage them to go on in the faith (4:1).

But Paul also wanted to correct certain doctrinal errors which had been reported by Timothy. Some of the believers were confused about Paul's teaching on Christ's second coming. Others were neglecting basic Christian morality. Paul writes to point out the need for watchfulness and holiness in anticipation of Christ's return.

What's the theme?

The theme of the book is "the need for holy living in light of Christ's coming" (3:11-13).

What's it about?

Paul's Relations with the Thessalonians 1-3	Paul's Instructions for the Thessalonians 4-5

What does it teach us?

Paul had experienced persecution during his ministry in Thessalonica, and now the young church was going through it as well. It appears that their trials and troubles were so intense that some of the new believers had become confused regarding Paul's teaching on the Day of the Lord, a major theme in the Old Testament prophets. The Day of the Lord anticipates a day of wrath and judgment on the disobedient (Joel 1:15, Zeph. 1:14-18), followed by deliverance and restoration for the righteous (Joel 3:18-21, Amos 9:11-15).

Paul writes that the Day of the Lord will come "like a thief in the night," unannounced and unexpected. He uses the figure of birth pangs (5:3) to describe how sudden destruction will come upon the wicked with increasingly intense pain and sorrow. But he goes on to contrast the destiny of believers with that of unbelievers. He describes believers as "sons of light" and "sons of the day" who will not encounter the darkness and destruction of the Day of the Lord but can anticipate instead deliverance and blessing (5:4-5). Paul explains in 5:9 that God has not "destined us for wrath" [the divine wrath of the Day of the Lord] but for "salvation" (or "deliverance") through Jesus Christ. God's promise of deliverance from the wrath of the Day of the Lord is a strong scriptural basis for hope and encouragement (5:11).

Where's Jesus?

Where's Jesus in First Thessalonians? The answer is found in 4:16-17 where Paul describes the moment when believers will see with their own eyes the resurrected, glorified Jesus. Here Paul describes a series of events associated with Jesus' return. First, the Lord will descend from heaven to the clouds. Next, the dead in Christ will be raised. Then, the living believers will be "caught up" to the clouds to meet their Lord (4:17). Have you thought about how you will greet Jesus when you see Him for the first time? Paul concludes with this assurance, "So we shall always be with the Lord."

SECOND THESSALONIANS

You've heard the expression, "same song, second verse." Well that may be an apt description of Second Thessalonians. Paul had sent his earlier letter (First Thessalonians) to correct some misunderstandings regarding the prophetic Day of the Lord. But we often need to hear the same lesson several times in order to grasp new truths completely.

Someone has said, "Repetition with variety is the key to learning." Paul's second letter to the believers at Thessalonica is a review lesson, but it is review with *variety*.

What's the title?

The title is taken from the name of the city where the readers resided. This is the second epistle Paul wrote to the Thessalonian church.

Who wrote it?

Paul claims to have authored the epistle (1:1, 3:17) and the authenticity of the letter was recognized by Irenaeus, an early church leader, around A.D. 170. Silvanus (Silas) and Timothy are associated with Paul in writing this letter as they were associated with him in ministering to the church.

To whom was it written?

The epistle is addressed to the "church of the Thessalonians" (1:1). In Paul's day, Thessalonica was a teeming metropolis--the largest city of Macedonia. Paul's founding of the church at Thessalonica is recorded in Acts 17:1-10.

When was it written?

Second Thessalonians was written from Corinth perhaps two or three months after Paul wrote First Thessalonians. Second Thessalonians should be dated in the summer of A.D. 51.

What is the historical setting?

The immediate occasion of the writing of the second letter was a report which Paul received concerning the Thessalonian believers, brought to him perhaps by those who had delivered the first epistle.

Apparently false teachers at Thessalonica who claimed to have Paul's teaching had persuaded the believers that they were living in "the Day of the Lord." (2:2). In response to this teaching some had given up their work and were idly waiting for the Lord's return (3:6-12).

Paul wrote his second letter to the believers at Thessalonica to commend them for their progress in the faith and to instruct them in concerning the Day of the Lord.

Why was it written?

The letter was intended to the believers' growth in faith and love (1:3) and to encourage their steadfastness under severe persecution (1:4-12). Paul's primary purpose, however, was to correct their misconception that the Day of the Lord had already come.

What's the theme?

"Corrections concerning the Day of the Day of the Lord" (2:1-2).

What's it about?

Consolation in a Time of Affliction 1	Corrections Concerning the Day of the Lord 2	Requests for Prayer and Discipline 3

What does it teach us?

The church at Thessalonica was going through such severe trials that some believers actually thought they were enduring the judgments of the Day of the Lord. Paul attempts to correct this confusion in verse 3, "Let no one in any way deceive you, for it [the Day of the Lord, v. 2] will not come unless the apostasy comes first, and the man of lawlessness is revealed, the son of destruction." The "man of lawlessness" is an obvious reference to the "little horn" of Daniel 7:8, the anti-Christ of the end time (see Dan. 9:27, Rev. 13:1-10). His appearance is one indicator of the beginning of the Day of the Lord.

The meaning of "apostasy" in verse three is somewhat debated, but it is doubtful that it refers to doctrinal defection. Doctrinal defection was already going on it Paul's day and would not have been a sufficiently specific event to indicate that the Day of the Lord had come. The Greek word *apostasia* is derived from a verb meaning "depart from." *Apostasia* literally means "departure." While the word can be used metaphorically of departure from doctrine, context must ultimately determine the meaning.

In 2 Thessalonians 2:1 Paul is writing about "the coming of our Lord Jesus" and particularly that aspect of the event which relates to "our gathering together with him." A comparison with 1 Thess. 4:17 suggests that this refers to the removal of the church from the earth at Christ's coming.

The Thessalonians (and persecuted believers today) may rest assured that they are not experiencing the judgments of the Day of the Lord since neither the *departure* of the church nor the *appearance* of the anti-Christ have occurred.

Where's Jesus?

Jesus can be found near the end of the letter where Paul offers a brief prayer for the readers, "Now may the Lord of peace Himself continually grant you peace in every circumstance. The Lord be with you all" (3:16). Peace in every circumstance! That's what Jesus promised his disciples in John 14:27. Jesus promised a peace not based on changing circumstances, but on an unchanging relationship with God through His Son. This is not the peace that the world offers, but the peace that is available only to those who have welcomed Jesus into their lives. Have you?

FIRST TIMOTHY

I'll never forget my first experience as the pastor of a church. I had just finished my seminary studies and was beginning my ministry as a Bible teacher at Western Seminary. A little church just south of town was in need of an interim pastor and invited me to candidate. The small congregation seemed satisfied with my preaching and so I began my first pastoral ministry. And although I had been trained in Bible and theology and had notebooks full of valuable information from my classes in church administration and pastoral duties, I was a young and inexperienced pastor.

Somehow I survived that initial immersion into pastoral ministry and have served many other churches since then. But how helpful it would have had an older man who could mentor me through my first six months of pastoral ministry. Even a couple of *letters* would have helped. And that is what we have here--Paul's letters to a young, inexperienced pastor who needed Paul's counsel, encouragement and support.

What's the title?

This letter takes its name from the addressee, Timothy, Paul's apostolic associate.

Who wrote it?

Although the Pauline authorship of the Pastoral Epistles (1 and 2 Timothy) has been contested in recent times, Paul claims to be the author of each (1:1) and this view was accepted by the early church. Those who deny the Pauline authorship of 1 Timothy argue that the vocabulary and content is different from Paul's other writings. They fail to consider that Paul is writing an individual, not a single church, and that style and vocabulary can vary according to the author's subject and purpose.

To whom was it written?

The letter is addressed to Timothy, the young man whom Paul encountered on his second journey when revisited Derbe and Lystra (Acts 16:1-3). Although his father was a

Greek, his mother Eunice and grandmother Lois were devout Jewesses who taught Timothy the Word of God when he was a child (2 Tim. 3:14). Paul's reference to Timothy as "my true child in the faith" (1 Tim. 1:2) suggests he came to faith in Jesus under Paul's ministry.

Timothy accompanied Paul on his third missionary journey (Acts 19:22, 20:4) and was with Paul in Rome during his first imprisonment (Phil. 1:1, 2:19-24). Paul mentions Timothy as his associate in writing Philippians (1:1), Colossians (1:1), and Philemon (1). Timothy's imprisonment is mentioned in Hebrews 13:23, but we have no details.

After Paul's release from prison and return to Ephesus, Timothy was appointed to guide the church there while Paul traveled on to Macedonia (1 Tim. 1:3). In Philippians 2:20-22 Paul commends Timothy as a man of God who was genuinely concerned for others and served the Lord with diligence.

When was it written?

The date of First Timothy depends on one's solution to the problem of where the Pastoral Epistles (1 & 2 Timothy and Titus) fit into Paul's ministry. The evidence suggests that First Timothy was probably was written soon after Paul's release from his first Roman imprisonment, after his visit to Ephesus. The letter was written by Paul from Macedonia, probably in the autumn of AD 62.

What is the historical setting?

Paul invested more of his time and energy in Ephesus than any other city he visited. During his third missionary journey (A.D. 53-57), Paul spent three years (Acts 20:31) there preaching the gospel and teaching his disciples (Acts 19:9-10). Later, Paul warned the elders of Ephesus that difficult times would come when false teachers would come among God's flock like savage wolves (Acts 20:28-30). Those times had come, and Paul had returned to Ephesus after his release from prison to strengthen and encourage the church.

After doing what he could, Paul traveled on to Macedonia (1 Tim. 1:3) leaving Timothy at Ephesus as Paul's representative. Since there was the possibility of his return to Ephesus being delayed (3:14-15), Paul wrote Timothy to provide information and direction that would help him lead the church at Ephesus in Paul's absence.

Why was it written?

Paul wrote to inform Timothy on matters of church polity (government) and practice, and to back up his leadership with Paul's apostolic authority (1 Tim. 3:14-15). The letter is also intended to encourage in the work of the ministry and to alert him to the dangers of false teaching at Ephesus.

What's the theme?

The theme of First Timothy is "the government and practice of the New Testament church" (3:14-15).

What's it about?

Doctrine of the Church 1	Teaching in the Church 4
Worship in the Church 2	Care for Members 5:1-6:2
Leaders of the Church 3	Charge to Timothy 6:3-21

What does it teach us?

1 Timothy presents us with a theology of church leadership. Paul presents qualifications for two church offices in

1 Timothy 3, "overseer" and "deacon." The term "overseer" emphasizes the responsibility of a church leader to have spiritual oversight over members of the congregation. The term "elder" is another term used for the same office (Titus 1:5-7, Acts 20:17,28) and emphasizes the spiritual maturity and experience necessary for church leadership.

The spiritual oversight of the overseer/elder includes visiting the needy (James 1:27), feeding the flock (1 Pet. 5:2), being an example (1 Pet. 5:3), protecting the church from false teaching (Acts 20:29-31), and leading God's people (1 Tim. 5:7).

Paul provides Timothy with a list of qualifications for those who would aspire to church leadership. The first and last mentioned qualifications serve as brackets for the others, "without reproach" (v. 2) and "a good reputation" v. 7). Taken together, these two qualifications refer to integrity. A person in church leadership must be someone others can trust–a person of integrity. No one can lead God's people spiritually if they are vulnerable in their private character.

The origin of the office of "deacon" (3:8) can be traced to Act 6:1-6. Although the title "deacon" does not appear there, the verbal form (*diakoneo*) is found in 6:2. The nature of the office is indicated by the word "deacon" which is from the verb "to serve." The word can be used in a general sense of anyone who serves (Eph. 6:21), but is used in 1 Tim. 3:8-13 of the church office of deacon. The qualifications for the office of deacon are no less spiritual than the qualifications for elder. Deacons must be men of spiritual maturity and integrity who are committed to following Christ's example (John 13:1-20) in serving the church.

Where's Jesus?

You will find Jesus in 1 Timothy 2:5 where Paul declares there is "one God, and one mediator also between God and men, the man Christ Jesus." A mediator is one who stands between two parties to remove a disagreement and reach a common goal. In order to be fair and just, a mediator must be able to represent the concerns of both parties. Jesus can do this perfectly since in Him deity and humanity have been united forever in one person. The Jesus of Scripture is not a mere man. He is fully God and fully human, and remains so forever as the resurrected, glorified Savior.

SECOND TIMOTHY

At home in an old family trunk I have some letters that are very precious to me. One is a letter from my grandmother Laney who died on her 102 birthday. It is the last letter my grandmother wrote to me. The writing is difficult to read because of her old age and arthritic condition, but I like to hold the letter and remember the loving words she wrote to me.

I sense a similar feeling when I read 2 Timothy knowing it was the last letter in the New Testament written by the Apostle Paul. He was aged and imprisoned when he wrote this letter to Timothy, and I'm sure that his very handwriting must have reflected those conditions. In 2 Timothy Paul testifies to the fact that he has "finished the course" of his life and ministry. Now he awaits the heavenly "crown of righteousness," which Christ will award him. He concludes the letter with the simply but profound words, "Grace be with you." I wonder how many times after Paul's death Timothy opened and reread this letter, letting Paul's words of exhortation sink deeper into his soul. May these words of grace sink deeply into your soul as well.

What's the title?

Like First Timothy, this letter is named for Paul's apostolic associate, Timothy.

Who write it?

The apostle Paul claims to have authored Second

Timothy (1:1) and the autobiographical remarks (3:10-11, 4:10-11,19-20) fit his life.

To whom was it written?

The letter is addressed to Timothy, Paul's young associate. Timothy was from Lystra (Acts 16:1-3). His father was a Greek and his mother (Eunice) and grandmother (Lois) were devout in their Jewish faith. Timothy joined with Paul on his second and third missionary journeys and was with Paul in Rome during his imprisonment. Timothy ministered as Paul's representative in Ephesus (1 Tim. 1:3) and may have been with the apostle during the last days of his final imprisonment (2 Tim. 4:1,21).

When was it written?

Second Timothy was written by Paul shortly before his death (4:6-8). Since Paul died in the spring of AD 68, the epistle was probably written in the autumn of AD 67.

What's the historical setting?

During Paul's first imprisonment in Rome he was able to have his own rented quarters and receive visitors. His second imprisonment was quite different. Paul was in Rome, having been arrested as a criminal (2:9). His death was imminent (4:6-8). Some of his fellow-workers had deserted him (4:16). Paul wrote Timothy, who was still in Ephesus, to bring Mark and join him before winter (A.D. 67/68). Paul was sending Tychicus to replace Timothy at Ephesus (4:12).

Why was it written?

Second Timothy was written to encourage Timothy in the ministry and outline the course of Christ's servant during a time of doctrinal confusion.

What's the theme?

The theme is "defending the faith in a time of doctrinal confusion and defection" (1:13-14).

What's it about?

Encouragement for Ministry 1	Directives for Service 2	The Coming Last Days 3	Charge to Timothy 4

What does it teach us?

In 2 Timothy 3, Paul warns Timothy of the spiritual confusion and decline which will characterize people in the last days before the return of Christ. How shall believers respond? What guidance can be offered? Is there anything solid that Christians can grasp when the world is slipping deeper and deeper into the quicksand of spiritual apostasy?

The answer Paul gives is "the sacred writings" (3:15) which Timothy was taught from childhood. The Word of God is a safeguard against spiritual confusion and an answer for spiritual error. In his classic statement on Scripture, Paul writes that "All Scripture is inspired by God and profitable for teaching, for reproof, for correction, for training in righteousness; that the person of God may be proficient, equipped for every good work" (3:16, author's translation).

The word "inspired" is actually the word "expired." This means that Scripture is the "breathing out" of the truth of God. Notice that Paul said, "all Scripture," not part of it, is inspired by God. The clear teaching of this text is that the books of the Old and New Testaments contain the very words of God and can be trusted to teach, reprove, correct, and train us in righteousness.

The truths of the Word of God are not simply pleasant to

read; they equip Christians to do God's will and work on earth. What a blessing to know that God's Word is a completely reliable guide which will never prove false or mistaken.

Where's Jesus?

The end of Paul's life we find him in a Roman prison cell, abandoned by nearly all his friends and ministry associates. But he is not alone! Toward the end of his second letter to Timothy he writes, "But the Lord stood with me and strengthened me, so that through me the proclamation might be fully accomplished" (2 Tim. 4:17). Where's Jesus? He's with Paul, of course! And the Apostle Paul is confident that Jesus will remain at his side to escort him safely to His heavenly kingdom (2 Tim. 4:18).

TITUS

Have you ever lived on an island? I lived on the small Pacific island of Guam for a summer serving as interim pastor at Bayview Baptist Church. It was quite an adventure! Guam is an island just six miles wide and thirty miles north to south. Everyone living in Guam is just a few minutes from the sea. It was a great place for my family to spend a summer!

But living on an island has its drawbacks. After several weeks on Guam we began to realize how isolated it is to live on a remote island in the Pacific. Mail took weeks to arrive from the States and phone calls were expensive. Most of the food we bought at the store had to be flown to the island! Since there were no cows on Guam, the milk we bought at the store was reconstituted powdered milk! Ugh! Service personnel stationed on Guam called it "the Rock," and spent most of their free time planning trips to somewhere else.

Perhaps Titus had similar feelings about being left by Paul on the island of Crete. It was a great place to visit, but maybe not a place to stay. Yet Paul had given Titus a strategic assignment on the island, and we can be assured that in spite of the difficulties of living on an isolated Mediterranean island, Titus fulfilled his ministry duties well.

What's the title?

The title of the letter is taken from the name of the addressee, Titus, Paul's disciple and son in the faith.

Who wrote it?

The Pauline authorship of Titus is indicated by internal evidence (1:1) and supported by the testimony of the church fathers. The personal tone of the letter and consistence with Paul's teachings elsewhere lend support to its authenticity.

To whom was it written?

Titus is referred to by Paul as his "true child in a common faith" (Titus 1:4), a designation which would indicate that Titus was one of Paul's converts. Titus was a Greek Christian (Gal. 2:3) and one of Paul's companions in some of his apostolic journeys (Gal. 2:1) and assistant in church planting work (1:5).

About four years after Paul's release from his first Roman imprisonment, Titus accompanied Paul to the island of Crete. He was left to set things in order and appoint elders while Paul went on to Asia Minor (1:5, 2 Tim. 4:13,20). Eusebius (A.D. 339) reports that Titus returned to Crete where he was made bishop and remained there until his old age.

When was it written?

The date of this epistle depends on the arrangement of the biographical material on Paul's life between his release from Roman confinement (A.D. 62) and his death (A.D. 67 or 68). The letter was probably written by Paul after his visit to Spain and Crete. He wrote Titus from Asia Minor in the summer of AD 66 before traveling on to Nicopolis (3:12), where he spent the winter before his arrest and return to Rome.

What is the historical setting?

The island of Crete, considerably larger than Guam, is 156 miles long and 7 to 30 miles wide. A mountain range in the center of the island features 8,193 foot Mt. Ida, the legendary birthplace of Zeus. The culture and history of Crete was filled with myth and legend (cf. Titus 1:14). The character and philosophy of the Cretans is illustrated by a line from the Cretan poet Epimenides (600 B.C.) which Paul quotes, "Cretans are always liars, evil beasts, lazy gluttons" (cf. Titus 1:12).

Jews from Crete were present at Pentecost (Acts 2:11) and may have carried the gospel back to Crete.

Titus had traveled to Crete with Paul, probably on his return voyage from Spain (A.D. 66). Titus was left on Crete after Paul's departure that he might set the church in order and appoint elders in every city (Titus 1:5).

Titus was facing a difficult assignment in Crete and needed encouragement as to how to deal with the problems of church order and doctrine. Titus needed Paul's instruction on how to deal with disorderly conduct and false teaching in the church. Apollos and Zenas were going to Crete (Titus 3:13) and Paul took the occasion to write Titus.

Why was it written?

Paul's letter to Titus was designed to encourage Titus to keep on teaching sound doctrine and provide further direction regarding church leadership (1:5-9). The letter emphasizes the need for purity in leadership and soundness in doctrine.

What's the theme?

The letter emphasizes the relationship between sound doctrine and good works. The theme is "the need for consistency between confession and conduct" (1:16).

What's it about?

| The Administration for Sound Doctrine 1 | The Proclamation of Sound Doctrine 2-3 |

What does it teach us?

The official slogan of the Boy Scouts of America is, "Do a good turn daily." Every day a Boy Scout is expected to find an opportunity to do good to someone in need. As evidenced by his letter to Titus, I'm quite sure that the Apostle Paul would have endorsed the Boy Scout slogan.

Five times in his letter to Titus, Paul encourages the doing of "good deeds." Paul urges the young men to be an "example of good deeds" (2:7). He explains that God has redeemed us and claimed us as a people "zealous for good deeds" (2:14). Paul tells Titus to remind the Cretans to be "ready for every good deed" (3:1). Those who have believed should be careful "to engage in good deeds" (3:8). Participation in "good deeds" is something Paul wants Christians to learn (3:14).

Paul is quick to emphasize that doing good deeds is not the basis for our salvation. God saved us, "not on the basis of deeds which we have done in righteousness, but according to His mercy" (3:5). Good deeds are the fruit, not the foundation of our salvation. As Paul explains to the Ephesians, "For we are His workmanship created in Christ Jesus for good works, which God prepared beforehand that we should walk in them" (Eph. 2:10).

Good deeds don't need to be extraordinary or heroic for them to reflect our faith and honor God. They may be something as simple as washing dinner dishes, folding the family laundry, or handing a homeless man a sack lunch. Peter recalls in his sermon to Cornelius that Jesus "went about doing good" (Acts 10:38). May we follow His example.

Where's Jesus?

If we were to ask Paul, "Where's Jesus in Titus?" he might direct us to 2:14 where he explains the Savior's redemptive work. Jesus "gave Himself for us to redeem us from every lawless deed, and to purify for Himself a people for His own possession, zealous for good deeds." What a great summary of the Christian message! Jesus came to redeem us, to purify us, and to prepare us for a life of service to others. In a nutshell, that's what Jesus is all about.

PHILEMON

The institution of slavery provides the background for Paul's letter to Philemon. Slavery was taken for granted in the first century world of the Bible. It was practiced in Jewish, Roman and Greek cultures alike. Although many people were born into slavery by birth, others were sold into slavery to pay off debt or as punishment for a crime. Many slaves were prisoners taken by the Roman army who were sold for revenue at a public auction. Although many slaves died as a result of mistreatment by their owners, Roman law made it illegal to take the life of a slave without a court order.

The rights of a master over a slave were absolute and were not affected by his running away. It was the duty of civil authorities to aid in the recovery of slaves whenever possible. Under Roman law it was a serious offense to harbor runaway slaves–the equivalent of holding stolen property.

We discover this short letter that Onesimus had run away from his master Philemon and had traveled to Rome. Somehow he had met Paul and came to faith in Jesus. Paul knows that Roman law requires that Onesimus be returned to his master. But how can that best be accomplish apart from legal action? Paul's letter to his beloved brother and fellow-worker Philemon is intended to pave the way for the reconciliation of a runaway slave to his rightful owner,

What's the title?

The title of the letter is taken from the name of the principal addressee, Philemon, owner of the runaway slave Onesimus.

Who wrote it?

The Pauline authorship of Philemon is clearly indicated by these letter itself Philemon. Writing in the first person, the author identifies himself as "Paul" (9). He uses his name again at the end of the letter where he mentions that he is writing with his "own hand" (19).

To whom was it written?

The letter is addressed to Philemon, Apphia, Archippus, and "to the church in your house." Philemon is a slave owner who appears to have been converted under Paul's ministry. He was at least indebted to Paul in some way (19). The term "fellow-worker" (1) suggests that he had ministered with Paul in some way. Since the church met at Philemon's house (2) he must have been a person of substance and influence.

The letter to Philemon, while being personal in content, is also addressed to the "church" which met at Philemon's house (2) at Colossae. It seems that Paul considered the matter of Onesimus worthy of the congregation's attention.

When was it written?

The close connection of Philemon with Colossians indicates that they belong to the same period. The reference to Archippus and Epaphras, both residents of Colossae (Col.

4:12,17), indicates that both letters were sent by Paul to the same Christian community. It is probable that Tychicus, accompanied by Onesimus, carried both letters to Colossae at the same time. The letters were probably written in the early spring of AD 62, shortly before Paul's release from his Roman imprisonment.

What is the historical setting?

The gospel was introduced to Colossae during Paul's long ministry at Ephesus (Acts 19:10,26), but Paul had apparently not visited the church (1:4, 2:1). The occasion of writing was the arrival of Epaphras from Colossae (1:7-9, 4:12) who brought news of theological error circulating in the church. The primary problem was a deficient view of Christ and His redemptive work. Paul immediately sent Tychicus back to Colossae with two letters—one for the church and one for Philemon, the master of Onesimus, a runaway slave who had been converted under Paul's ministry (4:7-9, Philemon 10).

Why was it written?

The purpose of the letter was to encourage the reconciliation between Onesimus and his master, Philemon. Paul urged Philemon to accept Onesimus as he would Paul, promising to pay any loss suffered when Onesimus fled.

What's the theme?

The subject of the letter is reconciliation. The theme is "reconciliation is possible through the merit of a mediator" (verses 17-18).

What is it about?

Paul's Prayer for Philemon 1-7	Paul's Petition for Onesimus 8-20	Paul's Plea for Himself 21-25

What does it teach us?

The little letter of Philemon presents us with a classic illustration of reconciliation. The relationship between Onesimus and his master Philemon was broken when Onesimus ran away, perhaps damaging or stealing some of his master's property.

Having befriended Onesimus and led him to faith in Christ, Paul wants to help bring an end to the enmity between two dear friends. As a mediator, he stands between Philemon and Onesimus seeking to encourage them to set aside their differences and embrace each other as brothers. To accomplish this end, Paul asks Philemon to "accept him [Onesimus] as you would me" (17). He also invites Philemon to charge the debt of his runaway slave to Paul's account (18). Paul assures his friend Philemon, "I will pay!"

Paul's intervention in behalf of Onesimus serves as a theological illustration. As Onesimus had wronged his master, so our sinful actions have wronged God. But Christ stands between God and humanity offering reconciliation by paying our debt of sin on the cross. With our debt having been paid, Jesus asks God to accept us, forgiven sinners, as He would welcome His own Son. There is great theology packed into this little book!

Where's Jesus?

If you asked Paul, "Where's Jesus?" I'm fairly confident that he would say, "Jesus is right here with me in this prison." Twice in this short letter Paul describes himself as a "prisoner of Christ Jesus" (1,9). Paul uses this phrase to stress the fact that he *belongs* to the Lord. Even while under the custody of Rome, Paul was Jesus' prisoner, not Caesar's. Paul was engaged in His service and imprisoned for Jesus' sake. Paul wasn't alone that Roman prison because Jesus, his Jailer, was with him.

CHAPTER NINE

The General Epistles

The next chapter in our Bibles is called the "General Epistles." This is the traditional designation given to the eight New Testament letters which were not written by the Apostle Paul. The first of these was probably the Epistle of James which may have been written as early as A.D. 49. James, the half-brother of Jesus, became an important leader in the Jerusalem church. Observing that many new believers were lacking in fervor for good works, James wrote to exhort his readers to live out the ethical implications of their faith.

First Peter was written by the Apostle Peter from Rome, perhaps in A.D. 63 or 64. His readers were going through the sufferings which were so common to first century Christians. Peter exhorted the believers to conduct themselves in accordance with their living hope! He encouraged them in their submission to authority and joyful response to suffering.

The Epistle to the Hebrews is the longest of the general epistles. It was written in the 60's, probably before the emperor Nero begin persecuting Christians in the summer of A.D. 64. In the face of hardships and persecution, these believers were in danger of drifting back into the shadows of Judaism. The writer presents the person and work of Christ, urging the readers to move on to spiritual maturity.

Second Peter was written shortly before the Apostle's death in Rome during the summer of A.D. 64. Peter realized that false teachers had come into the church who were advocating an abandonment of moral standards and denying Christ's second coming. Believing that his death was imminent, Peter wrote to remind his readers of the orthodox teachings and to encourage their growth in the knowledge of the Lord Jesus.

The Epistle of Jude appears to be written after Second

Peter, but before the destruction of Jerusalem. Jude addresses the same problem which concerned the Apostle Peter, an outbreak of false teachers who were denying Christ and perverting the doctrine of grace. Jude wrote his letter to encourage the readers to stand firm in Christian orthodoxy in the face of rampant apostasy.

The general epistles include three which were written by the Apostle John. First John was probably written late in the first century, around A.D. 90. John was concerned about false teachers who were drawing true believers into their theological error. As an eyewitness of the life and ministry of Jesus, John combats false teaching with a clear presentation of the truth about His person and work.

Second and Third John were written shortly after First John, and both emphasize the importance of "walking in the truth."

HEBREWS

When I was a boy I enjoyed reading books in the Hardy Boys mystery series. I remember reading *The Mystery of the Old Mill* and others books in the series which had just the right amount of intrigue and drama for a young reader without causing sleepless nights!

If you like a good mystery, you are going to *love* the Book of Hebrews! Everything about it is something of a mystery. *Who wrote it?* We don't know. *To whom was it addressed?* Well, we are not sure. *When was it written?* Again, we can't be too certain.

We don't know if or when these mysteries will be resolved. But what *isn't* a mystery in the book of Hebrews is its message. This is a book about Jesus Christ and how He is God's full and final revelation to humanity!

What's the title?

The title of this letter is taken from the name of the addressees, the Hebrews.

Who wrote it?

The author is not identified. The epistle has been ascribed to Paul, but Hebrews 2:3 presents a major problem for this viewpoint. Whoever authored the book received his teaching from others–second hand. Paul claimed to have received his gospel directly from Jesus Christ (Galatians 1:12). Suggested possible authors include: Barnabas, Apollos, Clement of Rome, Luke Silas, Philip, John Mark, and Priscilla (with or without her husband Aquila). The question of authorship remains a mystery. Origin confessed, "Who the author of Hebrews is, God truly knows."

To whom was it written?

Another mystery! The ancient title designates the readers as "Hebrews," but the letter does not mention the readers as either Jews or Gentiles. Internal evidence suggests that they were Hebrew Christians, perhaps at Rome (13:24).

When was it written?

The writer refers frequently to the Jewish sacrificial system as still in operation (7:8, 8:4, 10:1, 10:2,8,11). This would demand a date prior to A.D. 70 when the Jerusalem temple was destroyed. The reference in 12:4 ("You have not yet resisted to the point of shedding blood") would suggest a date prior to Nero's persecution of Christians which began in A.D. 64. A date of writing in the sixties accords well with the available data, perhaps before A.D. 64.

What is the historical setting?

Although they had been Christians for some time, the

readers were making no spiritual progress (5:11-12). They had failed to grow in the Lord, and this was reflected in their Christian conduct (10:25, 13:2-17). These Hebrew Christians were looking backward to their Jewish ways instead of forward to Christ (12:2). In the face of the hardships of the Christian faith they were in danger of drifting away (2:1) from the substance, Christ, to the shadows of the Jewish sacrificial system (10:1).

Why was it written?

The letter was written to (1) teach concerning the superiority of Christ, (2) warn against drifting to sin and disobedience, and (3) encourage the readers to move on to maturity in Christ.

What's the theme?

"The Person and work of Christ—a Christian's incentive to maturity and service" (12:1-3).

What's it about?

The Superior Person of Christ 1-7	The Superior Work of Christ 8:1-10:18	The Superior Life of Faith 10:19-13:24

What does it teach us?

The Epistle to the Hebrews is really a book about Christ. The book uses the word "better" to emphasize that Christ is better than prophets (1:1-3), better than angels (1:4-2:18), better than Moses (3:1-4:13), and better than Aaron (4:14-7:28). He goes on to explain that Christ is not only superior to all those who preceded Him, His work is better than all the rituals and traditions which the Old Covenant had to offer. He is a minister in a better sanctuary (8:1-5), the mediator of a better covenant (8:6-13), a priest of a better tabernacle (9:1-12), and the offer of a better sacrifice (9:13-10:18).

The writer of Hebrews points out that while the Old Covenant sacrifices had to be continually repeated, Christ has offered a full and final sacrifice that was sufficient for all time. Notice the words that emphasize the completed work of Christ: "having been offered once" (9:28); "offering the body of Jesus once for all" (10:10); "for all time" (10:12); "perfected for all time" (10:14); "there is no longer any offering for sin" (10:18).

While the Temple (or Tabernacle) had various articles of furniture for ritual use, one item that was always quite absent was a chair. The High Priest never sat down while officiating before the Lord. The writer of Hebrews contrasts this with Christ who, "after offering one sacrifice for sins…sat down at the right hand of God" (10:12). He sat down because the work of redemption was finished! There is nothing left to be done except to receive His gracious gift of salvation.

Where's Jesus?

The answer is easy in Hebrews. Jesus is in every chapter! But you will find Him particularly emphasized in Hebrews 1:2-3. The writer of Hebrews contrasts God's past revelation through the prophets with the full and final revelation given through Jesus.

Then the writer presents seven descriptive phrases which highlight the character, power and majesty of Jesus, God's Son. He is (1) Heir of all things, (2) Creator of the world, (3) Radiance of God's glory, (4), Revealer of God's nature, (5) Sustainer of creation, (6) Redeemer of mankind, and (7) Intercessor for believers.

The rest of the book goes on to expand these statements revealing who Jesus is and what He has accomplished.

JAMES

I went to the store to buy some groceries, and when I got to the check-out station, I put two fifty dollar bills on the counter. The clerk glanced at the bills and looked up at me.

"You can't pay for groceries with that money," he said.

"Why not?" I asked.

"Why, that is Monopoly Money! You use it in playing a game, not buying food!"

I picked up the two fifties and held them out to him.

"These say 'fifty dollars' each and since my groceries are $65, I expect to get back $35 dollars in change!"

Other shoppers in the line were looking with curiosity at the mini-drama being played out before them. I could read the expressions on their faces. "What kind of nut case is this who wants to pay for his groceries with Monopoly Money?" When the clerk threatened to call the store manager, I gave in and pulled out my debit card.

Most people would agree that while genuine U.S. dollars and Monopoly Money look similar, there is a vast difference between "legal tender" and "funny money."

And so James points out that there is a vast difference between genuine, regenerating faith and mere intellectual assent to certain facts. James insists that true faith is a working faith, proving its genuineness by what it does.

What's the title?

The title of this letter is taken from the name of the author, *Jakobos*, which comes into English as "James."

Who wrote it?

The author of the epistle identifies himself as "James, bond-servant of God and of the Lord Jesus Christ." Four men by the name of James are mentioned in the NT: James the father of Judas (not Iscariot), James the son of Zebedee, James the son of Alphaeus, and James the half-brother of Jesus (Matt. 13:55, Gal. 1:19). The traditional view is that the epistle was authored by James the half-brother of Jesus. This James was an important leader in the Jerusalem church (Acts 12:17, 15:13-21, 21:8) and needed no further identification.

To whom was it written?

The letter is addressed to Hebrew Christians scattered throughout the Roman Empire (1:1-2). Their scattering was probably the result of persecution which broke out in Jerusalem after the stoning of Stephen (Acts 8:1, 12:1-23).

When was it written?

The epistle of James must have been written before A.D. 62, the date of James' martyrdom according to Josephus (*Antiquities* 197-203). The lack of reference to the controversy addressed by the Jerusalem council (Acts 15) seems to indicate a date prior to A.D. 49. The mention of severe economic conditions (2:15-16) may allude to the famine predicted by Agabus in A.D. 44 (Acts 11:27-28). If so, James was the first New Testament epistle and should be dated between A.D. 45 and 49.

What is the historical setting?

James was a resident of Jerusalem and recognized as a "pillar" of the early church. In writing to scattered groups of Jewish believers, he apparently draws upon the situation in Judea as the basis for his exhortations and examples. The letter indicates that the readers were suffering persecution and trials (1:2-4,12, 2:6, 5:4). They were also lacking in fervor for good works and the practical application of truth to Christian living (1:26-27, 2:14-26). James addressed his letter to Hebrew Christians who, having been freed from the law, needed to be reminded that Christian performance must accompany Christian profession.

Why was it written?

James is a practical epistle. James insists that saving faith is a working faith, proving its genuineness by what it does. The author writes to exhort his readers to live out the ethical implications of their faith.

What's the theme?

The theme of James is, "Tests of a living faith" (1:3). James insists that a saving faith is an active faith, proving its genuineness by what it does.

What's it about?

Attitude toward Trials 1:1-8	Good Works 2:14-26	Prayerless Planning 4:13-17
Evaluating Wealth 1:9-12	Demonstration of Self-Control 3:1-12	Patience in Trials 5:1-11
Temptation 1:13-18	True Wisdom 3:13-18	Constant Honesty 5:12
Obedience to God's Word 1:19-27	Reaction to Worldliness 4:1-10	Resort to Prayer 5:13-18
Partiality 1:1-13	Refusal to Slander 4:11-12	Correcting Sinners 5:19-20

What does it teach us?

At first glance it appears that James is in flat contradiction with Paul on the doctrine of justification. Paul insists that "a man is not justified by the works of the Law but through faith in Christ Jesus" (Gal. 2:16). James, however, argues that "a man is justified by works, and not by faith alone" (James 2:24). How can these two apparently contradictory viewpoints be reconciled?

It seems that James and Paul were confronting different issues. Their words are similar, but their concepts are very different. Paul was refuting those who advocated the observance of Jewish ceremonial law as necessary for justification. James, on the other hand, was challenging those who presumed the adequacy of mere intellectual assent to dead orthodoxy.

Paul uses the word "faith" to denote one's personal acceptance of the Gospel ("trust") and commitment to Christ. James acknowledges this meaning (2:1), but in 2:14-26 uses the word to refer to mere intellectual assent to doctrine. Similarly, Paul uses the word "works" to denote the works of the law--ceremonial rites added to the work of Christ.

In James, "works" are moral deeds, such as acts of charity, which flow naturally from a genuine faith. Again, Paul uses the term "justify" in a forensic or legal way, "to declare to be just or righteous," while James uses the term in a manner more in keeping with the Old Testament sense, "show to be righteous."

Paul and James are not in disagreement on the matter of faith and works. Both agree that people are declared righteous (justified) by faith, not by works. Both also agree that the faith which saves is not *alone*. Ethical actions are the natural outflow of a genuine, saving faith.

Where's Jesus?

While there is no major teaching *about* Jesus in the Epistle of James, in almost every section of the letter James brings out and expands on the teachings of Jesus. This is particularly evident as you compare James with Jesus' Sermon on the Mount. They have similar teachings on trials (James 1:2; Matt. 5:12), giving (James 2:14-17; Matt. 5:24); judging others (James 4:11; Matt. 5:22-24); oaths (James 5:12; Matt. 5:33-37) and prayer (James 5:13-18; Matt. 6:5-13). This is just a sampling. As you read James, look for more of the highlights from the teachings of Jesus.

FIRST PETER

I received a newsletter from missionary friends serving in Indonesia that began, "It's time for Christians to pray!" The letter went on to detail six attacks on Christians which had occurred in the past two weeks. These included Indonesian churches being forcibly closed by Islamic extremists, a church attacked and their pastor hospitalized with injuries, and three Christian Indonesian women sentenced to three years in prison for teaching Sunday school.

As the trial for the three Sunday school teachers began, 150 angry Islamic extremists took over the courtroom and made murderous threats against the defendants and others present. The letter went on to explain that the Indonesian courts often give heavy sentences to Christians to keep radical Muslims from rioting.

Can you imagine being arrested, tried, convicted and imprisoned for teaching Sunday school? While I am thankful that this doesn't happen in America, such persecution is a fact of life for many Christians living in hostile environments around the world. And such was the case in Peter's day when he wrote his letter to Christians who were suffering for their faith.

What's the title?

The title is taken from the name of the author, Peter. The letter is called "First Peter" to distinguish it from Peter's second canonical epistle.

Who wrote it?

The author of the letter is named in the first verse as "Peter, an apostle of Jesus Christ," and there is no reason to question this assertion. The writer demonstrates an intimate acquaintance with the life and teachings of Jesus (2:19-24, 3:18, 4:1, 5:1,5) and was an eyewitness of the sufferings of Christ (2:19-24, 3:18, 4:1, 5:1) as Peter was. The remarkable similarities between Peter's speeches in Acts and his words in this epistle (Acts 2:32-36 with 1 Peter 1:21) confirm that Peter wrote this letter.

Simon Peter was originally from Bethsaida in Galilee (John 1:44). He and his brother of Andrew (John 1:40) were partners in a fishing enterprise in Capernaum. Peter first met Jesus at Bethany beyond the Jordan and was given the name Cephas (Aramaic) or Peter (Greek) meaning "rock" (John 1:42). Peter was later chosen by Christ to become an apostle (Mark 3:16).

Peter was a natural leader and often a spokesman for the twelve (Matt. 16:15-16). He was present with Jesus at the raising of Jairus' daughter (Mk. 5:37), the transfiguration of Jesus (Matt. 17:1-2) and in the Garden of Gethsemane (Matt. 26:36). And Peter saw the empty tomb (John 20:6) and the resurrected Jesus (Luke 24:34).

After Christ's ascension Peter took a position of leadership among the disciples and was the keynote speaker on the Day of Pentecost (Acts 2).

Later on Peter was God's instrument to open the way of salvation to the Samaritans (Acts 8) and the Gentiles (Acts 10-

11). He was also a prominent spokesman in behalf of Gentile believers at the Jerusalem Council (Acts 15:7-11). According to early Christian tradition Peter went to Rome and was crucified there during Nero's persecution in A.D. 64.

To whom was it written?

The epistle is addressed to the believers scattered throughout the provinces of Pontus, Galatia, Cappadocia, Asia, and Bithynia (1:1). Most of the readers were of Gentile background, although some may have been Hebrew believers (2:10,12, 4:3).

When was it written?

Peter's concern for impending persecution suggests that the epistle was written not long before his death (A.D. 64). Peter arrived in Rome in A.D. 62 and probably wrote this letter in A.D. 63 or early 64.

What is the historical setting?

Prominent in the background of 1 Peter is the theme of suffering due to persecution (1:6-7, 2:11-20, 3:13-17, 4:3-5,12-19, 5:8-10). Some believe that the sufferings and persecutions were those which began due to Nero in A.D. 64. It is also possible that the sufferings of these readers were of a general nature, common to the experience of first century Christians.

Peter, probably in Rome (5:13, cf. Rev. 17:5,9, 18:2,10,21), was anticipating more intense persecution, and wrote to the believers in the provinces to encourage them in their present struggle.

Why was it written?

The epistle was written to exhort the readers to conduct themselves in accordance with their living hope. The letter confirmed their knowledge of salvation and encouraged them in their submission to authority and joyful response to suffering.

What's the theme?

The theme of First Peter is "suffering as a Christian and how to endure it triumphantly."

What's it about?

The Believer's Salvation 1:1-2:10	The Believer's Suffering 3:13-4:19
The Believer's Submission 2:11-3:12	The Believer's Supervision 5:1-14

What does it teach us?

First Peter has much to say about submission to authority. This is not a popular topic since most of us would rather *be* the authority than to *submit* to authority. And yet Peter makes it very clear that all of us must relate to those in authority. Four specific areas of authority are mentioned– government (2:13), work or employment (2:18), the home (3:1), and the church (5:5).

The Greek word "submit" means "to be under command." A Christian in submission is under the command or authority of another. The word implies support of the authority, not a foot-dragging, reluctant submission.

All believers are called upon to submit to those who govern us. Interestingly, Peter doesn't limit this submission to good governments or democratic governments. In fact, a rather evil emperor–Nero–ruled when Peter was writing this instruction. The second area of submission is that of servants to their master. This has application today in the employer–

employee relationship. An employee must recognize and submit to the requirements of the boss—or find another job. The third area of submission is the home. The authority figure in the home is the husband who exercises loving and gentle authority over his wife and children. It is clear that the mother also shares in the authority of the home as she cares for and trains her children (Eph. 6:1-4). The fourth area of authority discussed by Peter is the church. In the church the elders have spiritual authority over the congregation (5:5, also Hebrews 13:17). And the elders themselves are under the authority of the Chief Shepherd, Christ.

Submission to authority isn't always easy. Sometimes it is difficult and painful, especially when the authority figure is unreasonable or unjust. But Christ provides us an example to follow when submission results in suffering (1 Peter 2:21-25).

Where's Jesus?

You will find Jesus in 1 Peter 2:21-25 where Peter uses Him as an example of how to endure unjust suffering. Peter explains how Jesus suffered innocently and graciously during His trial, scourging and crucifixion. "While being reviled, He did not revile in return; while suffering, He uttered no threats" (v. 23). Peter declares that through His suffering, Jesus has given us an example so that we might "follow in His steps."

SECOND PETER

Have you ever had a full-fledged encounter with a false teacher? It usually includes a process which begins with questionable teaching, then false teaching, followed by extreme dogmatism and often an immoral lifestyle. Neale Donald Walsch, author of the popular book, *Conversations with God*, is a contemporary example of what I'm referring to. He teaches his readers that they must let go of "yesterday's" omnipotent and transcendent God and embrace "tomorrow's" God who doesn't even require you to believe in him. Tomorrow's God is one who talks to everyone all the time and is unconditionally loving, non-condemning and non-punishing. The guru of "tomorrow's God" explains that God is not a singular being but a "process called life."

We shouldn't be that surprised. New and different views about God have been with us a long time. They were present in ancient Israel and in the early church. In his second epistle, the Apostle Peter tells us what to expect and how to respond when false teachers show up in your church.

What's the title?

The title of the letter is taken from the name of the author, Simon Peter (1:1), the fisherman from Galilee who became a follower of Jesus.

Who wrote it?

Differences in style between 1 and 2 Peter and the lack of external evidence for Petrine authorship have led to questions regarding the authenticity of this epistle. But there is no doubt that the author intended to identify himself as the Apostle Peter.

The author refers to himself as "Simon Peter" (1:1). He writes of his approaching death (1:14) which was predicted by Jesus (Jn. 21:18-19). He claims to be a witness of Jesus' transfiguration (1:16-17) as was Peter (Matt. 17:1-4). The evidence points to this epistle being a genuine work of the Apostle Peter.

To whom was it written?

The readers are of the epistle are believers (1:1). They are apparently the same group of Christians addressed in 1 Peter (2 Pet. 3:1). Most were of Gentile background, though some may have been Hebrew believers.

When was it written?

When Peter wrote this letter, he believed his death to be imminent (1:14-15). Since Peter died in A.D. 64 during the Neronian persecution which began after Rome's burning (July 18, A.D. 64), the epistle was probably written shortly before Peter's death in late A.D. 63 or early A.D. 64.

What is the historical setting?

The problem facing the readers of Second Peter was false teaching. As had been the case in ancient Israel, Peter anticipates the coming of false teachers within the church introducing destructive heresies (2:1-3). Advocating a complete abandonment of moral standards (2:10), they would promise freedom to others, while they themselves remained enslaved by their own lusts (2:19). One of the major doctrinal deviations addressed by Peter was a denial of Christ's second coming (3:4). Peter devotes most of the third chapter to this problem.

Why was it written?

Peter writes to warn his readers against the false teaching within the church (2:1-2, 3:17). Peter intends the letter to stir the readers to remember the orthodox teachings, and thus encourage growth in *true* knowledge of the Lord Jesus (3:1-2,18).

What's the theme?

The theme of Peter's second letter is found in the last verse, "Growing in the knowledge of Christ" (3:18).

What's it about?

The Nature of True Knowledge 1	The Peril of False Teaching 2	The Coming of the Lord Jesus 3

What does it teach us?

For a little book, 2 Peter contains lots of theology! Peter presents a theology of Scripture (1:20-21), a theology of divine judgment (2:4–10), and a theology of Christ's Second Coming (3:3-10). Within this last section we learn something about the character of God. Peter writes, "The Lord is not slow about His promise, as some count slowness, but is patient toward you, not wishing for any to perish but for all to come to repentance" (3:9).

Here we are reminded that God is a promise keeper. He is not one to forget a promise. What God has revealed about the Second Coming of Jesus will be fulfilled according to God's reliable word. This verse also reveals that God is patient. His patience is evidence of His desire that none should perish! The delay of Christ's return has a redemptive purpose in allowing more people to come to faith *before* the day of judgment.

God is compassionate. His heart's desire is that none perish, but that all should come to repentance. Contrary to popular belief, God must someday judge the world, but He is patiently and compassionately waiting to give each person an opportunity to hear and respond to the Gospel message.

Where's Jesus?

You'll Him in 2 Peter 1:16-18 where Peter recounts his experience with Jesus on the Mount of Transfiguration (Matthew 17:1-8). Peter insists that his teaching about the Lord Jesus was not based on clever tales or worldly fables. Rather, he was an "eyewitness" of a wondrous event when Jesus displayed His majesty and glory. Peter was there on "the holy mountain" when Jesus was transfigured and heard God speak from heaven declaring, "This is my beloved Son with whom I am well pleased."

FIRST JOHN

Christians should never underestimate the power of God's love to break down and transform the most hardened individuals. This is beautifully illustrated in Victor Hugo's classic novel *Les Miserables*. Jean Valjean becomes a hard and bitter man after being sentenced to nineteen years of hard labor for stealing a loaf of bread. Released from prison, he struggles to survive, but is welcomed one night into the home of a kind bishop. While the bishop is sleeping, Valjean slips out of the house with the family silver. After being arrested by the police, Valjean is taken back to the bishop who greets him warmly and says, "I am delighted to see you. Had you forgotten that I gave you the candlesticks as well. They are silver like the rest. Did you forget to take them?"

Jean Valjean is released and the police withdraw. Then the bishop charges him to use the money from the silver to become an honest man. Valjean's life is changed by forgiveness and compassion. This is the power of love–God's love mediated through a kindly Christian. First John provides us with a study of the life-changing power of *agape* love. John writes, "We love because He first loved us" (1 John 4:19).

What's the title?

This epistle is named after the traditional author, John the Apostle. It is the first of three of John's canonical epistles.

Who wrote it?

Although the epistle is anonymous, both internal and external evidence support the view that the author is John the Apostle and author of the Fourth Gospel. The author claims to have been an eye witness of the life and ministry of Jesus (1:1) and was a man of spiritual maturity and authority (2:1,12,18, 3:7,18, 4:4, 5:21). The similarity in thought, vocabulary and style between the Gospel of John and 1 John confirm that both were written by the same author, the Apostle John.

To whom was it written?

The readers are believers of Gentile background 3:1-2, 5:21). Since John spent his later years at Ephesus, it is likely that the epistle was written from that city to a nearby group of Asian churches with whom John was personally acquainted.

When was it written?

The epistle was probably written after the Fourth Gospel since the author seems to assume an acquaintance on the part of his readers with the facts of the gospel. The absence of any reference to suffering would indicate that the letter was written before the persecution of Domitian around A.D. 95, perhaps around A.D. 90.

What is the historical setting?

First John is written to churches in which false prophets had appeared (4:1) who were drawing Christians from fellowship with the true believers (2:19). The false teachers claimed a special illumination by the Spirit (2:20,27) and claimed to have reached a state of moral perfection (1:8-10).

The chief theological error tempting the readers was a denial of the incarnation of Jesus (2:22, 4:2). John combats this error by claiming to have been an eyewitness to the life and ministry of Christ (1:1-4,8, 2:2, 3:16, 4:10).

Why was it written?

In his epistle, John combats false teaching with a clear presentation of the truth. The primary purpose in writing is to promote fellowship (*koinonia*) in the family of God (1:3).

What's the theme?

The theme of First John is "Fellowship in the family of

God" (1:3).

What is it about?

First John is one of the most difficult books in the New Testament to outline because the structure of the letter is not readily apparent. The following outline is based on the major themes of light (1:5), love (4:8), and faith (5:4).

Walking in the Light 1-2	Abiding in Love 3-4	Overcoming by Faith 5

What does it teach us?

The chief theological error circulating among John's readers was a denial of the incarnation of Jesus (2:22, 4:2). This reflects the view of an early heresy known as docetism, from the Greek word *dokeo*, "to seem or appear." The docetics believed that since material things were evil, God could not have come into contact with the material world in the person of Jesus Christ. And so they denied the incarnation–that God in the person of Jesus took on humanity. They claimed that the body of Christ was only an "appearance" and was not real. Jesus only *seemed* to take on earthly, human form. Many docetics went on to deny the reality of Christ's sufferings.

John combats this error by claiming to have been an eyewitness to the life and ministry of Jesus (1:1-4). John claims to have "handled" Jesus' body, thus refuting the view that He was just a phantom. The incarnation–that God became a man in the person of Jesus–is a great mystery, but a solidly biblical doctrine. Jesus is truly human. At the same time, He is truly divine. Because of the incarnation, Jesus Christ remains forever both God and man (Rom. 9:5, 1 Tim. 2:2).

Where's Jesus?

Where do we find Jesus in 1st John? I'm confident that the Apostle would direct us to consider the love of God. John writes, "By this the love of God was manifested in us, that God has sent His only begotten Son into the world so that we might live through Him" (1 John 4:9). The supreme demonstration of God's love for mankind was the giving of His "only begotten" (better translated "unique" or "one of a kind") Son as the Savior of the world. The amazing thing is that God loved us and sent His Son to save us while we were yet sinners (Romans 5:8). That's called grace–*amazing* grace!

SECOND JOHN

The most exciting and significant archaeological discovery of the 20th century was the discovery of ancient scrolls in caves near the site of Qumran by the Dead Sea. The discovery of the Qumran Scrolls provided biblical documents in the Hebrew language that are a thousand years older that the most ancient Hebrew manuscripts existing to date. But with the discovery of the scrolls came a storm of controversy. Who wrote them? Why were they left in caves? Were the scrolls copied by the Essenes? Was John the Baptist an Essene? Was Jesus familiar with the people of Qumran and their teachings? Were there New Testament manuscripts at Qumran?

To respond to these and other questions, Professor William LaSor wrote a book, *Dead Sea Scrolls and the New Testament* (Eerdmans, 1972). In the first chapter LaSor expresses his desire to go wherever the facts lead. He writes, "We have nothing to fear from truth; only ignorance can hurt us" (p. 27). Then he adds, "New truths always challenge old opinions. But new truths never destroy old truths; they merely separate truth from falsehood."

I have read these words countless times to my students in the seminary classroom as we have explored controversial subjects. And I am confident that the writer of Second John would heartily endorse LaSor's remarks. For his goal in writing this letter is to help his readers keep "walking in the truth" (v. 4).

What's the title?

The title of this brief letter is "Second John," distinguishing it from John's two other canonical epistles.

Who wrote it?

Both internal evidence and early church tradition indicate that this letter was written by the Apostle John. However, the reference to the author as "the elder" (v. 1) has led some to conclude that the epistle was written by someone else. Yet the title "elder" would have been a fitting designation for John since he was advanced in years at the time of writing. Since the letter bears a close resemblance in language and thought with First John, it is clear that Second John was also authored by the Apostle.

To whom was it written?

John addressed his second letter to the "elect lady." Is John referring to an individual or a church? The use of the second person plural, rather than the singular in verses 8, 9, and 12, may suggest that a community of believers is in mind.

The personification of the church as a lady may be consisted with the idea of the church as the bride of Christ (Eph. 5:19-32). The most literal and straight forward understanding of the term "lady" would interpret it as referring to a Christian lady within the church. Perhaps a local body of believers meeting in her home would also benefit from John's letter.

When was it written?

The false teaching mentioned in the letter links it closely

with the circumstances of First John. Second John was probably written after First John had been sent, perhaps around A.D. 90.

What is the historical setting?

While living in Ephesus late in his life, John had apparently become acquainted with the children of a Christian lady and was pleased to find them believing and living the God's truth. It may have been from them that John learned of the false teachers who were denying the humanity of Jesus (v. 7). These false teachers were traveling among the churches taking advantage of the hospitality offered by Christian people (verses 10-11). John warns of such men and their ideas (verses 7, 9), instructing the believers how to respond to such deceivers.

Why was it written?

The purpose of the letter is to warn the readers of the dangerous error infiltrating their community by presenting in clear terms the nature of the false teachers and their doctrine.

What's the theme?

The theme of the epistle is "walking in truth" (v. 4).

What's it about?

John's Greeting 1-3	John's Instructions 4-11	John's Visit 12-13

What does it teach us?

During the trial of Jesus, Pontius Pilate asked the question that has hounded philosophers through the ages,

"What is truth?" (John 18:38). Sadly, he didn't wait for the answer, for *the* "Truth" was standing before him. John's writings contribute significantly to a biblical theology of truth, using the word 25 times in his Gospel and 20 times in his three Epistles.

The Greek word "truth" (*aletheia*) refers to the objective reality behind the appearance of things. Appearances can be deceptive, but the reality is always certain and reliable.

A layer of material called "Bondo" can be used to cover dents in a car fender. Scrape away the "Bondo" and you have the bare metal–the objective reality; the truth! The Bible refers to the "truth of the Gospel" (Gal. 2:5) in contrast to heretical distortions. Romans 1:25 refers to "the truth of God," that is, the truth concerning God.

In John 14:6 we discover that Jesus is the very embodiment of truth. He told His disciples, "I am the way, the truth, and the life." Jesus is the ultimate reality supporting all certainty. The Apostle John knows the truth (v. 1) and is pleased that he has found young believers who also know Jesus as the ultimate reality and are ordering their lives according to the reality He lived and taught (v. 4).

Where's Jesus?

The Apostle John says that we will find Jesus with those who abide in His teaching. He explains in verse 9, "Anyone who goes too far and does not abide in the teaching of Christ, does not have God; the one who abides in the teaching, he has both the Father and the Son." Some "deceivers" circulating among the believers were demonstrating by their false doctrine that they had no association with Jesus.

True believers, on the other hand, demonstrate by their adherence to the teaching of Jesus that they share an intimate fellowship with both the Father and the Son.

THIRD JOHN

I spoke with a church leader who told me about a man who had left his church. Then he added, "It is the best thing that could have happened to our congregation!" Perhaps you have encountered a similar troublemaker in your church, a Christian who seems wreak havoc in every area he touches. Often it begins with petty issues which are blown totally out of perspective. Then a lack of understanding, tolerance, and forgiveness brings disruption to the fellowship. When the offending individual finally resigns and leaves the church, everyone breathes a sigh of relief! Such was the case with Diotrephes, a troublemaker in the church of Gaius who was a well-loved friend of the Apostle John. John's third letter reveals how he intended to deal with such a trouble maker.

What's the title?

The title of the letter is taken from the name of the traditional author, the Apostle John. It is designated "Third John" to distinguish it from John's two other canonical letters.

Who wrote it?

Although the author of the epistle is not named, he refers to himself as "the elder" and this would indicate that the same individual authored who authored Second John. The vocabulary and style also unite it with Second John and point to the Apostle John as the author. Both writers rejoice over those who are "walking in truth." We may be confident that the Apostle John authored all three of the letters which are associated with him.

To whom was it written?

The addressee of the epistle is the "beloved Gaius." Although three other men in the New Testament are known by this name (Rom. 16:23, 1 Cor. 1:14, Acts 19:29, 20:4,5), it is not likely that this Gaius should be identified with any other.

The Gaius in this letter was a consistent Christian (3), known for his generous hospitality (5), and a well-loved friend of the Apostle John. The letter was apparently intended to be shared with others in the church community (14).

When was it written?

Although Third John does refer to a previous letter (v. 9), this does not appear to be a reference to either First or Second John, so no sequence of communication can be established. The epistle was probably written about the same time as Second John, around A.D. 90.

What is the historical setting?

John the Apostle had received a report from those who had visited the community where Gaius lived (3). John had learned of the faithful character and hospitality demonstrated by Gaius (3,5) as well as the problem with Diotrephes (9-10) who had usurped authority and was abusing the brethren. John urges his readers not to imitate the evil actions of Diotrephes.

The Apostle enlists the help of Gaius to assure a welcome and support for the co-workers who had been rebuffed by Diotrephes (5-8). John expresses his desire to visit Gaius soon and to deal with the troublemaker in person (10). Demetrius, who is so highly commended in verse 12, may have served as the carrier of the letter.

What's the purpose?

John writes to commend Gaius for walking in the truth and to encourage the practice of hospitality so that the messengers from John might receive a proper welcome when they visit the congregation.

Third John is also intended to censure the conduct of Diotrephes and reveal John's plans to deal with the situation in person.

What's the theme?

The theme of Second and Third John is the same, "walking in truth" (3).

What's it about?

| Commendation of Gaius 1-8 | Condemnation of Diotrephes 9-11 | Commendation of Demetrius 12-14 |

What does it teach us?

The practice of hospitality is a time honored tradition in the church. New Testament writers frequently urge believers to demonstrate hospitality toward others (Rom. 12:10, 1 Thess. 4:9, 1 Pet. 1:22, Heb. 13:1). Being hospitable is a character quality required for church leaders (1 Tim. 3:2, Tit. 1:8). It is also a qualification for widows receiving church support (1 Tim. 5:10).

Hospitality is not just inviting friends and family over for dinner. The Greek word actually means "love of strangers." You practice hospitality in the biblical sense when you invite *strangers* into your home as guests. Gaius is commended by the Apostle John for welcoming traveling missionaries into his home (5-6).

John goes on in the following verses to list several reasons why believers should show hospitality to traveling preachers and missionaries (7-8). First, their lives are dedicated to Christ. John says, "they went out for the sake of the Name," a reference to their dedicated service for Christ. Second, they have separated themselves from the world by "accepting nothing from the Gentiles." They have declined help from unbelievers since it might suggest they were willing to compromise the gospel for personal gain. Third, by showing hospitality we become "fellow-workers with the truth" (8).

Showing hospitality is actually an opportunity to enlarge your ministry! By providing food and housing for traveling teachers, evangelists and missionaries, you actually have a share in their ministry! Hospitality is not simply an obligation, it is a strategic opportunity to become more involved in God's kingdom work!

Where's Jesus?

Where is Jesus to be found in 3rd John? A quick read through the book will reveal that the name of Jesus is not even mentioned! So is He on a holiday? Not a chance! You will find Jesus in the phrase, "walking in the truth" (v. 4). In John 14:6 Jesus declared that He was "the truth." By this Jesus meant that He was the full revelation and embodiment of the redemptive purposes of God. To know Jesus is to embrace God's truth. And to "walk in the truth" is to embrace Jesus and His teachings. There's no greater joy in life than this!

JUDE

No one is immune to being taken advantage of by a false teacher. One of my students has had firsthand experience with this. He shared with me that as a young Christian he had become attracted to the teaching of a seminary graduate who had great knowledge of the Bible and was a persuasive teacher. There was a small group of Christians who had come under his teaching and influence. The doctrine which received the most emphasis was grace.

Now, God's grace is a good thing and a very biblical doctrine. But this teacher exploited and perverted the doctrine of grace to say that what may be sin to others was not sin to their enlightened group. There was sufficient "grace" and freedom to abuse alcohol, smoke marijuana, even steal money for drugs. Living in a communal living situation, the leader had sexual privileges with other members' wives.

My young friend and his family were taken in by the false teacher and remained in the group for several years before facing the reality of their deception. Then one night they left the community, literally with their clothes on their backs. By the grace of God, the family stepped out of the darkness and into the light. Jude knew of the potential for spiritual deception and instructs his readers to beware.

What's the title?

The title of the book is taken from the name of the author, Jude.

Who wrote it?

The author identifies himself as "Jude [Gk. *Judas*], a bond-servant of Jesus Christ, and brother of James." It is unlikely that the author was Judas the apostle (Lk. 6:16), for he seems to distinguish himself from the apostles (Jude 17). Both internal evidence and the testimony of the church fathers indicate that the epistle was written by Jude (or Judas), the half-brother of Jesus (Matt. 13:55, Mk. 6:3), who came to faith after the resurrection (Jn. 7:5, Acts 1:14). His spiritual life was no doubt influenced by his devout parents and the personal contact he had with Jesus.

To whom was it written?

Jude wrote to believers (v. 1), but gives no indication as to their specific location. They had heard of the words of the apostles and were acquainted with the teachings of Paul (18,19). The readers had some knowledge of Jewish intertestamental and apocryphal literature, but this does not demand a Jewish setting. It is probable that the readers were first century Christians, both Jews and Gentiles.

When was it written?

Jude appears to have been written after 2 Peter (A.D. 64) and before the destruction of Jerusalem (A.D. 70). The letter was probably written not long after A.D. 64 when the error Peter had predicted had come to fruition. The book may be dated around A.D. 65-68.

What is the historical setting?

Jude writes to deal with an outbreak of false teaching (3-4). He addresses himself to the same problem which concerned Peter (2 Pet. 2:1-2,10), and encourages the readers to contend earnestly for orthodox Christianity (v. 3). The false teachers were denying Christ and perverting the doctrine of grace. They were ruled by their passions (vv. 4,16) and scoffed at the accepted Christian way (v. 17).

Why was it written?

The purpose of the letter is to encourage the readers to contend for Christian orthodoxy (v. 3), to remind them of God's judgment on the ungodly (v. 5), and to instruct the readers how to offset the evil effects of the false teachers (17-23).

What's the theme?

The theme of the letter is "Contending for the true faith in the face of apostasy" (v. 3).

What's it about?

Jude's Purpose 1-4	Examples of Judgment 5-7	Character of the Apostates 8-16	Response of the Believers 17-23	Jude's Prayer 24-25

What does it teach us?

My daughter worked as a paramedic, responding to emergency calls to help injured people and save lives. She was given a pin by her employer for saving the life of a woman by using a defibrillator to restart her heart. Each of us should be ready to serve as "spiritual paramedics" when we become aware of someone whose spiritual life is in grave danger.

Jude identifies three groups of people who have become ensnared by false teaching–the doubters, the deceived, and the confirmed heretics (v. 22-23). For those who are doubting and questioning their faith, Jude says we must *convince* them of the truth with a spirit of gentleness and mercy. Some texts read *have mercy* rather than convince. But convincing the doubters (probably new believers) would seem to be more necessary.

Jude refers to "others" who have been led into error, but are not beyond the point of no return (v. 23a). These are the deceived. For these, Jude urges drastic action. No effort should be spared to rescue deceived believers from spiritual destruction.

The last group mentioned by Jude is the saddest of all–those who are confirmed in their false teaching. These probably refer to the teachers and leaders of pagan religions and deceptive cults. Out of regard for one's own spiritual well-being, Jude instructs believers to separate from them as you would from a defiled or contaminated garment. While ever effort must be made to convince doubters and rescue the deceived, Jude seems to leave little room for dialogue with a cult leader. Concern for one's own spiritual well-being demands separation.

Where's Jesus?

You will find Jesus in the closing prayer at the end of Jude's letter where Jude declares, "To God be the glory!" Jude insists that there is only one God, and He is "Savior" (v. 25). Jesus is called "Savior" sixteen times in the New Testament. Through Jesus Christ and His sacrifice on the cross God saves those who call out to Him for help and forgiveness of sin. After His ministry in Samaria, the people of that region concluded that Jesus is not just the Savior of the Jews, but "is indeed the Savior of the world" (John. 4:42).

CHAPTER 10

The Final Revelation

There is something very satisfying about coming to the last chapter in a book. It is always nice to find out how the story turns out and how the issues and conflicts are resolved. And that is what we have in the final chapter in the story of the Bible–the Book of Revelation. Here we learn that God's kingdom rule on earth has been reestablished after Satan's challenge. We learn that salvation has been provided through the redeeming work of Savior Jesus and many have embraced His wonderful gift. And finally, we learn in Revelation how Satan and his followers have been judged. It is at this point in the story of the Bible we can say, "Mission accomplished!"

A comparison of the first three chapters of Genesis with the last three chapters of Revelation illustrates how the problems which came about because of sin will be resolved:

Genesis 1-3	Revelation 20-22
God created the heavens and earth	God prepares a new heaven and earth
Satan appears as deceiver of mankind	Satan disappears in the lake of fire
Sin and defilement enter the garden	Nothing defiled will enter the city
Walk with God interrupted by sin	Walk with God resumed by grace
Initial triumph of the serpent	Ultimate triumph of the Lamb
Pain multiplied because of sin	No more tears, pain or death
Paradise closed because of sin	Paradise open to all believers
Access to the tree of life lost	Access to the tree of life regained
Fallen people driven from God's presence	Redeemed people shall see His face
The ground is cursed because of sin	There shall be no more curse

If you enjoy a story with a happy ending, then the last chapter of the Bible won't disappoint you. The Great Story ends with the removal of the effects of sin and an end to the curse which resulted from mankind's fall. With the curse of sin removed, and God's blessing will be restored–not just for a moment, but forever.

REVELATION

It was a starry night at Arrowhead Springs in the San Bernardino Mountains. I had spent the evening at a college conference listening to a lecture by a speaker who would eventually write the bestselling book, *The Late Great Planet Earth*. Hal Lindsey, a staff member of Campus Crusade for Christ had given an evening message introducing a crowd of college students to God's program of biblical prophecy. He had talked about the Rapture of the church, the seven-year Tribulation, and the Second Coming of Christ. Although I had been raised in the church and had been in Sunday School since I was old enough to walk, biblical prophecy was a whole new world to me. I was both thrilled and fascinated by what I had heard.

Returning to the University of Oregon after the conference, I began a study of the Book of Revelation and the events of prophecy. My study of biblical prophecy has continued for the last forty-five years. And I have not ceased to be thrilled and fascinated by what I have learned. But I have discovered that the Book of Revelation is not so much about biblical prophecy as it is a book about Jesus Christ. Here in the last book of the Bible, God reveals who Christ is, what He has accomplished, and what He will do in the future.

What's the title?

The book is titled by the author as "The Revelation of Jesus Christ" (1:1). The book is often called the *Apocalypse*, which is the first word in the Greek text and means "unveiling" or "disclosure."

Who wrote it?

The author of Revelation calls himself "John" (1:1,4,9, 22:8). The only John who would have been so clearly known to the seven churches of Asia would have been John the Apostle. There are many similarities between the Fourth Gospel and Revelation which serve to confirm that John wrote the Revelation. Only in Revelation 19:13 and John 1:1,14 and 1 John 1:1 is the Greek word "logos" used in a personal sense to refer to Jesus. Jesus is referred to as "Lamb" in John 1:29,36 and 28 times in Revelation. Early church tradition confirms the view that the Apostle John wrote the Revelation.

To whom was it written?

The book is addressed to seven churches of Asia (1:4) which were leading centers of the province and connected by major travel routes. The churches include Ephesus, Smyrna, Pergamum, Thyatira, Sardis, Philadelphia and Laodicea. The individual letters in Revelation 2-3 are directed to the "angels" or "messengers" of the churches. The Greek term *aggelos* may refer to either, but is best understood to refer to the human messengers of the seven churches. These church messengers may have been sent to Patmos to learn of John's situation and subsequently carried his letters to the seven churches.

When was it written?

Some scholars date the Revelation during the reign of Nero (A.D. 54-68) or shortly thereafter on account of the reference to Jerusalem as though it were still standing (11:1-13). But such an early date does not allow for the historical developments within the churches John addresses in chapters 2-3. Irenaeus, a second century church leader, writes that Revelation was recorded "at the close of the reign of Domitian" [A.D. 81-96] (*Against Heresies* V.xxx.3). This is confirmed by the early church historian Eusebius (*Historia Ecclesiastica* 3:18). The weight of evidence points to a date of writing toward the end of the reign of Domitian, around A.D. 95 or 96.

What is the historical setting?

The Revelation was received by John while he was in exile on the island of Patmos late in the reign of Domitian. Patmos was a small, rocky island in the Aegean Sea off the coast of Asia Minor, about 35 miles SW of Miletus. The island, measuring only six by ten miles, served as a place of banishment in Roman times. It may have been John's refusal to submit to the imperial decree of emperor worship that led to his exile. Domitian took the title *Dominus et Deus* ("Lord and god") and proclaimed his infant son a god and his mother a goddess. Christians refused to worship Domitian and suffered severe persecution under his reign. Persecution of believers is reflected in the message of Revelation (1:9, 2:10,13, 6:9).

Why was it written?

The book of Revelation was written to encourage believers under the shadow of Roman persecution by showing them the ultimate victory of Christ over His enemies and to warn the churches of the dangers of spiritual lethargy and apostasy. The book brings Old Testament prophecy and promises to consummation and presents the glorious Christ directing the churches, judging the world, and ruling His kingdom.

What's the theme?

The theme of Revelation is "the glory, judgment, and triumph of Christ" (19:10).

What is it about?

The outline of Revelation is suggested in 1:19 where the glorified Christ instructs John concerning the message he is about to record.

| Things Seen: John's Vision of Christ 1 | Things Which Are: Letters to Seven Churches 2-3 | Things Which Shall Be: Day of the Lord 4-22 |

What does it teach us?

The Bible teaches that God is king of the universe and rules over His creation. But His sovereignty challenged by a spirit being referred to in the Bible as "Satan." This evil being rebelled against God and through his influence on Adam and Eve drew humanity into his rebellion. As a result, the world is now under Satan's sway, standing against God and His will. But God did not give up on His creation and fallen creatures. He established a plan to redeem fallen humanity, reclaim His kingdom in the face of Satan's challenge, and execute judgment on all sin and evil.

The Book of Revelation teaches how God will accomplish His plan. Genesis begins the Bible, recording that a curse fell on the earth because of sin (Gen. 3:17). Revelation concludes the Bible, recording the removal of the effects of sin and an end to the curse (Rev. 22:3). In summary, this is God's plan for the ages–to reverse the curse!

Today, believers in Jesus are living between the first and second comings of Christ. As people submitted to the King, they are participating in God's present spiritual kingdom. But they are living in anticipation of Christ's return and the full consummation of God's earthly kingdom when Jesus will sit on David's throne and rule the world from the holy city, Jerusalem (Isa. 2:2-4, Rev. 20:4-6))

How encouraging to know that God has a plan. He

knows the end from the beginning. All history and human existence is under His sovereign rule and progressing according to His design, all to His honor and glory!

Where's Jesus?

People are often surprised to learn that the Book of Revelation is not so much about prophecy as it is about Jesus. This is nowhere more evident than in chapter one where John records his opening vision (1:12-16). Here he describes "one like a son of man" standing among seven golden lampstands (representing the seven churches).

Jesus is described with a number picturesque similes. His hair is white "like snow." His eyes are "like a flame of fire." His feet are "like burnished bronze." His voice was "like the sound of many waters." His face was "like the sun shining in its strength." When confronted with this heavenly vision, John did the only logical thing. He fell at His feet in an act of humility and worship. May we do the same as Jesus reveals Himself to us through God's Word.

CHAPTER 11

The Most Asked Questions about the Bible

In the previous ten chapters I have introduced the Bible, section by section, book by book. I have provided important background for each book of the Bible. But you may still have some questions. The goal of this chapter is answer some of the most asked questions about the Bible.

1. What is the Bible?

The Bible is a collection of books written by many different authors over a period of 1,500 years. The Hebrew Scriptures, known to Christians as the Old Testament, records God's dealings with the nation of Israel. It contains 24 books (divided into 39 in the Christian Bible). The literature of the Hebrew Bible includes historical narrative, poetry, and prophecy.

The New Testament contains 27 books including the four gospel narratives of the life of Christ, an account of the activities of the apostles (Acts), 21 early church letters, and Revelation, disclosing the prophetic future.

Roman Catholics and those of Greek Orthodox tradition include additional Old Testament books known as the Apocrypha. The name "Apocrypha" means "hidden" and refers to the fact that these books were not considered suitable for public reading because of their questionable content. They are also called "Deuterocanonical" (second canon).

The Apocrypha or Deuterocanonical books (Tobit, 1-2 Maccabees, Baruch, Ecclesiasticus, etc.) were declared a part of Scripture by the Council of Trent in 1546.

2. What does the word "Bible" mean?

The word "Bible" is derived from the name of the ancient Phoenician city of Byblos. It was there that the papyrus plant was cut and dried in strips for use as writing paper. The manuscript material was called *biblos* after the place of its manufacture. The word "Bible" means "little books," derived from the Greek word *biblia,* a diminutive form of *biblos.*

3. Who wrote the Bible?

The Bible contains the writings of many different authors. Some of the authors are identified in the writing itself. Other authors are known only by ancient tradition. Some of the books of the Bible are anonymous. Major contributors of the Bible include the following:

Moses–The largest contributor to the Hebrew Bible was Moses, author of the Torah or Pentateuch (Genesis, Exodus, Leviticus, Numbers and Deuteronomy).

Luke–Although he wrote only two books, Luke wrote a greater volume of material than any other New Testament writer.

David–Gifted with both musical and poetic abilities, David authored 73 psalms.

Solomon–Noted for his great wisdom, Solomon wrote Ecclesiastes, Proverbs and the Song of Solomon.

Jeremiah–The prophet wrote the Book of Jeremiah and his Lamentations over the destruction of Jerusalem.

Paul–The apostle Paul authored 13 of the 27 New Testament books.

4. Is the Bible an "inspired" book?

Many believe that the Bible is unique among the sacred writings of the great religions. Most Christians believe that the Bible is divinely inspired. This belief is based on what the Bible says about itself. "All Scripture is inspired by God...." (2 Tim. 3:16). The word *inspired* literally means *God-breathed*. The doctrine of inspiration means that God so directed the human authors of Scripture that the truth He desired to reveal was recorded in the original manuscripts without error.

5. Must one believe that the Bible is divinely inspired?

Many people who have no particular religious convictions have read, studied, and enjoyed the Bible. The Bible is recognized as a sacred book by the Jews, Christians, and Muslims.

The Bible contains some of the greatest literature ever written–captivating stories, dramatic poetry, elevating prayers, mysterious parables, engaging allegories, powerful sermons, and memorable letters. Biblical laws and ethical principles form the foundation of our own American legal system. A truly educated person should not be unfamiliar with the Bible. For many, the Bible is simply great literature. For others of us, it is the Word of God.

6. When was the Bible written?

Although some would place them later, the Bible chronology indicates that the books authored by Moses were written around 1400 B.C. The Book of Job may have been written even earlier. Malachi, the last of the Old Testament books, was written around 432 B.C.

The first New Testament book was probably the Epistle of James, written around A.D. 45. Paul's letter to the Galatians was probably next, around A.D. 49. Although debated, I suggest that Matthew's Gospel was probably written about A.D. 50. Paul's letters were completed by A.D. 67. The Apostle John finished off the New Testament with the Book of Revelation around A.D. 90. And so the books of the Bible were written over a period of about 1500 years.

7. Is the Bible the world's oldest book?

During the last century, archaeologists have found the remains of several ancient libraries which contain clay tablets written long before the oldest books of the Bible. Enuma Elish, the Babylonian Creation account discovered in the excavation of Asherbanipal's library at Nineveh, was probably composed about 1800 B.C.

The Gilgamesh Epic recorded on clay tablets found in Asherbanipal's library is said to date from around the beginning of the second millennium B.C. It records the adventures of Gilgamesh and contains a flood account which has numerous parallels to Genesis 6-9. The Code of Hammurabi, dating around 1723 B.C. is the longest Babylonian document ever found. It records the laws of Hammurabi, sixth king of the First Dynasty of Babylon.

In 1875 archaeologists discovered the remains of an ancient library at Ebla (Tell Mardikh). There they found over 15,000 clay tablets, many of which date from the third millennium B.C. They give us a detailed picture of the laws, science, mathematics, religion, and economic life in the Middle East one thousand years before the time of Abraham. This evidence makes it clear that the Bible is not the world's oldest book, but of all ancient writings, it is the most well-known.

8. In what language was the Bible originally written?

Most of the Hebrew Bible was written in classical Hebrew, a Semitic language spoken by the ancient Israelites.

Small portions of the Old Testament were written in Aramaic, a dialect spoken in Syria and Mesopotamia which is closely related to Hebrew. The Aramaic sections of the Bible include Daniel 2:4-7:28, Ezra 4:8-6:18, 7:12-26, and Jeremiah 10:11. The New Testament books were written in Koine (*common*) Greek, the international language of the Roman world in the first century.

9. When was the Bible first translated?

The first translation of the Bible was made in Alexandria, Egypt about the middle of the third century B.C. There was a large Jewish population there and many of the younger generation no longer understood classical Hebrew. According to the Letter of Aristeas (preserved for us in Josephus *Antiquities* XII), an ancient writer, Egypt's ruler Ptolemy Philadelphus was engaged in gathering books for Alexandria's famous library. He requested that the Jewish High Priest send 72 translators (six from each tribe) to Alexandria to translate the Hebrew Scriptures.

This earliest translation of the Bible is known as the Septuagint (*seventy; LXX*) from the approximate number of the translators. The Septuagint was a very influential translation. It was essentially the Bible of the Greek-speaking Jews of the first century. Many of the Old Testament quotations in the New Testament are from the Septuagint.

The next major translation of the Bible was Jerome's Latin Vulgate. Jerome was commissioned by the bishop of Rome to translate the Scriptures into the common language of the Latin speaking people of the church. Jerome completed his work in Bethlehem between 385 and 405 A.D.

The Church of the Nativity in Bethlehem honors the traditional cave where Jerome is said to have done his translation work. We don't have another major translation of the Bible from the original languages until William Tyndale in the 1500s.

10. Do we possess the original copies of the books of the Bible?

Not a single original copy of any biblical book has survived. Ancient copies of the books on papyrus and parchment have been preserved in Jewish synagogues and libraries like the one at Saint Catherine's Monastery at Mt. Sinai. The standard text of the Hebrew Bible we have today was given its final form by the scribal copyists known as Masoretes in the 7th to 9th centuries A.D. They standardized the Hebrew text by recording the vowels which had been agreed upon by oral tradition. (Like modern Hebrew, the original Hebrew manuscripts were written without vowels.)

Before 1947, the oldest complete copies of the Hebrew Bible dated from the 9th and 10th centuries. Then the Dead Sea Scrolls were discovered! These scrolls included parts of every book of the Hebrew Bible except Esther. The whole book of Isaiah was found on a parchment (animal skin) scroll. The Qumran texts date from around the first century B.C.

The oldest manuscripts of the New Testament date from the 4th and 5th centuries A.D. These include:

Codex Vaticanus (4th century), located in the Vatican Library. This manuscript omits Hebrews 9:14 to the end of the book, the Pastoral Epistles, Philemon and the Revelation.

Codex Sinaiticus (4th century), located in the British Museum.

Codex Alexandrinus (5th century), located in the British Museum. This manuscript is fairly complete, including most of the Septuagint and the book of Revelation.

The Greek manuscripts in existence total nearly 5300. If you don't read Greek, you can be especially thankful that the ancient biblical manuscripts have been translated into English!

11. What is meant by the *canon* of Scripture?

The Greek word *canon* means a straight stick by which something is ruled or measured. The term *canon* refers to the standard or measurement by which books were included or excluded from the final list of authoritative Scripture.

The tests for determining which books should be included in the canon of Scripture include the following:

Was it written by a biblical figure?
Does the author write with God's authority?
Is the book in agreement with other revelation?
Is the book universally accepted by those of like faith?

The Old Testament canon was officially recognized at an assembly of eminent rabbis and Jewish leaders who met about A.D. 90 in the village of Jamnia (Yavneh). The complete canon of Scripture as we know it today was formally certified at a council of church leaders who met at the North African city of Carthage in 397 A.D. Most of the books of the Bible had been recognized earlier, but the canon was officially recognized at this time.

12. What does the term *testament* mean? How do the New and Old Testaments differ?

The word *testament* is a synonym for *covenant* which refers to an agreement or promise. The Hebrew Bible places a great emphasis on the covenant established between God and Israel at Mt. Sinai when the Law was given to Israel. When the people broke the rules of the agreement, God disciplined His people. The ultimate consequence of breaking the covenant was exile from the Promised Land. In light of this impending judgment, the prophet Jeremiah began to speak of a New Covenant (Jer. 31:31) which God would inaugurate with His people.

Christians believe that Jesus, the promised Messiah, inaugurated the New Covenant at the time of His sacrificial death for mankind (Heb. 8:13). At the Last Supper, Jesus passed the cup and said, "This cup which is poured out for you is the New Covenant in My blood" (Luke 22:20, cf. Matthew 26:27-28). In 2 Corinthians 3:7-11 Paul contrasts the glories of the Old Covenant with the surpassing glories of the New!

To Christians, the Hebrew Scriptures deal with the Old Covenant, so this part of the Bible is referred to as the "Old Testament." The writings of the Apostles deal with the New Covenant, hence the designation "New Testament." Tertullian (160-215), an early church teacher and theologian, was the first to use this designation for the Christian Scriptures around A.D. 200.

The term "Old Covenant" should not lead us to conclude that the Hebrew Bible is antiquated, outdated or irrelevant. To avoid such implications I prefer to refer to the Old Testament as the *Hebrew Scriptures*. Jewish readers used the term Tanakh to refer to their Bible. Tanakh is an acronym which uses the first Hebrew letter for each of the three divisions of the Hebrew Bible—The Torah (Pentateuch), Neviim ("Prophets") and Ketuvim ("Writings").

13. Why should someone who is not Jewish study the Old Testament?

The Apostle Paul was writing to a predominately non-Jewish audience in his first letter to the Corinthians. After citing a series of examples from the Hebrew Scriptures, Paul writes, "Now these things happened to them as an example, and they were written for our instruction, upon whom the ends of the ages have come" (1 Cor. 10:11). It is very clear that Paul appreciated the instructional value of the Old Testament. Here are five other reasons we should study the Hebrew Bible:

(1) The Hebrew Bible reveals the origins and history of

the Jewish people whom God chose to bring spiritual light and salvation to the world.

(2) The Hebrew Bible contains some of the greatest literature ever written. A thorough education should include a basic appreciation and understanding of this literature. Many of the images used in art and literature cannot be understood without a reasonable familiarity with the Hebrew Bible.

(3) Judaism, Islam and Christianity all recognize the books of the Hebrew Bible as part of their religious heritage. To understand and appreciate these people, a study of the Hebrew Bible is necessary.

(4) The Hebrew Bible lays a foundation for any study of the life of Christ and New Testament theology.

(5) The Hebrew Bible provides answers to many of the fundamental questions of life. Where did we come from? Where are we going? What is our greatest need? What is the purpose of our existence? The wisdom and insights of the writers of Scripture provide guide to living life successfully–according to the plan of God, the Author of life.

Appendix 1

HOW TO STUDY THE BIBLE

Introduction

There is a considerable difference between reading and studying the Bible. One who studies the Bible follows an established order and procedure, endeavoring to learn from Scripture rather than impose one's own ideas into the text. As a baker carefully follows a cooking recipe to produce a tasty dessert, so a wise Bible student must follow certain steps to insure an accurate interpretation an application of the biblical text. Believers are commanded by God to be good students of the Bible (2 Tim. 2:15), and are given the assurance that such an endeavor is profitable (2 Tim. 3:16-17).

The steps presented here may be used to guide a careful student of Scripture in asking the right questions about a biblical text and to follow a logical procedure in studying that text.

The three basic steps of this inductive method of Bible study are (1) observation, (2) interpretation, and (3) application. These three-fold steps are beautifully illustrated by the observations made by Solomon in Proverbs 24:30-34.

Since Bible study is a spiritual exercise, we must always ask the Lord to guide our thoughts and teach us through His Word. "Open my eyes that I may see wonderful things from Your *Torah*" (Psalm 37:18).

I. OBSERVATION - WHAT DOES A TEXT SAY?

The Bible student must begin by setting aside all preconceived notions about what a passage may or may not teach. Careful study is inductive (asking questions as to the meaning) rather than deductive (looking for proofs of a certain interpretation or doctrine).

A. Background Questions

    1. What is the historical setting?
    2. Who are the persons involved?
    3. What place names am I unfamiliar with?

B. Composition Questions

    1. What is the literary form used in this text?

        Discourse - a speech (Sermon on the Mount)
        Narrative - a historical development (Acts)
        Poetry - parallel ideas, figures of speech (Psalms)
        Legal - specific commands, case law (Exodus 20-24, Deut. 22:22-29)
        Proverb - wisdom for life expressed by analogy (Proverbs)
        Parable - teaching kingdom truth by analogy (Matthew 13)
        Prophetic - confronting God's people for breaking the covenant (Isaiah)
        Apocalyptic - visionary literature ("I saw . . ."); (Ezekiel 40-48)

    2. What do the figures of speech mean? Explore the nature of the figure.

    3. What does the grammar indicate? Is the writer describing past, future, accomplished, or presently occurring events?

C. Content Questions

    1. Ask the six interrogatives:

Who? - persons	Where? - places
What? - facts	Why? - reasons
When? - time	How? – means

2. What words don't I understand?
   Consult a dictionary, Bible dictionary or concordance.

II. INTERPRETATION - WHAT DOES IT MEAN?

Interpretation is the important step in Bible study which helps the student bridge the linguistic, cultural, geographical, and temporal gap between the biblical writers and 20th century Christians. Faulty interpretation is the basis for the doctrines of the cults, making the Bible a book of confusion rather than a source of light. The basis of our interpretation is faith in the verbal (Exod. 20:1, 1 Thess. 2:13), plenary (full in all respects), inspiration of the Bible (2 Tim. 3:15-16).

The doctrine of verbal, plenary inspiration may be expressed like this: "God so directed the human authors of Scripture that using their own individual personalities, His complete revelation for humanity was recorded without error in the words of the original manuscripts." The aim of our interpretation is to discover the *one* true meaning of the text and to recognize its contribution to the revelation of God's intention to save the fallen human race through His Son, Jesus Christ.

A. Literal Interpretation

1. Am I interpreting the word or sentence according to its normal, customary, and basic meaning?

2. What is the meaning of the figure of speech?

   a. Look for the plain, literal meaning behind the figure.
   b. Note the inherit contradiction (Gal. 2:9).
   c. Look for the explanation in the context (John 3:37-39).
   d. Look for the lesson taught by the figure (Jer. 2:13).

B. Cultural Situation

   1. What is the physical background?
      Bible geography; climate
   2. What is the temporal background?
      Bible history, political history
   3. What is the social background?
      Bible culture and institutions

C. Contextual Setting

   1. What is the immediate context? Examine the book, sections, paragraphs

   2. What is the parallel context? Note the parallel gospel accounts or parallel teachings of Paul.

   3. How does my text advance the flow of thought in the immediate and extended context (the whole book)?

   4. How would the message of this book be diminished if this text were absent?

D. Biblical Message

   1. How does this little story or event advance the big story of Scripture, namely God's purpose to redeem the human race through the Promised One, Jesus?

   2. How do the prophets, priests, and kings in the Hebrew Bible point to and anticipate Jesus, the One who ultimately fulfills these offices for Israel?

   3. How does the story or text contribute to our understanding of the great themes of Scripture– kingdom, redemption and judgment?

III. APPLICATION - HOW DOES IT APPLY TO ME?

Application is the final and most important step of Bible study, yet it is often the most neglected. Ezra set an example of being one who studied and *practiced* the law of the Lord (Ezra 7:10). Christ warned of the inevitable defeat of the one who fails to act upon the truth of God's Word (Matt. 7:24-27). James commands believers to be "doers" of the Word and not "forgetful hearers," for it is the "doer" of the Word that is blessed (James 1:22-25).

A. <u>Evaluation</u>   Look for the principles, the timeless truths

   1. Is the passage addressed to Israel, or to a specific Old Testament situation? To evaluate the Old Testament passage, look to the New Testament.

      a. Does the NT nullify the OT teaching? (Israel's dietary laws)

      b. Does the NT modify the OT teaching? (Jesus' Sermon on the Mount)

      c. Does the NT verify the OT teaching (truths about God; life principles)

   2. Is the passage addressed to a specific New Testament situation or specific individuals? See Acts 18:9-10, 1 Cor. 11:1-16, Jn. 16:13

   3. Is the passage addressed to a historical situation *and* to others as well? This would include the timeless truths like the truths Jesus told Nicodemus (John 3).

B. <u>Application to My Life</u> (theoretical)

   1. Is there a fact I should know? (Cognition) Gal. 1:17

2. Is there a truth I should believe or be convinced of? (Persuasion) Jn. 10:10

3. Is there something I should do? (Action) 1 John 1:9

   a. A sin to confess?
   b. A promise to claim?
   c. A command to obey?
   d. A temptation to avoid?
   e. A truth to apply?

C. <u>Application to a Contemporary Situation</u> (practical)

   1. Develop a principle from the passage.
   2. Observe a need in an area of your life.
   3. Do something in application of the passage.
   4. Give proof of the application in some tangible way.

IV. RECORD - PRESERVE WHAT YOU HAVE LEARNED

The final step of Bible study is to record your discoveries, interpretation, principles and applications so that you will have this information for future reference. What you don't record will eventually be forgotten.

V. REVIEW - BIBLE STUDY IS AN ON-GOING PROCESS

Bible study is an on-going process not a one-time event. The Apostle Peter recognized and emphasized the importance of review (1 Peter 1:12-13). Moses taught this principle as well (Deut. 6:7-9). Repetition with variety is the key to learning!

V. BIBLE STUDY TOOLS

Study tools and reference works can help the careful student answer many of the questions raised in the process of Bible study. Keep these to a minimum since you want to develop your own study skills, not simply depend on the study and research of others. It is more exciting to discover biblical principles through your own study of the text than to find these truths in a commentary. Commentaries can be used to check the results of your work and to explore possible solutions to problem texts. It can be very helpful to consult Martin Luther's commentary on Romans and read his thoughts about Romans 1:17. But go to the "pros" only after doing your own work so you won't miss out on the joy of being led by the Holy Spirit in discovering for yourself the truths of the Bible.

Suggested study tools include a Bible dictionary, Bible encyclopedia, a Bible concordance, Old Testament and New Testament word books, a dictionary of theological terms, a Bible atlas, a history of the biblical world, a book on the cultural background of the biblical period, and a Bible handbook or introduction (like the one you are reading!) to provide background for the book or passage being studied.

I have written other Scripture resources which you may find helpful in your study of the Bible. Some of these books are out of print but can still be found on www.Amazon.com/books.

> *A Guide to Church Discipline* (Wipf and Stock) 1985
> *Answers to Tough Questions* (Wipf and Stock) 1997
> *Biblical Wisdom* (CreateSpace), 2018
> *Concise Bible Atlas* (Hendrickson Publishers) 1999
> *Commentary on John* (Moody Press) 1992
> *Discipleship* (CreateSpace) 2018
> *Ezra and Nehemiah* (Moody Press)1982
> *First and Second Samuel* (Moody Press) 1982
> *God* (Word Publishing) 1999
> *Messiah's Coming* Temple (Kregel) updated ed. 2014
> *The Divorce Myth* (Bethany House) 1981
> *Tyndale Concise Bible Commentary* (Tyndale) 1990.
> *Zechariah* (Moody Press) 1984

May the Lord bless you as you dig deep into the rich treasury of God's Word!

Appendix 2

THE MOST IMPORTANT EVENTS OF THE BIBLE

If you were asked to identify the twelve most important events in your life, which events would you choose? Your birth would be a good place to begin. You can't go anywhere without that! Your high school graduation would be another significant milestone. You would probably identify some events that were formative in your spiritual life and development. Your marriage, first child, a major career change would no doubt be included in your list.

What would you identify as the twelve most important events of the Bible? Answers would vary, no doubt. Out of hundreds of important events recorded in the Bible, I have selected thirteen (a baker's dozen!) which I consider *essential* to the story of the Bible. As you read and study the Bible, these are the events you don't want to miss!

1. Creation

The first of the most important events of the Bible is creation (Genesis 1-2). Although God was absolutely complete in Himself and needed nothing, God created the heavens to display His glory. He then created mankind to bear His image, reflect His glory and enjoy His grace. All that God made was totally perfect and complete. At the end of His creative work God Himself recognized that it was "very good."

2. Fall of Mankind

Although mankind was placed in a perfect and sinless environment, it didn't stay that way long. God gave mankind the freedom to choose to obey or disobey their Creator. Sadly, mankind was tempted by an evil spirit being named "Satan" and fell into sin (Gen. 3). Just as God had warned Adam and Eve, sin resulted in death–immediate spiritual separation from God and eventual physical death. Although God had purposed to bless His creation, a curse came upon creation because of sin. But mankind is not left without hope. In Genesis 3:15 God promised the coming of a Promised One who would share in humanity and sacrifice himself to achieve victory over Satan.

3. Destruction by the Flood

The next essential event in biblical history is the world flood which constituted God's severe judgment on mankind's persistent wickedness. Since the whole earth was filled with violence and sin, God determined that all flesh must die (Gen. 6-8). Only God, the Creator, has the authority to execute such judgment. But God demonstrated His grace by preserving Noah, his family, and pairs of animals by means of a great boat, the ark. After the flood had resided, Noah and his family were directed to be fruitful and replenish the earth. The rainbow was placed in the sky to symbolize God's promise that He would not bring another world judgment by flood. This promise provided time for God to bring about the fulfillment of an earlier promise made in Genesis 3:15.

4. God's Promise to Abraham

The promise to Abraham in Genesis 12:1-3 reveals how God will restore blessing to mankind which was lost because of sin. Here God announces that He will bless Abraham, make his descendants a great nation, and use these people as a channel of blessing to all the nations of the earth. God has a plan to restore blessing to the world and He is using the people of Israel to do it. One doesn't have to look too far to see how the Jewish people have contributed so much to the betterment of humanity. Golda Meir, George Gershwin, Albert Einstein and Sandy Koufax are just a few examples. But the ultimate blessing has come to the world through Abraham's ultimate descendant, Jesus, who provided a means of salvation for all mankind. It is through Jesus that the blessing of Abraham extends to all the nations of the earth.

5. Exodus and 1ˢᵗ Passover

Israel's first Passover (Exodus 12) was followed by their exodus from Egypt after 430 years of bondage. Together, these events mark the beginning of the people of Israel as a nation. The young nation of Israel received its constitution and government at Mt. Sinai and its land in the conquest of Canaan. The Passover is to the Jews what the resurrection of Jesus is to Christians--the defining event that makes them who and what they are. The Passover is the key to God's redemptive program because it provides the pattern for redemption which will be followed in the future. Passover looks ahead and anticipates the redemptive work of Christ on the cross. Jesus is the [Passover] Lamb of God (John 1:19) who gave His live that those under the sentence of death might have life in Him.

6. God's Promise to David

2 Samuel 7:12-16 records the next essential event in biblical history–God's promise to David and his family. Here God promises that David's family line will always be the royal line in Israel. Although some of David's descendants would be chastened for disobedience and sent into exile, the right to rule Israel would always belong to David's descendants. On the basis of this promise, David's royal line, his throne, and His kingdom are secure. According to the angel Gabriel's announcement to Mary, Jesus is the descendant of David who will ultimately sit on David's throne and rule his kingdom forever. The promise in 2 Samuel 7:12-16 and Luke 1:31-33 assures us that Jesus will someday return to take David's throne and rule God's kingdom. Little wonder that Jesus began his ministry with the announcement, "Repent, the Kingdom of heaven is at hand" (Matt. 4:17).

7. The Birth of Jesus

The birth of Jesus (Luke 2:1-20) may not be the most important event in biblical history, but it is right up there. His birth came in fulfillment of many prophecies which had prepared the way for His arrival. In the time of Noah God had promised that He would "dwell in the tents of Shem" (the Semitic people; Gen. 9:27). That promise was further detailed by the announcement of Isaiah that He would be born of a virgin (Isa. 7:14) and Micah that He would be born in Bethlehem (Micah 5:2). The birth of Jesus is the ultimate miracle of the Bible because in that wondrous event God took on humanity and came to live on this earth with us. The Apostle John summarizes this event with the words, "The Word became flesh and dwelt among us" (John 1:18). So significant was this moment in time that the two history are divided by His birth–before Christ (B.C.) and "in the year of our Lord" (A.D.).

8. The Death of Jesus

The death of Jesus (Matt. 27:50, John 19:30) was God's means of providing atonement for the sins of the world–the sins which the blood of previous sacrifices had only covered. Through His sacrifice, Jesus paid the penalty for all sins–past, present and future. Like the "scape goat" on Israel's Day of Atonement, Jesus took mankind's sin upon Himself and carried it away. His death was the culmination of all God's preparation to deliver people from the curse of death that came upon all mankind because of sin. With Jesus' sacrifice, God's wrath on sin was fully and finally satisfied so that He can now be just in offering forgiveness and cleansing from sin through faith in Jesus.

9. The Resurrection of Jesus

Of all the essential events of the Bible, the resurrection of Jesus is the *most* important (John 20). For without the resurrection there would be no historical or factual basis for Christianity. Paul writes to the Corinthians saying, "And if Christ has not been raised,… your faith is in vain" (1 Cor. 15:14). The resurrection of a dead man after three days in the grave has been viewed by some as a "faith" event rather than something historically verifiable. But the historical evidence for the resurrection of Jesus is quite strong. The Gospel record the accounts of his appearances to his disciples and family members. Paul records how on one occasion Jesus appeared to more than 500 people who were gathered together. Most of Jesus' apostles died for their belief that the resurrection was an actual, historical event.

10. The Ascension of Jesus

All churches celebrate Jesus' birth and honor His death, and resurrection. But many give little if any notice to Jesus' ascension back to heaven (Acts 1:9-11). And yet, this is a very important event. The ascension was prophesied by Isaiah (52:13). Luke anticipates Jesus ascension as the goal of His journey to Jerusalem (Luke 9:51). Jesus spoke about His ascension to the disciples (John 16:10, 20:17). The ascension of Jesus demonstrates that His mission on earth was complete. His return to the Father in heaven is evidence of Jesus' abiding righteousness. His personal holiness was not tarnished during His stay on earth.

11. The Day of Pentecost

A birthday is a special day, a time when family and friends help celebrate the beginning of your life on earth. The church also has a birthday–the day of Pentecost. "Pentecost" is Greek for "fiftieth," and refers in the Bible to the Jewish feast that was celebrated fifty days after the feast of First Fruits. The particular day of Pentecost recounted in Acts 2 is the day when followers of Jesus, both Jewish and Gentile, were united together as one body of believers by the ministry of the Holy Spirit (Acts 2:4, 1 Cor. 12:13). The miracle of speaking in other languages (literally "dialects") gave evidence of the work of God's Spirit and prepared the believers for the world-wide proclamation of the Gospel.

12. Paul's Encounter with Jesus

Before His ascension to heaven, Jesus instructed the

apostles that they should be His witnesses in Jerusalem, Judea and Samaria, and to the ends of the earth. Acts 9 records God's preparation of the witness who would fulfill the third part of this commission. Saul of Tarsus was a zealous Jewish rabbi who sought to defend traditional Judaism by severely persecuting Jews who had embraced Jesus as their Messiah. But when Saul was confronted by the risen Jesus on the road to Damascus and his life was forever changed (Acts 9:1-22). He suddenly realized that the God whom he had sought to serve was Jesus whose followers he was persecuting! Saul of Tarsus became the Apostle Paul, a vigorous evangelist, proclaiming that Jesus was Israel's Messiah. Paul is regarded by many as the most significant Christian of the church age. His teachings and writings were providentially used to bring about the expansion of the Kingdom of God and the theological formulations of the early church.

13. The Jerusalem Council

Acts 11 records how Peter reported to the Jerusalem church the conversion of Cornelius, a Gentile. Later Paul and Barnabas went preaching to the Gentiles and many came to faith in Jesus (Acts 13-14). But there arose some opposition to the practice of accepting Gentiles into the church on an equal basis with Jewish believers. It was argued by those who embraced Jewish traditions that a Gentile was not acceptable to God without adopting Jewish practices (like circumcision and obeying Jewish dietary laws). Could a Gentile get saved as a Gentile, or did he have to become Jewish first? It was a crucial issue which would define the nature of the church. The leaders of the early church, including Paul, Barnabas and other leaders from Antioch, gathered in Jerusalem to resolve the matter (Acts 15:1-31). After much debate, the council finally agreed that God's plan of salvation included Gentiles *as* Gentiles. It was not necessary to make them into Jews in order to become part of the people of God with full standing and acceptance in the church. This decision safeguarded the truth of the gospel which offers the gift of salvation to all who believe apart from the traditional requirements of Judaism.

Appendix 3

"WHO'S WHO?" IN THE BIBLE

Who would you identify as the most important people in American history? George Washington, Thomas Jefferson and Abraham Lincoln would probably be high on your list. But could you name the most important people in the Bible? Here are some of the most significant heroes of the faith, introduced in order of appearance:

Adam - The first man and the father of the human race.

Eve - The first woman and the best gift God ever gave to Adam.

Noah - The man who obeyed God and built the ark even though he'd never seen rain or witnessed a flood.

Abraham - The man who demonstrated his faith by offering God his most precious possession—the life of his son.

Sarah - The barren wife of Abraham who gave birth to Isaac in her old age.

Isaac - The son of Abraham and Sarah who distinguished himself as a man of peace.

Rebekah - The wife of Isaac and mother of twin boys—Esau and Jacob.

Esau - The older twin brother of Jacob; became the chief ancestor of the Edomites.

Jacob - Father of twelve sons who became heads of Israel's twelve tribes. Jacob was given the name "Israel" after wrestling with God.

Judah - Jacob's 4th son by Leah. His tribe became the line of David and the Messiah.

Joseph - The first son of Rachel. Sold into slavery by his brothers, Joseph rose to power in Egypt and was used by God to preserve Jacob's family through famine.

Moses - The adopted son of Pharaoh's daughter who led Israel out of Egypt and mediated the covenant between God and the Israelites at Mt. Sinai.

Aaron - The older brother of Moses and first High Priest of Israel.

Miriam - The older sister of Moses and the first prophetess in the Bible.

Joshua - The successor of Moses who led the Israelites in the conquest of Canaan.

Deborah - The only female judge; she accompanied Barak in his campaign against the Canaanites.

Jael - The heroine who drove a tent peg through the head of Sisera, Israel's enemy.

Samson - The long-haired judge who is remembered for his daring exploits against the Philistine.

Samuel - The last of the judges and first of the prophets; anointed both Saul and David.

Saul - The first king of Israel, but was rejected by God because of his disobedience.

David - The first of a dynasty of kings from the line of Judah; a man after God's own heart.

Solomon - David's son by Bathsheba and successor to the

throne; author of Proverbs, Ecclesiastes, the Song of Solomon, and two psalms (72 and 127).

Elijah - A prophet who ministered in the Northern Kingdom as an antagonist against Baal worship and idolatry.

Elisha - Elijah's successor; he continued the prophetic attack on paganism in the North.

Josiah - The most godly king of Judah; he loved God "with all his heart and with all his soul and with all his might" (2 Kings 23:25).

Isaiah - The prophet who warned God's coming judgment through the Assyrians. He called God "the Holy One of Israel."

Daniel - The prophet who served in the royal court of Babylon's King Nebuchadnezzar and is noted for his unique ability to interpret dreams visions about the future.

Ezekiel - The priest turned prophet who served the community of exiles in Babylon. His unusual symbolic actions justify calling him "the prophet of pantomime."

Jeremiah - The prophet who ministered in Jerusalem at the close of the Judean monarchy and witnessed the capture and destruction of the city by the Babylonians in 586 B.C.

Ezra - The priest and scribe who returned to Jerusalem from Babylon in 458 B.C. to teach the people and support the ministry of the temple

Esther - A young Jewish woman who providentially became the wife of Persia's king and heroically used her influence to intercede in behalf of her people.

Nehemiah - After leading a small group of Jews back to

Jerusalem in 444 B.C. Nehemiah organized and led the people in rebuilding the city walls!

Malachi - The last of the Old Testament prophets who spoke against the abuses which had arisen in Jerusalem during the time of Nehemiah.

John the Baptizer - The first prophet in the four hundred years since Malachi, John called people to repent and prepare for the coming of the Messiah and the inauguration of God's kingdom.

Mary - Although there are many different Mary's in the Bible, the most prominent is Mary, the virgin mother of Jesus.

Joseph - A quiet and somewhat obscure figure, Joseph was the husband of Mary and adopted father of Jesus. No spoken words of Joseph are recorded in the Bible.

Jesus - The most important question in life is, "Who is Jesus?" Many would say that He was a teacher and a healer. But the Bible says He was more than that. His name "Jesus" means "salvation." The Bible presents him the promised Messiah of Israel and the divine Son of God.

Peter- A Galilean fisherman who became a follower of Jesus and a prominent leader in the early church. He is often remembered for his enthusiastic but sporadic faith.

James - One of the inner circle of Jesus' apostles, James became the first of the Twelve to die for his faith.

John - The most prolific author of the Twelve Apostles, John wrote the Fourth Gospel, First, Second and Third John, and the Book of Revelation.

Matthew - A tax collector before me met Jesus, Matthew became the first apostle to write the story of the life of Jesus in his Gospel.

Stephen - Having been appointment by the apostles to assist in the distribution of food to the poor, Stephen became a powerful evangelist and the first Christian martyr.

Saul - Trained as a rabbi and hard line Pharisee, Saul persecuted the followers of Jesus until he experienced his own conversion on the road to Damascus. As the Apostle Paul, he became an evangelist, church planter, and author of thirteen New Testament letters.

Barnabas - After commending the converted Saul to the Apostles in Jerusalem, Barnabas invited him to Antioch of Syria where he served as a teacher until the two left together on a missionary journey to Cyprus and Galatia.

John Mark - The son of Mary of Jerusalem, John Mark accompanied Paul and Barnabas on their first missionary journey. Later he authored the Gospel of Mark.

James, brother of Jesus - Clearly distinguished form James the Apostle, this James was a half-brother of Jesus and became a leader in the Jerusalem church. He is the author of the Epistle of James.

Aquila & Priscilla - This couple joined Paul in a tent making business at Corinth and later accompanied him to Ephesus where they had a significant ministry in the life of a young Jew named Apollos.

Luke - Although not an apostle, Luke accompanied Paul during many of his travels. As a capable researcher and historian, Luke became the author of the Gospel of Luke and Acts of the Apostles.

Timothy - This young man accompanied Paul on his third missionary journey and was with him in Rome during his first imprisonment. Later Timothy was appointment to guide the church at Ephesus during Paul's absence.

Titus - A Greek Christian and traveling companion of Paul, Titus accompanied Paul to the island of Crete and was left there to lead the church while Paul went on to Asia Minor.

Philemon - A leader in the church at Colossae, Philemon was a slave owner. Paul wrote Philemon on behalf of his run away servant Onesimus, encouraging him to welcome Onesimus back as a Christian brother.

Jude, brother of Jesus - Like James, Jude was another half-brother of Jesus. We know little about him except that he became the author of the Epistle of Jude.

I'm sure that there are important people from the Bible that have been omitted here. Did I miss any of your favorites? If so, add them to this list!

Appendix 4

IMPORTANT DATES TO REMEMBER

Nobody really likes memorizing dates! And yet knowing important dates can be useful. Think of where you might be sleeping should you forget your wife's birthday or anniversary! Think of the consequences as a United States citizen of forgetting or ignoring April 15th. Dates are like a hat rack. If you place your hat on a hat rack, you will always know where to find it when you need it. And knowing the most important dates in the Bible will help you locate and keep track of some of history's most significant events.

Dates can be divided into two eras–B.C. (Before Christ) and A.D. (Anno Domini; Latin for "in the year of our Lord"). Frequently Jews and non-Christian publications will use the designations B.C.E (Before the Common Era) and C.E. (the Common Era).

2166 B.C.	The birth of Abraham--the first datable event in biblical history.
1876	Jacob and his family enters Egypt–the start of the 430 year Egyptian sojourn.
1446	The Exodus--Moses leads the people of Israel out of Egypt.
1406	The Conquest–Joshua leads the people of Israel into the Promised Land.
1375	Death of Joshua and beginning of the 325-year period of the judges
1050	The beginning of the Israelite Monarchy. Saul is anointed by Samuel as Israel's first king.

1010	David, the first Judean king, takes the throne and establishes Jerusalem as the Israelite capital.
966	King Solomon builds the first Israelite temple in Jerusalem.
931	The monarchy divides into the Northern Kingdom of Israel and Southern Kingdom of Judah.
722	The conquest of the Northern Kingdom by Assyria and exile of the Israelites to Mesopotamia.
605	Nebuchadnezzar, king of Babylon, comes to Jerusalem and deports Daniel and members of the royal family to Babylon.
597	Nebuchadnezzar invades Judah, ransacks the Temple, and deports 10,000 Judeans (including Ezekiel) to Babylon.
586	The conquest of the Southern Kingdom by Babylon and exile of the Judeans to Mesopotamia.
539	Babylon is captured by Cyrus who decrees that the Jews can return to Jerusalem to rebuild their Temple.
537	The first return of the Jewish exiles to Jerusalem to build the Second Temple.
473	Queen Esther intervenes in behalf of her Jewish people and the Feast of Purim is established to their deliverance from destruction.
458	The second return of the exiles under Ezra to support the Temple and strengthen worship.
444	The third return of the exiles under Nehemiah to

	rebuild the walls of Jerusalem.
432	The ministry of Malachi, the last prophet before the coming of John the Baptizer.
332	The conquest of Persia and the Holy Land by Alexander the Great.
198	Antiochus III defeated the Ptolemaic army at Panias bringing Israel under Seleucid (Syrian) rule.
175	Seleucid ruler Antiochus Epiphanes IV assumes the throne.
167	The revolt of the Maccabees against the rule of Antiochus IV Epiphanes who had desecrated the Jerusalem temple.
164	The cleansing of the Temple and reestablishment of Jewish worship in Jerusalem–events commemorated by the celebration of Hanukkah.
142	The priestly descendants of the Maccabees (Hasmoneans) establish Jewish rule over Palestine.
63	The coming of Pompey and the beginning of Roman rule in Palestine.
40	The Parthians invade Syria and Palestine; Herod escapes to Rome where he is appointed "King of the Jews."
37	King Herod begins his rule in Jerusalem as a puppet potentate for Rome.
5/4	The birth of Jesus, the promised Messiah of Israel, in Bethlehem.*

A.D. 1	The beginning of the present (common) era–the year of the Lord (A.D.)
33	The crucifixion of Jesus by the Romans in Jerusalem.
35	The Apostle Paul's life changing encounter with Jesus on the road to Damascus.
48-49	Paul's first missionary journey (Acts 13-14)
49	Jerusalem Council (Acts 15)
50-52	Paul's second missionary journey (Acts 15-18)
53-57	Paul's third missionary journey (Acts 18-21)
59-60	Paul's voyage to Rome (Acts 27-28)
68	The death of the Apostle Paul in Rome.
70	The destruction of Jerusalem and the Second Temple by the Romans.

*Could you be wondering why Jesus was born B.C., before Christ? Here is an interesting bit of trivia. The present Christian Era is a dating system invented by a monk named Dionysius at the request of Pope St. John in A.D. 525. Dionysius placed Christ's birth 753 A.U.C. (*Anno urbis conditae*, Latin for "from the foundation of the city of Rome). He failed to take into account that King Herod died in 750 A.U.C.

The dating by Dionysius was questioned in the 8th century and was rejected in the 9th century, but tradition is hard to change and the flawed dating has continued to the present day. To calculate the *actual* number of years since Jesus' birth, just add four years to the current year.

Appendix 5

THE BEST BIBLE QUOTATIONS

The Bible has had a profound impact on the English language and literature. Many people quote phrases from the Bible without even realizing it. Poems frequently contain images and phrases that come right from the pages of the Bible. Here are a few examples:

"The hand writing on the wall"

This phrase comes from Belshazzar's feast in Daniel 5 where God announced judgment on the king of Babylon through a hand written message on the wall. The phrase is used in literature of an ominous warning.

"Escaped by the skin of his teeth"

This phrase was spoken by Job in Job 19:20 where he complains during his great suffering that he has escaped death only "by the skin of my teeth." The phrase is used to refer to a "close call" or narrow escape.

"The apple of his eye"

David prayed in Psalm 17:8, "Keep me as the apple of the eye." God speaks to the prophet Zechariah regarding His people, "He who touches you, touches the apples of His eye" (Zech. 2:8). The "apple" refers to the pupil of the eye, a part of the body that needs extreme care and protection. The phrase is used in literature to refer to someone who is the subject of special favor and protection.

"A man after his own heart"

God revealed to Samuel that he would replace king Saul with another ruler who would be "a man after His own heart" (1

Samuel 13:14). He was referring to the psalmist David who had a heart that was committed to following and obeying God. The phrase is used in literature to describe someone who has a heart for God or shares a common commitment.

"A merry heart is good medicine."

This familiar phrase comes right out of the book of Proverbs. Solomon writes, "A joyful heart is good medicine, but a broken spirit dries up the bones" (Prov. 17:22). This bit of folk wisdom is often cited as a justification for a little fun and laughter. Modern medicine supports the truth of this proverb. Joy, laughter, and a positive attitude do affect the body's chemistry in ways that promote healing.

"A stranger in a strange land"

After naming his son Gershom (which means "a stranger here"), Moses explains "I have been a stranger in a strange land" (Exodus 2:22). The phrase is used in literature to describe someone who is in an unfamiliar situation–a land or experience that is completely foreign.

"Eat, drink and be merry."

While most people would link this phrase with hedonistic philosophy, it actually comes from the Bible. Ecclesiastes 8:15 recommends pleasure, good food and joy as a means of coping with life's inevitable frustrations. But these earthly joys and pleasures are to be received as a blessing from God. The phrase is used in a negative context in Luke 12:19-20 where Jesus warns the rich man against exploiting earthly pleasure and neglecting the priority of God. The phrase is commonly used in literature to refer to an Epicurean lifestyle which focuses on the physical while neglecting eternal realities.

"The love of money is the root of all evil."

This biblical phrase is often misquoted to say, "money is the root of all evil." But Paul used the phrase in 1 Timothy 6:10 to describe the situation of those who pursue riches at the expense of their personal integrity and morality. As a consequence they plunge into ruin and self-destruction. Money is morally neutral and can be used for good or evil. According to Paul, it is the *love* of money that destroys people. The phrase is properly used as a warning against the pursuit of riches by wrongful means.

"A house divided against itself cannot stand."

Contrary to popular opinion, Abraham Lincoln was not the first to use this memorable phrase. When Lincoln spoke these words in the Gettysburg Address, he was actually quoting Jesus (Mark 3:25-26). In the original context, Jesus was arguing his exercising authority over demons was to by Satan's power because Satan doesn't work against himself. The phrase is used in our literature as a basis for an appeal for unity, as Lincoln used it in his address.

"You can tell a tree by its fruit."

This phrase is used by Jesus in Matthew 12:33 (see also Matthew 7:16-20). Jesus was teaching his disciples that what one actually does tells more about their spiritual condition than what one says. It is not the profession of righteousness, but the fruit of righteousness that truly pleases God. The phrase is used in literature to make the point that what I *see* counts more than what you *say*.

"The poor are with you always."

Jesus spoke these words to his disciples after Judas Iscariot upbraided Mary for pouring out a costly ointment on Jesus' feet. Jesus explained that Mary was honoring Him in anticipation of His death and burial. Then he added the words, "For you always have the poor with you, but you do not always have me with you" (John 12:8). These words are often quoted to point out the fact that the poor and their needs will always be with us and are an on-going, not a momentary concern.

"You can't play with fire and not get burned."

This phrase is often quoted to little boys who are found playing with matches. In its original context it Proverbs 6:27, it was given as a warning against adultery. "Can a man take fire in his bosom and his clothes not be burned?" Verse 29 makes the application, "So is the one who goes into his neighbor's wife whoever touches her will not go unpunished." This very practical principle applies in a variety of contexts. There are serious consequences to our decisions and actions.

"The patience of Job"

When early Christians were suffering persecution and various trials, James counseled them to endure these trials, reminding them of the example of Job. He writes, "You have heard of the endurance of Job and have seen the outcome of the Lord's dealings, that the Lord is full of compassion and is merciful" (James 5:11). Job patiently endured his suffering and was eventually vindicated and restored. The phrase is often used in literature to describe someone who is extremely patient and longsuffering.

"The salt of the earth"

In His Sermon on the Mount, Jesus challenged His listeners regarding the conduct appropriate for those anticipating His kingdom. He described them as "the salt of the earth" (Matthew 5:13). Salt was used in ancient times to preserve foods. It is also a seasoning that creates thirst. Jesus may have been saying that the disciples were to be a preserving influence, or that they were to create spiritual thirst for God's kingdom. The phrase is commonly used in literature to describe someone who is a preserving or stabilizing influence.

"Skin for skin"

This obscure phrase comes from the mouth of Satan as his explanation for why Job has maintained his piety and faith in God after the loss of his possessions and family. Satan was saying, "people will give up a little skin on their hands to save the skin on their chin." According to Satan, Job was maintaining his piety hoping that it would protect him from further suffering. Interestingly, a Latin translation of this phrase (*Pro pelle cutem*) was used as the motto for the Hudson's Bay Company which bought furs from trappers in the Pacific Northwest during the early 1800's. The motto implied, "We risk our skins to get skins (furs)." The phrase is used to describe sacrifices people will make to protect themselves or improve their situation.

"Your reap what you sow"

This quotation from the Bible can be found in Paul's letter to the Galatians 6:7-9 where he is reminding them of a biblical principle that is repeated many times in the Bible. Proverbs 22:8 says, "He who sows iniquity will reap vanity." Eliphaz in the book of Job says, "Those who sow trouble harvest it." The prophet Hosea exhorted the Israelites, "Sow with a view to righteousness, reap in accordance with kindness" (Hos. 10:12). And Paul reminded the Corinthians, "He who sows sparingly will reap sparingly, and he who sows bountifully will also reap bountifully." This principle is known as "the law of the harvest." If you plant carrot seeds, you will harvest carrots. The Bible applies this principle as a reminder of the consequences of both good and evil actions.

As you read the Bible, look for phrases that have made their way into English literature and expression. I am sure you will find more of them!

Appendix 6

CLASSIC PRAYERS OF THE BIBLE

Prayer can be defined simply as "communication with God." It is the spreading out of our helplessness before a gracious God who hears and understands; cares and answers. The Bible contains many examples of prayer which can serve as models or guides for our own prayers. If you want to improve your own prayer life, try reading some of the prayers recorded for us in the Bible.

Here is a listing of the *classic* prayers of the Bible:

Abraham's prayer for the people of Sodom: Genesis 18:22-33

Moses' prayer for the people of Israel: Numbers 14:11-20

Hannah's prayer at the dedication of Samuel: 1 Samuel 2:1-11

David's prayer for forgiveness and pardon: Psalm 51

Solomon's prayer at the dedication of the Temple:1 Kings 8

Ezra's prayer of confession for marital unfaithfulness: Ezra 9:5-15

The Judean's prayer of confession of sin: Nehemiah 9:1-38

Daniel's prayer of praise and confession: Daniel 9:4-19

Habakkuk's prayer for God's mercy: Habakkuk 3

Jesus' example of prayer for His disciples: Matthew 6:9-13

Jesus' prayer in the Upper Room: John 17:1-26

Jesus' prayer in the Garden of Gethsemane: Matthew 26:39-44

Paul's prayer for the Ephesians: Ephesians 1:15-23

Paul's second prayer for the Ephesians: Ephesians 3:14-21

Paul's prayer for the Colossians: Colossians 1:9-14

Appendix 7

BIBLE DEFINITIONS YOU SHOULD KNOW!

Don't you hate it when someone starts throwing around words you don't know or understand? It happens frequently in technical fields. Your doctor says, "Well, I see you have a case of Gametogenesis on your vena cava. But no cause for alarm! A daily application of rodenticide for several weeks will take care of that." Or your son who is a computer geek starts talking about defragmenting his hard drive. And preachers do it too. They talk about propitiation, substitutionary atonement, and supralapsarianism. This kind of talk goes right over most of our heads!

So here is your guide to some of the essential words of the Bible. Familiarity with them will help you avoid feeling totally lost the next time you hear one of them in a sermon. You can even throw a word or two into a conversation to impress your friends! The definitions presented here are intended to be clear and concise. A Bible dictionary or commentary will provide more detailed discussion.

Antichrist

The word *Antichrist* is used by the Apostle John to refer to false teachers who deny the true nature of Christ (1 Jn. 2:18,22; 4:3, 2 Jn. 7). The Greek *anti* can mean "in place of" or "opposed to." The term Antichrist is popularly used to describe the false "messiah" who opposes God and will be judged by Christ at His return (Dan. 7:25-26; 9:27, 2 Thess. 2:4-8; Rev. 19:19-20).

Apostle

Apostle is a Greek word which means "sent one." The

word is used specifically of the twelve apostles (Mark 3:16-19) whom Jesus "sent" out to proclaim the good news. The word can be used generally of someone like Barnabas (Acts 14:14) who was a missionary, a "sent one."

Atonement

This important word is used 150 times in the Bible, 49 times in Leviticus. Although traditionally associated with the concept of "covering," more recent studies of the Hebrew root suggest that the basis meaning is "ransom." To make atonement means to remove sin or defilement by the payment of a ransom. Through a sacrifice the life of the animal (symbolized by its blood) is exchanged for the life of the worshiper." The ultimate and final atonement is through the sacrificial death of Jesus (Heb. 10:1-18).

Baptism

The Greek word *baptizo* means "to dip or immerse." It was used in the dye trade of dipping or immersing fabrics. The fabrics which were immersed became identified with the dye into which they were dipped.

In the New Testament the word "baptize" is used metaphorically of the *identification* of a new believer as a follower of Christ through the ritual of water baptism (Matt. 28:19, Acts 2:41). The word is also used of a spiritual identification–the baptizing work of the Holy Spirit (Acts 1:5, 1 Cor. 12:13).

Benediction

The benediction is the act of blessing that occurs at the close of worship or at the end of a letter. Although not a biblical word, concluding blessings, usually in the form of a prayer, appear frequently in scripture (Num. 6:24-26; Rom. 15:23; Phil. 4:23).

Blood

Blood refers to the red body fluid that circulates in humans and animals. But in the Bible, the term takes on a metaphorical usage. We read that "the life of the flesh is in the blood" (Lev.17:11). This means that "blood" represents *life*. When the blood of an animal offered in a sacrifice, this means that a life has been given. God designated blood as a means for atonement and cleansing from sin.

Born again

The expression *born again* (1 Pet. 1:3) is a metaphor for spiritual rebirth. Nichodemus had been born *physically*. But Jesus said that in order to enter God's kingdom he must be born again *spiritually* (John 3:3,7, lit. "born from above").

Communion

Communion refers to the act of communing or sharing. Communion is the fellowship believers share when they worship, pray, or observe the Lord's Supper together. "Taking Communion" the usual expression for observing the Lord's Supper (1 Cor. 11:23-26).

Canon

The word *canon* comes from a Greek word meaning "measuring rod" or "rule." Although not a biblical word, it is used to refer to the books of the Bible which are recognized and accepted by the church.

Conversion

Conversion refers to the act of "turning around" or changing your mind from unbelief to an attitude of faith (Acts 15:3). This concept is illustrated by the repentance of the Thessalonians who "turned to God from idols to serve a living and true God" (1 Thess. 1:9).

Covenant

A *covenant* is a solemn compact or agreement which can be conditional or unconditional. God made an unconditional promise to Noah to never again destroy the earth by a flood (Gen. 9:11). God's covenant with Abraham was unconditional. God promised Abraham that his descendants would become a great nation which would be a blessing to all the people of the earth (Gen. 12:2-3). God's covenant with Israel was conditional. God promised His blessings on the people and their land when they obeyed His law (Deut. 27-28). The New Covenant promises unconditional spiritual blessings on those who trust in the redeeming work of Jesus (Jer. 31:31-34, Heb. 8:6).

Deacon

The word *deacon* means "servant" (Greek *deaconos*). While anyone who serves can be considered a deacon (Matt. 20:26), the word is in a specialized sense to refer to the biblical office (1 Tim. 3:8-13, Phil. 1:1). Deacons assist the church elders in fulfilling their ministry responsibilities (see Acts 6:1-6).

Demon

Demons are spirit beings who serve as emissaries of Satan, the ruler of the demons (Matt. 12:24) in seeking to thwart God's purposes (Eph. 6:12; 2 Pet. 2:4). Demonic activity was quite prevalent when Jesus was on earth proclaiming God's kingdom (Mark 5:1-13).

Disciple

The word *disciple* refers to an "interested learner." The disciples who were following Jesus were learning by His words and example. A disciple can become a true believer in Jesus, but some disciples loose interest and turn away from Him before coming to saving faith (John 8:60-66).

Dispensation

The word *dispensation* comes from a Greek word which means "house rule" and refers to how the house is ruled or administered during a particular time. Paul uses this word to refer to the present dispensation or administration of God's grace (Eph. 3:2). Most Christians recognize at least two dispensations in Scripture–the Old Covenant and the New Covenant. Many recognize God's future Kingdom as a third dispensation.

Dispensationalism is a theological viewpoint which recognizes the distinctive ways in which God has worked and continues working through different periods of history. There are various forms of Dispensationalism including classic, progressive and ultra. Not all of those who identify themselves as dispensational are in agreement about the way God administers His rule.

Elder

The word *elder* can refer generally to one who is aged and mature, but is used most frequently in the New Testament to refer to a spiritual leader who holds the office of elder. Paul appointed elders in the churches he planted (Acts 14:23). Qualifications for the office of elder are found in 1 Tim. 3:1-7.

Election

Election refers to the biblical teach of God's sovereign selection of a nation or an individual to be brought into a relationship with Him. God chose Jacob as the ancestor of the nation of Israel (Rom. 9:11). God also chooses those who will be saved and become members of the body of Christ (Eph. 1:3). This biblical teaching does not negate the place and importance of personal faith as the basis for salvation (Acts 16:31).

Elohim

The Hebrew *Elohim* is the plural form of *El* meaning "God." The plural form is usually explained as the "plural of majesty." It may also reflect that God reveals Himself through many attributes. *Elohim* is not a proper name for God (as is *Yahweh*), but rather a designation for deity.

Foreknowledge

Divine *foreknowledge* is usually understood to mean that God has knowledge of people and events beforehand. While this is true, the word has more to do with relationship than a mere knowing of facts. Divine foreknowledge means that God foreknew in an intimate and personal way those who would enter into a relationship with Him (Matt. 7:23; Rom. 8:29-30; 1 Peter 1:1-2).

Glorification

The term *glorification* is used by Paul to refer to God's final step in the redemption of the believer's body (Rom. 8:23,30) when they are resurrected with immortal bodies (1 Cor. 15:50-54).

Gospel

The Greek word translated *gospel (euangellion)* means "good news" and is used over seventy times in the Bible to refer to the good news about Jesus Christ. In 1 Corinthians 15:1-5 Paul declares the principle points of the gospel he preached.

Heaven

Heaven is the place where God our Heavenly Father abides (Matt. 6:9) and the place where believers will join Him someday (John 14:2-3). Revelation 21:1-22:6 provides some insight into what heaven will be like.

Hell

Hell is the English translation of the Greek *Gehenna* which referred in ancient times to the Hinnom Valley of Jerusalem which had once been used as a place for burning children before the idol of the fiery god Molech (2 Kings 23:10). Hell is the eternal abode of the unbelieving (wicked) dead. It is described as a lake of fire which is prepared for the devil and his angels (Matt. 25:41; Rev. 20:14-15).

Hosanna

Hosanna is a Hebrew verb in the imperative form and means "save now!" The multitudes who cried out *Hosanna* when Jesus came into Jerusalem (Matt. 21:9) were quoting from Psalm 118:26.

Incarnation

The word "incarnation" is derived from Latin and means "in the flesh." While not a biblical word, it is used by Christians to describe what happened when Jesus took on humanity. According to the Bible, Jesus is God incarnate–"in the flesh" (Jn. 1:14).

Inspiration

Inspiration is a theological word used to describe the Bible as God's Word. The idea comes from 2 Tim. 3:16 which says that "all Scripture is inspired (literally *expired*) by God." This means that Scripture shares with God the quality of perfection and is therefore without error.

Immanuel

The word *immanuel* is Hebrew and means "God with

us." This word is used by Isaiah to describe the son to be born of a virgin (Isa. 7:14). While Jesus never went by this name, he fulfilled the meaning of the word as the divine Son of God.

Justification

Justification is one of the most important words in the Bible. To *justify* means to declare one to be righteous. Justification is the act of being "declared righteous." The Bible teaches people become righteous not be doing good works but through faith. Paul insists in Romans that both Jews and Gentiles are justified as Abraham was–on the basis of faith (Rom. 4:1-5:1).

Levite

A Levite is a descendant of Levi whose tribe was chosen to serve in Tabernacle and Temple worship. Aaron and his sons were chosen from among the Levites to serve as priests. Other members of the tribe (the Levites) assisted the priests, but only the priest were allowed to officiate at sacrifices (Num. 8:6-26, 18:1-3).

Logos

Logos is a Greek term which means "word." The word had philosophical implications among the Greeks and was understood to refer to a mediating principle between God and matter. Jews, on the other hand, thought of the *logos* as a personification of God's revelation. The Apostle John writes that the *logos* as more than a principle or personification. The *logos* is a divine Person–Jesus Christ (John 1:1).

Messiah

Messiah is a Hebrew word (*mashiach*) which simply means "anointed one." In the biblical period being anointed with oil was a religious act which set a person apart as representative of God. Kings were anointed. Priests were anointed. But God's ultimate representative is *the Anointed One* who fulfilled God's promises to His people and the prophecies of the Hebrew prophets. The Greek word "Christ" is not a personal name, but a title. It is the New Testament equivalent to the Old Testament term, "Messiah."

Millennium

The word *millennium* is Latin and means "one thousand." The Greek equivalent (*chilioi*) is used six times in Revelation 20:2-7 to refer to a period during which Satan is bound and Christ shall reign over the earth. While some theologians favor a figurative interpretation, there seems to be no reason in the text to suggest that the number should not be taking literally. After Jesus returns to the earth to judge the nations and assume the throne of David (Luke 1:32-33), the *Millennial* kingdom of Christ will commence. This period is also known as the *Messianic* kingdom which avoids the issue of whether or not it is a thousand years in duration.

Mosaic Covenant

The *Mosaic Covenant* is the agreement between God and Israel which was mediated by Moses at Mount Sinai. Unlike other biblical covenants, the Mosaic Covenant is conditional. God promised that He would bless the people of Israel if they would keep His law. No obedience, no blessing (Deut. 27-28)! The breaking of the Mosaic Covenant resulted in the destruction of Jerusalem and the Babylonian captivity. The prophet Jeremiah announced that God would establish a New Covenant with His people to replace the one which Israel broke (Jer. 31:31-34).

Offering

An offering (Hebrew *corban*) is something which is set apart as consecrated and devoted to God. Leviticus 1-7 discusses five different kinds of offerings which were presented for a variety of purposes. The Epistle of Hebrews shows how the offerings where ultimately fulfilled by Jesus in His sacrifice on the cross. New Covenant believers are encouraged to offer themselves as a "living sacrifice" (Rom. 12:1-2) and the fruit of their lips as a "sacrifice of praise" (Heb. 13:15).

Paradise

Paradise is a Greek word which refers to a park or a garden. It is used three times in the New Testament to refer to a place of blessedness (Luke 23:43, 2 Cor. 12:4, Rev. 2:7). Paradise is the eternal abode of the righteous (believers), a virtual synonym in the New Testament for *heaven*.

Passover

Passover is the Jewish Feast which celebrates Israel's deliverance from Egyptian bondage. Exodus 12 recounts the first Passover and explains how God promised to "pass over" they Israelite houses where blood of the lamb was applied. As the first-born sons of the Israelites were protected by the shedding of blood, so the blood of Jesus, the Lamb of God, provides deliverance from sin and death (1 Cor. 5:7).

Pharisee

The *Pharisees* were a sect of Judaism which were noted for their strict observance of the law and the Jewish traditions. Josephus, the Jewish historian, describes them as the "most accurate interpreters of the laws." Pharisees were laymen who were serious about their religion and were faithful in their attendance to the synagogue. They stressed individual responsibility to obey the law and emphasized ethics over theology. Jesus rebuked the Pharisees for their hypocrisy (Matt. 23). They had good doctrine, but their practice wasn't consistent with their profession.

Praise

The biblical word for *praise* means "to give public acknowledgment." And while you can thank God in private, biblical praise requires a forum where others can hear and appreciate what is being said about God (Psalm 22:22). The Book of Psalms presents two kinds of praise. Declarative praise declares God's actions. Descriptive praise declares God's attributes. We praise God when we tell others what God has accomplished and what He is like.

Prayer

Prayer can simply be defined as "talking to God." Prayer can take the form of personal requests, intercession for others, confession of sin. Prayer is the taking of our helplessness before a God who knows and cares, hears and answers. Truly one of the greatest privileges given to us as believers is the opportunity to talk with our heavenly Father–anytime, anywhere, about anything (Phil. 4:6)

Priest

The *priests* of Israel were descendants of Aaron who was appointed by God to be High Priest (Lev. 8). Aaron's oldest living son succeeded him as High Priest and had special responsibilities on the Day of Atonement. Other descendants of Aaron served at the Tabernacle and Temple officiating at sacrifices. The priests were also responsible to teach the law and judge difficult cases as a high court of appeals. Because Jesus was not a descendant of Aaron, his priesthood had to be of a different order. The writer of Hebrews explains that Jesus is a priest of the order of Melchizedek (Heb. 7; Psa. 110:4).

Predestination

To *predestine* means "to mark out the boundaries beforehand." The Bible teaches that God has predestined our lives as believers (Romans 8:28; Ephesians 1:11). While this biblical teaching emphasizes God's sovereignty and provides comfort and confidence for believers, it does not take away anything from the biblical teaching of human responsibility (John 3:16, 6:37). Properly understood, God's sovereignty and human responsibility are complimentary, not contradictory concepts.

Prophet

A *prophet* is one who speaks for another (Exodus 7:2). In the biblical sense, a prophet is one who speaks forth divine revelation from God. Not everyone who claims to speak for God actually does so. The Bible warns of the dangers of false prophets and how to identify them (Deuteronomy 13, 1 John 4:1-6).

Prophecy

Biblical *prophecy* is the message spoken by a genuine prophet. Much of biblical prophecy involved an announcement of judgment on Israel and Judah because of their disobedience to God's law. Often the prophets simply rehearsed before their hearers the judgments which God had promised on a disobedient people (Deut. 27-28). The prophets also had a message of hope for the future. God would judge His people but not destroy them. The prophets also spoke of God's future Kingdom and the blessings His people would someday enjoy (Isaiah 58-66; Ezekiel 40-48; Revelation 20-22).

Propitiation

The word *propitiation* refers to the satisfaction of God's wrath on sin through an offering or sacrifice. The good news of the Bible is God has provided the means of removing His own wrath. He sent His Son Jesus to be the "propitiation for our sins" (1 John 2:2, 4:10). Jesus has taken upon Himself our sin and satisfied God's wrath through His death on the cross.

Rapture

The word *rapture* doesn't actually occur in the Bible, but is a Latin based word which is used to refer to the event Paul describes in 1 Thessalonians 4:17 when believers are "caught up" in the clouds to meet the Lord in the air. The rapture is preceded by the resurrection of the believing dead. Then living believers will be "caught up together with them," joining the resurrected saints and the Lord Jesus for all eternity. The coming of Jesus for His people is described by Paul as "the blessed hope" Titus 2:13).

Reconciliation

Reconciliation is central to the message of the Bible. Sin separates people from a holy God. Reconciliation means that an attitude or relationship has changed. According to the Bible, God initiated the reconciliation through Jesus Christ (2 Cor. 5:9). Believers have received this reconciliation (Romans 5:11) and can now enjoy peace with God (Romans 5:1).

Regeneration

The Greek word translated *regeneration* literally means "new birth" and is used in the Bible to describe the spiritual renewal which takes place in the individual who believers (Titus 3:15).

The concept of regeneration can be traced to Jesus' instructions to Nicodemus that he must be "born again" (literally "born from above" (John 3:5-8). Regeneration is the spiritual "birth" that make a sinner into "new creation" (Gal. 6:15, 2 Cor. 5:17).

Repentance

The word *repentance* occurs 23 times as a noun and 34 times as a verb in the New Testament. Repentance was a prominent theme in the preaching of John the Baptizer and Jesus (Matt. 3:2,8; 4:17). The Greek word literally means "to change one's mind" and refers to a turning from an attitude of unbelief to faith, from spiritual darkness to light (1 Thess. 1:9).

Revelation

Revelation can be defined simply as "divine disclosure." General revelation refers to the divine disclosure of God and His truth through creation (Psa. 19:1-6, Romans 1:20), conscience (Rom. 2:14-15), and God's providential goodness to humanity (Acts 14:17). Special revelation refers to the revelation of God through His Son Jesus (John 1:18) and through Scripture (Psa. 19:7-11).

Sabbath

The Hebrew word *Sabbath* refers to Saturday, the seventh day of the week which God blessed and set apart as a day of rest from labor (Gen. 2:4). The Sabbath was particularly important for the people of Israel since it was the sign of God's covenant (Exod. 31:13). Although Christians are not under the Old Covenant requirement of Sabbath observance, the principle of a weekly day of rest for physical and spiritual refreshment is still relevant and applicable. The writer of Hebrews declares that all believers can all enjoy a "sabbath-kind-of-rest" in the finished work of Christ (Heb. 4:9).

Sacrifice

The Hebrew word for *sacrifice* is related to the verb "to slaughter," and refers to a particular kind of offering where blood is shed. All sacrifices are offerings, but not all offerings involve the shedding of blood. The offerings considered to be sacrifices include the burnt, sin and guilt offerings (Lev. 1, 4-5). Paul encourages believers to offer themselves as a "living and holy sacrifice" (Rom. 12:1). The writer of Hebrews encourages believers to offer God "a sacrifice of praise" (Heb. 13:15).

Sadducee

The *Sadducees* were an aristocratic sect of Jews who associated themselves with the priests and Temple. They were ultra conservative and rejected any teaching or traditions which didn't come from Moses including the resurrection, angels, and the persistence of the soul after death. Regarding the Sadducees, Josephus writes, "As for the persistence of the soul after death, penalties in the underworld, and rewards, they will have none of them" (Jewish War II. 165).

Salvation

The word *salvation* is used in the Bible to refer to physical deliverance from danger and distress (Acts 7:25, 27:31). But the more familiar use of the term is with reference to spiritual deliverance from divine wrath and eternal judgment (1 Thess. 5:9, Heb. 5:9). Salvation is a gift of God's grace which is received through faith in Jesus (Acts 16:30-31). .

Sanctification

The word *sanctification* is based on the word "holy" and literally means "to be set apart." *Sanctification* refers to the act or process of setting something or someone apart from common use and devoted to God. Believers are sanctified (set apart) by their faith in Christ (1 Cor. 1:2).

Believers undergo a process of sanctification as they yield to God's will and are transformed by the work of the Holy Spirit (Rom. 8:3-4, 1 Thess. 4:3).

Sanhedrin

The Sanhedrin was the supreme religious, political and judicial Jewish authority in the land of Israel. The origin of the Sanhedrin is traced back to the seventy elders appointed by Moses (Num. 11;16). Members of the Sanhedrin participated in the plot to arrest and kill Jesus (John 11:47-53). The Sanhedrin assembled to hear charges against Jesus and concluded that he was worthy of death (Mark 14:55-64).

Shaddai

The combination of *El Shaddai* is a familiar designation for God (Gen. 17:1, 28:3, 35:11). Some scholars have linked *Shaddai* with a word meaning "mountains," thus God of the mountains." Others suggest it comes from the word "breast," suggesting that God nourishes His own. In the Hebrew Bible *El Shaddai* stresses the might and power of God. He is sufficiently powerful to fulfill His promises and meet our needs.

Sheol

The Hebrew word *sheol* is often transliterated into the English text rather than being translated. The word basically means "the grave" or "the pit." It refers to the place of the dead–both the righteous and the wicked (Psa. 31:17). But Sheol has no lasting hold on believers who will be redeemed and delivered (Psa. 16:10, 49:14).

Sin

Sin is the "bad news" of the Bible. Both the Hebrew and the Greek words for *sin* mean "to miss the mark." Scripture teaches that all people "miss the mark" and fall short of God's righteousness and glory (Rom. 3:23). People sin by their thoughts, words, and actions. Romans 6:23 reveals that the payout for sin is death–spiritual separation from God for eternity. But the Bible presents a message of good news! The "good news" is that people don't have to remain in their state of sin and separation from God. Salvation from sin and its consequences is provided through faith in Christ (John 3:16, Rom. 5:8). The Apostle John writes, "If we confess or sins, He [Jesus] is faithful and righteous to forgive our sins and to cleans us from all unrighteousness" (1 John 1:9).

Synagogue

Synagogue is a Greek word for a Jewish institution which probably began when the Jews were deprived of their temple during the Babylonian captivity. The word means "gathering" or "assembly" and refers to the place where Jewish people gather for prayer and instruction from the Scriptures. Jesus taught in the synagogues (Luke 4:16-21) as did the Apostle Paul (Acts 17:1-2). The Hebrew term for a synagogue is *Bet Midrash*, "house of study."

Theophany

The word *theophany* means "appearance of God" and usually refers to a visible manifestation of God. The burning bush which Moses witnessed was a *theophany* (Exod. 3:1-6). Sometimes God appeared in human form as in the experience of Samson's father, Manoah (Judg. 13:9-22). The "Angel of the Lord" is usually understood to be God Himself, appearing in human-like form (Exod. 23:20-23).

Tithe

The Hebrew word *tithe* means one tenth. According the Mosaic law, the Israelites were to give one tenth of their crops to the Levites, who would in turn give a tenth to the priests (Deut. 14:22-27). While sacrificial giving is emphasized in Scripture, tithing is not required by the teachings of the New Testament. Instead, Paul taught that giving should be according to how one has prospered (1 Cor. 16:2). Those who prosper greatly should give generously. Paul sets forth the Macedonian believers as an example of grace giving (2 Cor. 8:1-5).

Tongues

When the Holy Spirit was given to the church on the Day of Pentecost, the apostles spoke in foreign languages, the dialects of the many visitors to Jerusalem (Acts 2). Paul later discusses the spiritual gifts of speaking in *tongues* that someone has not studied or learned. Paul explains that not all believers have the gift of tongues (1 Cor. 12:30) and those who do must recognize the intended purpose of this gift (1 Cor. 14:20-22) and follow the rules which apply (1 Cor. 14:27-33).

Tribulation

The Greek word *tribulation* means "pressure" and is used in Scripture to refer to the pressures and difficulties Christians experience living in an unbelieving world (John 16:33). But the term can be used in prophetic contexts to a seven-year period of Tribulation which will come upon the earth prior to the return of Christ. Jesus described characteristics of this Tribulation in his Olivet Discourse (Matt. 24:3-29). Revelation 6-19 also describes the events, judgments, and major personalities of this period.

Trinity

The word *Trinity*, although never used in the Bible, is used to signify that the God of Scripture is three-in-one. God is Father, Son and Holy Spirit (Matt. 28:18). Christians do not believe in three Gods, but in three separate but equal divine Persons who share together in a single God-head–a *Tri-unity*. While we may never completely understand this teaching, it is clearly revealed in both the Old and New Testaments (Isa. 48:16, 61:1, Matt. 3:13-17, 2 Cor. 13:14). By faith we accept the grand mystery of the *Trinity* as a biblical truth.

Yahweh

While there are many designations used to refer to God in Scripture, He has only one true name. God's name was revealed to Moses when God spoke to him at the burning bush (3:13-15). God's name is based on the Hebrew verb, "is." When God speaks of Himself, He says, "I AM." When Moses speaks about God he says, "HE IS." The revealed name of God is

YAHWEH which in Hebrew means "He is." Unfortunately, a fear of misusing God's name led to the tradition of avoiding it altogether (Exod. 20:7, Lev. 24:10-16). The name of God in Scripture is usually replaced by the designation "LORD" (Hebrew *Adonai*). But God's personal name, the name He wants to be known and remember by, is Yahweh.

Zion

The Hebrew term *Zion* has an uncertain etymology, but is first used in Scripture to refer to "the city of David" which was captured from the Jebusites (2 Sam. 5:7). Later, the term becomes used in the Psalms as general designation for the city of Jerusalem. During the exile, the Israelite nation came to be called *Zion* (Zech. 2:7) and those who eventually returned to their homeland are said to have "returned to Zion" (Psa. 126:1). The phrase "daughter of Zion" (Jer. 6:23) likens Jerusalem to a dear and beautiful young woman.

Appendix 8

AN INDEX OF BIBLICAL THEOLOGY

Many people love the Bible but have little interest in theology. "Too academic and dry," they say. Well, I'm sorry that some biblical scholars have made it seem that way. The word "theology" comes from the Greek words *theos* ("God") and *lego* ("to speak"). Theology is basically "talk about God." And I think God is a great subject for discussion! And since God is infinite, you will never run out of divine subjects for conversation.

There are two basic approaches to theology. Systematic theology organizes discussion about God around logical and philosophical categories. You can talk about God's existence, His attributes, His plan of salvation and His plans for the future. Most theology books approach the subject of theology from this systematic way. Biblical theology is not so organized and doesn't adhere to strict categories. Instead, biblical theology recognizes that certain books of the Bible highlight particular teachings about God.

The biblical theologian is more interested in the topics that bubble to the surface as you stir the pot of biblical truth. In the gospel of John, the topic of "belief" rises to the surface. Ninety-eight occurrences of the word "believe" confirm this! Paul's letter to the Romans highlights justification by faith. Proverbs focuses on the "fear of the Lord," and Ezekiel, "the glory of God."

For each book of the Bible I have searched for a prominent teaching about God and presented a brief summary to help you start thinking and discussing theology ("talk about God"). I have introduced these theological topics for all sixty-six books of the Bible. The following chart directs you to the book of the Bible where these topics are presented in your book, *Essential Bible Background*. These are great subjects for dinner conversations or family devotions. Become a theologian! Start talking about God!

The Theology	The Book
Belief; believe	John
Blessings	Daniel
Christ	Exodus; Hebrews
Circumcision	Galatians
Compassion	2 Chronicles; Jonah
Conduct	Ephesians
Davidic Covenant	Books of Samuel
Day of the Lord	Joel; Zeph. 1 & 2 Thess.
Deceived	Jude
Deliverance by God	Exodus
Discipline	Books of Kings
Doubt, doubters	Job, Jude
Election	Amos
Elijah	Malachi
Faith	Job; James
Faithfulness of God	Numbers; Joshua; Ezra
Fear of the Lord	Proverbs
Glory of God	Ezekiel
Grace	Jonah
Good deeds	Titus
Holiness	Leviticus; Joshua; Habukkuk

Holy Spirit	Luke
Hospitality	3 John
Humility	Philippians
Incarnation	1 John
Inspiration	2 Timothy
Israel	Daniel; Zechariah
Judgment	Kings; Chronicles; Daniel
Joy	Ecclesiastes
John the Baptist	Malachi
Justice	Micah
Justification	Romans; Galatians; James
Kingdom of God	Acts
Kinsman-Redeemer	Ruth
Law	Ruth
Leadership	Nehemiah; 2 Timothy
Long suffering	Nahum
Love of God	Deuteronomy
Loyal-love	Hosea
Marriage	Song of Solomon
Mercy	Judges; Chronicles
Messiah	Isaiah; Zechariah; Matthew
Ministry	2 Corinthians

New Covenant	Jeremiah
Passover	Exodus
Patience	Judges
Plan of God	Revelation
Praise	Psalms
Prayer	Luke
Presence of God	Haggai
Preservation	Zephaniah
Pride	Obadiah
Promise Keeper	Ezra; 2 Peter
Providence	Esther
Reconciliation	Philemon
Religion	Micah
Repentance	Judges
Resurrection	1 Corinthians
Retribution	Obadiah
Righteousness	Habakkuk
Sanctification	Leviticus
Scripture	2 Timothy 3; 2 Peter
Second Coming	2 Peter
Servanthood	Mark
Sex	Song of Solomon

Sovereignty of God	Genesis, Judg., Jon., Mal.
Submission	1 Peter
Suffering	Job
Sufficiency	Colossians
Theocratic Kingdom	Books of Samuel
Truth	2 John
Wrath of God	Numbers, Judges; Nahum

Appendix 9

FUN WITH BIBLE TRIVIA

The word "trivia" is defined as "insignificant and unimportant matters." While I would not want to trivialize the Bible itself, there are some details which are not essential to its message but quite helpful when attempting to puzzle or stump your friends. See if you can throw a few of these facts into your next table conversation!

What does the word "Bible" mean?
"Bible" comes from the Greek *biblia* ("books").

How many books are there in the Bible?
There are 66 books in the Protestant Bible, 80 in the Catholic Bible.

How many books are there in the Old Testament?
39 Old Testament books.

How many books are there in the New Testament?
27 New Testament books.

What does "New Testament" mean?
"New Testament" refers to the New Covenant which was inaugurated by Jesus' death (Jeremiah 31:31-34; Hebrews 8:6).

Who first used the term "New Testament" as a designation for the Christian Scriptures?
Tertullian (an early church teacher and theologian), around A.D. 200.

What is the shortest Old Testament book?
Obadiah (21 verses)

What is the longest Old Testament book?

Psalms (150 chapters)

What is the shortest New Testament book?
2nd John (13 verses). 3rd John actually fewer words but one more verse.

What is the longest New Testament book?
Acts (28 chapters)

What is the shortest verses in the Bible?
In the English, "Jesus wept" [*Edakrusen ho Jesous*] (John 11:35)

In the Greek, "Rejoice always" [*Pantote chairete*] (1 Thess. 5:16)

What is the longest verse in the Bible?
Esther 8:9

What are the original languages of the Old Testament?
Hebrew *and* Aramaic

What is the original language of the New Testament?
Koine (common) Greek

Where is the longest Aramaic passage in the Bible?
Daniel 2:4-7:28

Where is the shortest Aramaic text in the Bible?
Jeremiah 10:11

What is the oldest book of the Bible?
Most scholars would suggest "The Book of Job."

What is the last book of the Bible to be written?
Revelation (about A.D. 95-96)

What is the oldest Psalm?
Psalm 90, written by Moses (around 1450 B.C.)

What is the shortest Psalm?
    Psalm 117 (just two verses!)

What is the longest Psalm?
    Psalm 119 (176 verses)

Who wrote the most books of the Bible?
    The Apostle Paul (13 letters)

Who wrote the majority of the New Testament?
    Luke's Gospel and Book of Acts has slightly more text than Paul's 13 letters.

What is the most well-known verse of the Bible?
    John 3:16

What is the most obscure verse of the Bible?
    There is competition for this unusual honor! Here are the contenders:

    Galatians 3:20 "Now a mediator is not for one party only; whereas God is only one" (Gal. 3:20). One scholar notes that there are 250 different interpretations of this verse.

    1 Corinthians 15:29 "Otherwise, what will those do who are baptized for the dead? If the dead are not raised at all, why then are they baptized for them? There are at least 36 different interpretation of this verse!

    Revelation 22:11a "Let the one who does wrong, still do wrong; and let the one who is filthy, still be filthy" (Rev. 22:11a). I think this verse takes the prize!

Who has the longest name in the Bible?
    Isaiah's son, Mahershalalhashbaz (Isaiah 8:1)

What is the last word in the Hebrew Bible?
    "Curse" "And he will restore the hearts of the fathers to

their children, and the hearts of the children to their fathers, lest I come and smite the land with a *curse.*"
Malachi 4:6 NASV

What is the last word in the New Testament?
"Amen." Revelation 22:21 reads, "The grace of the Lord Jesus be with you all. *Amen."*

How many chapters are in the Bible?
1189 chapters; 929 in the Hebrew Bible and 260 in the New Testament

What is the middle chapter in the Bible
Psalm 118

What is the longest chapter in the Bible?
Psalm 119 (176 verses)

How many verses are there in the Bible?
31,173 verses; 23,214 in the Hebrew Bible and 7,959 in the New Testament

What is the middle verse in the Bible?
Psalm 118:8 "It is better to take refuge in the Lord than to trust in man."

What is the number of times the word "God" is used in the Bible?
3,358

What books of the Bible don't use the word "God."
Esther and the Song of Songs

What is the only book of the Bible named after a Jewish woman?
Esther (Ruth was Moabite)

What is the saddest verse in the Bible?
Revelation 20:15 "And if anyone's name was not found

written in the book of life, he was thrown into the lake of fire."

What is the most miss-referenced "Bible verse"?
"God helps those who help themselves." This proverb comes from Benjamin Franklin, not from your Bible!

How small is the world's smallest Bible?
The world's smallest Bible was engraved in Israel on a tiny silicon chip the size of a period on this page. The feat was accomplished to illustrate the science of nano-technology.

For more interesting facts about the Bible, go to the following web site, http://www.christiananswers.net/bible/about.html

Appendix 10

WHAT HAPPENED AFTER ACTS?

(Paul's Life after Acts 28)

The Book of Acts ends with a "cliff hanger." After a perilous voyage and ship wreck, Paul has been confined under house arrest in Rome for about two years. Based on his "appeal to Caesar" he has been awaiting a hearing before the Roman emperor. But none of Paul's Judean accusers have arrived in Rome to bring formal charges against him. Luke records that Paul stayed two full years in Rome welcoming visitors and teaching them about Jesus (Acts 28:30-31). And then the Book of Acts abruptly concludes. The end! Readers are left to wonder, "What came next? "What happened to Paul?"

It has been suggested by some biblical scholars that Luke intended to write another volume which would continue the story of Paul's life and ministry. But like many great book ideas, this one failed to materialize. Others speculate that Paul was executed after Acts 28 and Luke simply had nothing more to write about.

On the other hand, there appears to be strong biblical evidence for the continuation of Paul's ministry in the Mediterranean world after his release from confinement in Rome. It may be that since the Judean accusers against Paul never arrived in Rome to bring their charges against him, the case was simply dismissed. Or perhaps Paul's case exceeded the statute of limitations and the charges were dropped.

Whatever may have actually happened, many biblical references suggest that Paul continued his ministry after Acts 28. Paul's travels and ministry after Acts 28 may be reconstructed in various ways. The following is an attempt to reconstruct a likely itinerary based on the biblical data:

To Asia Minor:
Philemon 22, "prepare me a lodging" in Colossae

Paul's latest letters from Rome mention his desire to see the believers in Philippi (Phil. 1:25, 2:24) and Colossae (Philemon 22), so upon his release from confinement, Paul first traveled east.

To Ephesus:
1 Tim. 1:3, "remain on at Ephesus"

Since Paul had written Philemon requesting that he prepare him a lodging (Philemon 22), Paul probably sailed to Ephesus and then traveled up the Lycus Valley to Colossae. Paul probably retraced his steps to Ephesus after his visit with Philemon and the church at Colossae.

To Macedonia:
1 Tim. 1:3, "departure for Macedonia"

Paul wanted to go to Philippi (Phil. 1:25, 2:24) and left Timothy in Ephesus to lead the church in his absence. Paul wrote Timothy from Macedonia and visited churches there, including the church at Philippi.

To Philippi:
Phil. 1:25, 2:24, "coming shortly"

Evidence for Paul's planned visit to the church at Philippi is found in his letter to the Philippians where he wrote that he hoped to be "coming shortly" (Phil. 2:24).

To Ephesus:
1 Tim. 3:14, "in case I am delayed"

When Paul wrote Timothy from Macedonia, he wrote with the hope of returning to Ephesus soon (1 Tim. 3:14). But in case he was delayed, he provided Timothy with instructions concerning church practices and leadership. Perhaps Paul was able to return to Ephesus and minister again there as he planned.

To Spain:
Romans 15:24, "whenever I go to Spain"

At this point, Paul's itinerary becomes less certain. Perhaps at this time Paul was able to realize his desire to journey to Spain. He had mentioned this desire when he wrote his letter to the church at Rome (Rom. 15:28).

Evidence from early Christian writings appears to confirm that Paul did journey to Spain. Clement of Rome writes in his epistle to the Corinthians, "After preaching both in the east and west, he [Paul] gained the illustrious reputation due to his faith, having taught righteousness to the whole world, and came to the extreme limit of the west, and suffered martyrdom under the prefects" (1 Clement 5:7). Scholars believe that "the extreme limit of the west" refers to the Spanish peninsula. Another mention of Paul's journey to Spain is found in the Muratorian Canon (A.D. 170). It seems that Paul's journey to Spain was accepted by the early church as an historical fact.

To Crete:
Titus 1:5, "I left you in Crete"

It would be logical for Paul to have visited the island of Crete on his return voyage from Spain. After a successful ministry there, he traveled on leaving Titus to complete the follow-up work and appoint elders in every city (Titus 1:5).

To Asia Minor:
2 Tim 4:13, "the cloak I left at Troas"

The details of Paul's life are even less certain at this point, but references indicate that he visited Miletus (2 Tim.

4:20) and Troas (2 Tim. 4:13) in Asia Minor.

To Greece:
Titus 3:12, "come to me at Nicopolis"

Writing Titus from Asia Minor, Paul requested that he join him in Nicopolis (western Greece) for the winter. He was apparently on his way to Nicopolis when he wrote Titus. When Paul wrote Timothy from Rome during his last imprisonment, he mentioned that "Erastus remained at Corinth" (2 Tim. 4:20), indicating that Paul had been there also.

To Rome:
2 Tim. 1:16,17, "in Rome he searched for me"

Sometime around A.D. 67 Paul was arrested a second time and brought to Rome (2 Tim. 1:8,16, 2:9). During this imprisonment he was treated more harshly and anticipated his own death (2 Tim. 4:6-8). From the Mamertine prison adjacent to the Roman Forum he wrote Timothy requesting that he join him before winter (2 Tim. 4:21).

Paul's martyrdom probably took place late in A.D. 67 or early A.D. 68. According to tradition, Paul was beheaded with a sword just outside Rome on the Ostian Way and was buried in a catacomb south of the city. His tomb is traditionally located today under the Basilica of St. Paul Outside the Walls.

While parts of the itinerary I have reconstructed here are speculative, much of it rests on biblical references in Paul's writings. At least we know what *might* have happened after Acts 28. Perhaps this reconstruction is something like the story Luke would have told us had he written a third volume.

Appendix 11

WHAT IS THE APOCRYPHA?

Perhaps you have never even heard of the "Apocrypha." *Apocrypha* is a Greek word which means "things hidden" or "concealed." The term has been traditionally used to refer to fourteen books which appear in Catholic Bibles, but are not included in the Bible used by Protestants. Catholics usually refer to these books by the term *Deuterocanonical*, meaning "second canon" since these books were added later to the approved collection of books ("canon") included in the Bible. The Apocryphal or Deuterocanonical books were written between about 200 B.C. and 100 A.D. Unlike the Old Testament which was written in Hebrew, these books were composed in Greek.

Nearly all of the Apocryphal books were included in the Septuagint, the Greek translation of the Hebrew Bible. Around A.D. 90 a group of Jewish scholars endorsed the 39 Hebrew books of the Old Testament, but decided against including the Apocrypha with the Hebrew Scriptures. The early Christians recognized these books for their historical, literary and devotional value, but distinguished them from the rest of Scripture. This view was confirmed by Jerome who translated the Bible into Latin. He included the Apocrypha in the Vulgate believing that these books were helpful and even edifying, but should not be used to establish church doctrine.

Although Martin Luther incorporated the Apocrypha into his translation of the Bible into German (1534), he did not believe the Apocryphal books were equal to Scripture. As the Reformation continued, Protestants took steps to remove these books altogether from the canon of Scripture. The Roman Catholic Church, on the other hand, affirmed them as sacred and approved them at a church council that met at Trent (northern Italy) in 1546. That is why Catholic Bibles contain more books than the Bible used by Protestants. Not all the

Apocryphal materials appear as separate books. For example, the Prayer of Azariah, Song of the Three Men, Bel and the Dragon and Susanna all appear as supplements to the Book of Daniel.

Whether included in your Bible or not, the Apocryphal or Deuterocanonical books shed considerable light on the history, beliefs, wisdom and lore of the Jews during the intertestamental period. If you are not familiar with the Apocryphal books, you will find them included in Catholic Bibles such as the *Jerusalem Bible*. The following is a brief listing and description of the apocryphal books.

> Wisdom of Solomon: Like the book of Proverbs, this book encourages the pursuit of wisdom and a zeal for God by showing the blessings which will result.
>
> Ecclesiasticus: Another book of Hebrew wisdom showing that a successful life is based on reverence for God and observance of the law.
>
> Tobit: Like Pilgrim's Progress, the book of Tobit is an adventure story intended to show the spiritual rewards of piety, humility and obedience.
>
> Judith: The book of Judith is patterned after the heroic exploits of the book of Judges. Like the biblical Jael, Judith kills the enemy commander and delivers her people in a time of great peril.
>
> Esther: This material supplements the book of Esther providing a religious dimension to the story. Included are open references to God and expressions of devotion and piety.
>
> 1 Esdras: This book traces the history of the Jewish temple from the last great Passover under King Josiah to the restoration of temple worship under Ezra.

2 Esdras: Like the book of Revelation, 2 Esdras contains visions about the future. The seven visions were given to Ezra in order to justify God's actions toward sinful humanity.

Prayer of Azariah: The prayer of Azariah is a supplement to the account of Daniel's three friends in the fiery furnace (Daniel 3).

Song of the Three Men: Another supplement to Daniel 3, this is the song of praise sung by Daniel's friends after their deliverance (Daniel 3).

Susanna: This is a short story of Susanna, the virtuous wife of a Babylonian Jew who was caught by two elders bathing. She is falsely accused of adultery and condemned, but ultimately vindicated through Daniel's wisdom.

Bel and the Dragon: This story is a supplement to the book of Daniel and is intended as an attack against idolatry. Daniel exposes the idolatrous priests of Bel and destroys the cult of the dragon whom the people believed to be a god.

Letter of Jeremiah: The letter, supposedly sent by Jeremiah to the Jews in Babylon, attacks idolatry by showing the uselessness of idols and stupidity of worshiping them.

1 Maccabees: This is an excellent historical source recording struggles of the Maccabees against the Syrian ruler Antiochus Epiphanes who had outlawed Jewish worship and turned the Temple into a shrine for Zeus.

2 Maccabees: This is a supplement to 1 Maccabees providing a theological interpretation of some of the history recorded in 1 Maccabees.

Prayer of Manasseh: This book supplements the scriptural account of King Manasseh's repentance recording the prayer he prayed after turning from idolatry.

Baruch: Patterned after the Old Testament prophets, Baruch addresses the Jews in exile. The book presents prayers, confession of sin, a plea for God's pardon, and a promise of restoration and return.

While the Apocrypha is not recognized by all churches as authoritative Scripture, it does contain historical and devotional material that many Christians have overlooked. If you are looking for something a little different to supplement your Christian reading, consider one of the books from the "second canon"–the Apocrypha!

Appendix 12

IS THERE HUMOR IN THE BIBLE?

God is too holy and awesome to be trivialized as a cosmic Joker. Yet, there is biblical evidence that God takes delight in surprising His creatures with the extraordinary and unexpected. And this lies as the heart of good humor. Jokes are funny because of the unexpected ending or surprising twist.

I find a good deal of humor in the Bible. That a donkey spoke to Balaam is unusual. But the fact that Balaam spoke back without so much as a blink of an eye is funny (Num. 22:29)! And the fact that the donkey saw the angel blocking the path (22:27) while the "seer" (another name for a prophet) *didn't* adds another touch of humor to the story.

The story of Jonah has many theological lessons, but these are presented through the medium of humor. We are surprised by the fact that the fish was more obedient than Jonah. God commanded the prophet and he fled. But when God commanded the fish and it obeyed! This subtle contrast is certainly intended to elicit a chuckle.

If you find puns or wordplays humorous, don't miss Micah 1:10-15. Here Micah employed a number of puns in mourning Israelite towns being attacked by the Babylonians. He wrote things like, "Hightown will be laid low," and "Cannon Falls will fall by the cannon." Shaphir ("Beauty Town") will be made ugly and shameful as a result of the Babylonian attack, and Beth-ezel ("House of Removal") will be removed to captivity.

I find humor in the fact that Paul could not seem to recall how many people at Corinth he had baptized and he kept on correcting himself to make sure that his letter to the Corinthians was not in error (1 Cor. 1:14-17). Even the most sober soul smiles when reading Paul's comment that Christians who were requiring circumcision should emasculate themselves (Gal. 5:12). Jesus was certainly expecting his listeners to smile when

He spoke of religious leaders who would "strain out a gnat and swallow a camel" (Matt. 23:24).

While God has a sense of humor in that He enjoys surprising us with something unexpected, He Himself cannot be amused. This is because God is never surprised. He knows the end from the beginning. He knows the punch line before a story is ever told.

Solomon wrote in Proverbs that "laughter is good medicine." The following questions and answers are designed to keep you smiling and healthy. Enjoy!

Q. What kind of man was Boaz before he married?
A. Ruth-less.

Q. What time of day was Adam created?
A. A little before Eve.

Q. Where in the Bible is baseball mentioned?
A. Genesis 1:1, "In the beginning" (big inning).

Q. What do they call pastors in Germany?
A. German Shepherds.

Q. What kind of lights did they have on the ark?
A. Flood lights!

Q. Who was the greatest financier in the Bible?
A. Noah. He was floating his stock while everyone else was in liquidation.

Q. Who was the greatest female financier in the Bible?
A. Pharaoh's daughter. She went down to the bank of the Nile and drew out a little prophet.

Q. What kind of motor vehicles are in the Bible?
A. The Lord drove Adam and Eve out of the Garden in a "Fury." David's "Triumph" was heard throughout the land. Also,

probably a "Honda," since the apostles were all in one "Accord."

Q. Who was the greatest comedian in the Bible?
A. Samson. Because he brought the house down.

Q. What excuse did Adam give to his children as to why he no longer lived in Eden?
A. Your mother (Eve) ate us out of house and home.

Q. Which servant of God was the most flagrant lawbreaker in the Bible?
A. Moses. He broke all Ten Commandments at once!

Q. Which area of the Holy Land was especially wealthy?
A. The area around the Jordan. The banks overflowed every spring.

Q. Who is the greatest baby sitter mentioned in the Bible?
A. David. He rocked Goliath to sleep.

Q. Which Bible character had no parents?
A. Joshua, the son of Nun.

Q. Why didn't they play cards on the ark?
A. Because Noah was standing on the deck.

Q. Who was the shortest man in the Bible?
A. Many believe that Nehemiah (knee-high-miah) was the shortest man in the Bible. But I believe that honor is reserved for Bildad the Shuhite (shoe-hight).

Q. How do angels in heaven greet one another?
A. "Halo!"

Q. What did Noah do for a living?
A. He was an "ark-itech."

Q. What did the lion say when Daniel tumbled into the lions' den?

A. "Let us prey."

Q. What did Eve say when Adam asked, "Do you really love me?"
A. "There's no one but you."

Q. What did God say after making Adam?
A. "He looks pretty good, but I think I can do better!"

Q. What did the little boy say when he found a fall leaf pressed in the family Bible?
A. "Mom, I've found Adam's suit!"

Q. Why was Adam a world famous runner?
A. He was first in the human race.

Q. Did all the animals in on Noah's ark come in pairs?
A. No, the worms came in apples.

Q. How do you know when Enoch is at the door?
A. "E" knocks.

Q. How long did Cain hate his brother?
A. As long as he was Abel.

Q. When is meat first mentioned in the Bible?
A. When Noah took Ham into the ark.

Q. What do you call the wife of an apostle?
A. An epistle.

Q. Who was the most famous mathematician in the Bible?
A. Moses, because he wrote the book of Numbers.

Q. Where is the first tennis match mentioned in the Bible?
A. When Joseph served in pharaoh's court.

Q. Who is the straightest man in the Bible?
A. Joseph, because pharaoh made a ruler out of him.

Q. What do you call a sleep walking nun?
A. A roaming Catholic.

Q. Why were the cannibals the poorest people in the Bible?
A. They kept eating up all their prophets!

Remember the words of Proverbs 17:22, "A joyful heart is good medicine." And keep smiling! "For the joy of the Lord is your strength" (Nehemiah 8:10).

Recommended Bible Resources

John A. Beck, *Discovery House Bible Atlas* (2015).

Gorden D. Fee and Douglas Stuart, *How to Read the Bible For All Its Worth* (1981).

Wayne Grudem, C. John Collins and Thomas R. Schreiner, *Understanding the Big Picture of the Bible* (2012).

Walter C. Kaiser, Jr. *The Promise-Plan of God* (2008).

J. Carl Laney, *Answers to Tough Questions from Every Book of the Bible* (1997).

Leland Ryken, *How to Read the Bible as Literature* (1984).

Carl G. Rasmussen, *Essential Atlas of the Bible* (2013)

William Schlegel, *Satellite Bible Atlas* (2016).

John F. Walvoord and Roy B. Zuck, *The Bible Knowledge Commentary* (Two Volumes: OT, 1985; NT, 1983).

Made in the USA
Columbia, SC
01 January 2019